O.J.

THE
LAST
WORD

OTHER BOOKS BY GERRY SPENCE:

The Making of a Country Lawyer
How to Argue and Win Every Time
From Freedom to Slavery
Gunning for Justice
Of Murder and Madness
Trial by Fire
With Justice for None

O.J.

THE
LAST
WORD

GERRY SPENCE

ST. MARTIN'S PRESS

NEW YORK

Production Editor: David Stanford Burr
Book design by Gretchen Achilles

ISBN: 0-312-18009-8

First Edition: November 1997

10 9 8 7 6 5 4 3 2 1

To the unsung, unpublished, unrecognized, criminal defense lawyers of America. They abound in every village, every community across the land. They fight for the rights of the poor, the forgotten, the lost, the hated, and the damned, usually for a pittance, often for no pay at all. To them we owe a great debt for our freedom. . . .

and to Garvin Isaacs, one of the best of them.

CONTENTS

NO, NOT YOU, TOO, MR. SPENCE

I SPURNED THOSE O.J. books, the talking heads who never won a murder case, those D.A.'s who, in this perverse world, became famous because they lost the big one. I loathed this Barnum & Bailey of the justice system. I abhorred the media, of which I was a part, which became the loud-mouthed, mindless monster whose insatiable hunger was fed on the obscenity of race, and who laughed at pain and turned us all into the new tabloid people. I mocked the public as they ogled and leered like bawdy ghouls, ecstatic in this new pornography of blood and celebrity.

"Are you going to write an O.J. book?" the book writers asked, the others of the media as well, all seeking companions in this maddened business, as if the more who joined in the orgy the fewer apologies were in order. Everyone was writing an O.J. book. That made it all right. And like the gold rush of '49, everyone had packed it up and headed west to seek their fortune. Write a book. Get rich. Join us as we watch this sideshow where the freak is tortured and dissected a little at a time, and we howl with delight and then, raising eyebrows of the all-knowing, attempt to set the world straight about it—as if this were the most serious business of state.

"No, I am not, I repeat, *not*, going to write an O.J. book." I didn't say it but I thought, I have something more important to do with my life, like rocking in the old rocking chair, contemplating the ants crawling by on the floor. I mean, what is the ant's perspective? Do they ask, "What is the meaning of life?" So I said no. "No. I am not writing an O.J. book."

During the eons that our species has dominated this earth, one could, I imagine, fill the North Sea with the bones from the skeletons of women who have been murdered by men. Except for the celebrity ingredient attached to the murders, this case had occurred endlessly throughout the ages. But even though the magnitude of the tragedy had not fully registered, one began to know something—something—in uncomfortable deep places. The case would not go away. It had a life of its own, ugly, huge, noisy, something that crowded all else aside, something like a vulture hatched in a robin's nest. It had become an international event, something ironically bigger than the Gulf War. A lot bigger than the Gulf War. It was a new kind of war, a civil war perhaps, being fought all over again on a different turf, with different rules, rules often so subtle it became hard to recognize the war. The language was not the language of a battlefield. Instead the talking heads, and then the people at large, talked of witnesses and judges; they spoke of evidence, the loathsomely shallow performance of the lawyers. When the people talked about the flimflam of Judge Lance Ito, they were talking about a potpourri of other complaints that could not be discussed openly in this new, "politically correct" world. Misogynists and men haters and racists and bigots and the frightened and the abandoned and the alienated—all saw the case as standing for what they despised the most, feared the most. The O.J. Simpson case had become a symbolic war, a war belonging to every man and woman in America, of every race, every economic class, every walk of life, a case everyone could somehow relate to down to the blood and the bone. This was *their* case. It was Aunt Bessy's returning nightmare of her abduction as a child. It was the case of the redneck who hated blacks and saw the trial as proof that blacks get away with murder in this country and that they all ought to be shipped out or shoved in. It was the case of the rich guy's aloof, disdainful assessment of the justice system. It was the black person's confirmation that in America we are still lynching black men for "messing around" with white women. It was an astounding spectacle in which the masses of uninformed were learning the wrong things about trials and lawyers and judges. It was a celebrity case that titillated the gonads of those who had no life of their own. But at the bottom of the pile of emotional garbage the case created, it was a race case that permitted America to palpate once more the ugly scars left from nearly 250 years of overt slavery in this, "the land of the free and the home of the brave."

I saw the trial. I was in the courtroom daily. I knew the lawyers, some personally. I met the judge. I knew the major players in the media. I had been approached to try the case. I had talked to O.J. on three or four occasions. And during forty years in the courtroom, I had tried and won more murder cases than all of the members on the defense team put together, which is not a bragging matter but a fact, like one who has forded the river, nearly drowned, and then floated ashore. I knew something of what was on the other side. Moreover, I became one of those talking heads. I had observed the media firsthand, seen its purulent underside, heard its empty-headed voice spew out nonsense that turned a nation into a ranting mob squealing unintelligible protestations from horizon to horizon. But I was above it. Quite. No, I would not write an O.J. book.

Then I began to see that the books out there were not written by anyone who had ever forded much of a river, who had no stake in the case, who embraced no agenda to withdraw this so-called search for truth from that circus fantasia and bring it back to the real world. I began to wonder what a real trial lawyer would have said about the case. What would Clarence Darrow have said? Would he knowingly go to bed, yes, to his final bed, and be silent about this case that would eventually do more to do or undo the justice system in America than any in its history?

Not that I could ask Clarence Darrow to scoot over and let me occupy a little of his niche. But I began to question my obligation to set the O.J. case in some kind of credible perspective. Did I have a duty to speak? And then I began to think, what if I remain silent? What if terrible things happen to the justice system because of this freak of the courtroom, and I remained silent while it happened? What if someday I look back, and it is too late? Maybe if I had spoken, that grotesque mutant that grew out of the trial might have been held back. Maybe if I wait, what I have to say will be irrelevant, the opportunity will have passed, and I will have failed, as is my obsessive fear. Maybe I can't change anything, save anything, count for anything. Maybe I can do nothing more than satisfy my own need to speak out. And suddenly I needed to write an O.J. book.

—GERRY SPENCE
Jackson Hole, Wyoming
July 1997

O.J.

THE
LAST
WORD

CHAPTER 1

THE "DREAM TEAM"

I THOUGHT THAT if O.J. called me, called me and spoke to me in that voice as deep and pure as fresh hot pudding, I probably would take the case. In fact, when he did reach me, I thought he was probably innocent. The police, almost by reflex, accuse the husband when the wife has been murdered. You can look at the statistics: Husbands are the ones who kill wives. And in celebrity cases, the police have to look good—the whole world watching and all. The police have to make their public statements and take care of their jobs. They have to protect the politicians, their bosses— the mayor, the chief of police. Justice isn't the issue. Careful police work isn't imperative. The rights of the accused in such tabloid cases don't worry the officials. They play to our anger, our fear, our compassion for the victims, but justice—despite their deep, righteous, tearless cries—does not move them. A conviction is the issue.

The police need a conviction! Let us somehow, in some way, get the "twelve-headed monster," as Marcia Clark called the jury, to hate the defendant, to see in the jurors' frightened eyes the defendant covered with the blood of an innocent victim—the pretty, the powerless, the near perfect victim. Let us somehow get the court to order him up onto the executioner's gurney, where the state's masked killer will stick the needle in him, or let us at least put him away in some damnable dank hole for the rest of his life.

Yet when the case does not involve a celebrity, when the media is not covering the murder of a famous heiress or the wife of a superathlete, no one seems to care. "Willy" may have killed half his neighborhood in a crumbling ghetto somewhere, the bodies strewn across the rotting place, and the police remain calm, their eyes placid. When they get around to it, after the long morning coffee, they will haul in some snitch, make a deal with him, slap a crackhead up against the wall—just like in the movies—and get him to point the finger. And they'll make their arrest. Day after day we are still confronted with the same boring, senseless crime, the same swaggering gangs of kids, the violent talk, the hard faces of the young that should be open and innocent. The pain. The death. But no one gets excited. You can kill everyone in a fallen-down project somewhere, one person at a time, a couple at a time, and the jobs of the police remain secure. The mayor takes no heat. The media doesn't get excited. No one wants to read about how a mother with nine little snot-nosed kids living in a project got her brains blown out by some drugged-up puke. That's what some police call a suspect who doesn't live on the right side of town—a puke. When there's killing in these tough places, the police process is something like scooping up roadkill off the highways. The process doesn't enter our living rooms because *Hard Copy* can't make a story about it. No one cares about the puke or his victim. And in the morning the cops can have a third cup of coffee and a couple more cigarettes before they start smashing heads. But when a celebrity's wife is dead, that's another story. We gotta have justice.

"We are horrified," the D.A. says. "We are very concerned about the victims and the family." The D.A. makes his public statements. And the police and the D.A. begin what has become known as the "demonization process" always associated with a big media case. It's what you do to convict the accused before he goes to trial. You poison the well of justice. You leak the worst details to the press, factual or not. You play up the blood, the horror. You know the people will begin to get stirred up. If you've ever heard the chickens in the chicken house when an old raccoon gets in at night, you know how it sounds: like a freight train going through, thousands of wings beating, the crazy screeching, the poor things panicked in the night, afraid of their own sounds, and of the raccoon who has already stolen his dinner and gone off to feast.

I didn't believe O.J. Simpson could have committed this crime. Who would believe it? Not this smiling man, this good-natured man, this great athlete, this talented hurdler of objects in airports, this man whom we forgave for his poor acting because he was a decent fellow. "The Juice." God, I used to love to watch him run. I would go to sleep at night doing a Walter Mitty thing—I was the Juice. I would slip off left tackle, little hole, the swiveling hips—just give me a block, half a block even, and I'm gone. The Juice couldn't have done this thing, the slashing, the throat of the mother of his children cut down to the spinal cord, her head almost off, the other nameless kid, whoever he was, butchered, the blood at the front door like the blood on the floor of the slaughter shed at the packinghouse. The police must have gone wrong again. Couldn't find the murderer. Didn't have a clue. Charged the husband as they always do. Mindless. Automatic. But the statistics say they will be right most of the time. And predictably they had already started the demonizing process. You could foresee the rest, the evidence leaking to the media. You could recite the next steps you'd read about in the paper like the next line of bad verse. And *Hard Copy* and the others! What a story. What a sumptuous feast. They loved it. They had something to sell—this diamond of a man dunked in blood. You sell the crime. You sell the horror, the sex, the decadence. Oh, they loved the blood, the blonde, and the black. The best screenwriter in America couldn't have sold a racist screenplay like that. But this wasn't cheap Hollywood fiction, not yet. This was for real. *The Blood and the Blonde and the Black.*

So I hung on to the presumption of innocence in the case. The Juice couldn't have done it. That's what the presumption of innocence is about, among other things—the legal codification of the proposition that man is fundamentally good. And the presumption stops the police from smashing in the front door and pointing their long white fingers at you whenever it suits them. We have constitutional guarantees. Besides, I was the Juice—at least, just before I stepped over the goal line and dropped off to sleep.

By the time O.J. called me in Jackson Hole, the so-called Dream Team was mostly in place. My old friend Howard Weitzman had already left the case, and Robert Shapiro, whom I also knew, had been hired. From what I could tell, the high-school-football mentality was in operation. The hangers-on, the guys who couldn't carry the ball across the other side of the hall, were still clinging to the big letterman, soaking up his reflected glory. O.J. had his business lawyers, his business associates, his old friends, the inner circle, and they were making the decisions for him. His legal retinue consisted of men who wouldn't have been able to try a case if all they had to do was read it from a movie script. You see it all the time. These were the people calling the shots for the Juice—the elite in the country club who made deals but who had never been in court all day and then had lain awake half the night looking up at the ceiling, seeing their client being dragged off, his head shaved clean as an egg, sweating, his eyes wild, the chair waiting. These were the men who had never had to say to themselves, "It's my fault. If I had been a better lawyer, better prepared, if I had had a quicker wit, if I hadn't been so afraid, if I had been a *real* lawyer instead of this piteous, beaten bastard who made a bad final argument, maybe he wouldn't have to die."

Many of the people making the decisions for O.J. played golf with a generous handicap and drank their Tanqueray martinis. They knew a lot, all right, but most of it was about movie percentages. But some had money, and they hung out in the right restaurants and knew a lot of movie people and high flyers and flitted in the giddy air that is Hollywood. And O.J., who wouldn't make up his mind whether he should kill himself or not, wasn't thinking much about lawyers—not then. So the lawyer decisions were made by "the guys," the hangers-on who at that moment claimed O.J. was their best friend in the world.

The idea of a Dream Team was the media's invention. The notion prevails in America that if you have enough money and know the right people, you can buy whatever you want. You can buy happiness, buy the cute little blonde with the cute little whatever it is. You can buy a new liver if yours is rotted out after having filtered a tankerfull of whiskey through it. You can buy your way to heaven if, after having stolen from the poor and the middle-class mom-and-pop investors all your life, you give a small percent of it to charity. And of course, you may not always be able to buy justice, but a lot of money helps.

Yet some perverse power is at work here. You see it all the time. The rich are taken care of by the carriage-trade physicians. The fact that such doctors charge ten times what the doctor down the street charges is seen as a surefire indication of their worth. A doctor who bills twenty thousand dollars for a simple appendectomy must be a lot better doctor than one whose fee is under a thousand. It stands to reason—you are buying a Rolls, not a Honda. The problem is that what the carriage-trade doctors offer are the big reputations, not necessarily the big skill, the talented hands, a healer's genuine compassion. They, too, hang out with the so-called smart people, and that makes them smart. Besides, it's a lot easier to have a big reputation than it is to have had your hands in the bloody bellies of hundreds of anguished human beings, most of whom can't pay your bill. It's more profitable to office in the high-rent district and cater to the silk-underweared rich than to have sweat out the recovery of the maimed in those bleak rooms where people are weeping and dying, a place where the dead are being hauled off to the morgue. Who wants to look into the worn faces of old wives and the blank eyes of motherless children paralyzed with fear? So it is, as well, with carriage-trade lawyers.

Carriage-trade lawyers usually don't know very much about much that counts. At the same time, the rich think all they have to do is pull out their checkbook and everything will be all right and the charges will evaporate under the heat of money. All they have to do is hire the lawyer with the big reputation—the one they play golf with, or the one their golf partner plays golf with. The rich get mixed up. They think that because they have money, they must also be smart—that money is equivalent to brains. And of course, the more money they spend for a lawyer, the more brains the lawyer must have. The media thinks that, too, and therefore America thinks it. Money and talent, money and smarts, money and justice—all are seen as comparables. But when it comes to picking a doctor to save my life, let me have somebody with a bloodied gown who has stacked enough corpses up in front of his office to have finally learned how to do it right. And as for a lawyer, give me somebody who has sweated sweat as thick as syrup in the courtroom, somebody who can crawl into my hide and feel my fear because he knows his own. And you can't find those lawyers in the four-star restaurants, or on those pretty groomed golf courses. The carriage-trade boys, the hangers-on, the flitters in the high social places, the monarch butterflies of Hollywood, don't even know the good trial lawyers. Never heard of them. The only lawyers they know have a decent handicap and eat at the Eclipse.

So the Dream Team was a myth—the fictional child of the media. And America bought the myth. I am not saying that the lawyers who represented Simpson weren't good trial lawyers. I only say that they were a team picked by those who weren't. The Dream Team were lawyers whose skill could have been duplicated a hundred times over in L.A., and in countless other towns across the land. Robert Shapiro and Johnnie Cochran themselves never claimed they were the greatest trial lawyers in America. The media claimed it, and then as soon disclaimed it. They were the Dream

Team, and the next day they were paraded across the screen as lawyers who had pulled a fast one on America. One day they were the best lawyers money could buy, and the next they were vilified by every author who had a book to sell.

America buys whatever America is told to buy—Bud or Big Macs or Bugle Boy pants—and so it was with this Dream Team. You have to believe what you hear on TV with your own ears, and what you see on TV with your own eyes. What else is there to believe? The trouble is that the people who create our conventional wisdom and fuel our daily fantasies are mostly kids under thirty. Most are underpaid producers working ungodly hours who have rarely been encouraged to hatch an original thought of their own because they don't have time, and if they did the result might be too frightening to behold. They are also people who are frantically, pathetically driven by the invisible whip of ratings. And things get distorted through the media's ratings glasses. How can news be news when ratings, and the advertisers who buy time accordingly, govern what will make the news? The producers believe that simple, hard, unvarnished truth won't sell. People want to hear the bad and the horrid—about husbands who get their penises amputated and baby beauty queens who get murdered, and Lord knows what else. People want to chortle and gasp. People want to believe that Shapiro and Cochran are fancy lawyers who can be bought for big money but who, somehow, are less than ethical, less than competent, or whatever at the moment will sell.

My experience with Bob Shapiro tells me he is a caring man who is deeply aware of his public persona. Who isn't? I'll fight at the first words insinuating I'm dishonest or disingenuous. As proclaimed in Proverbs: "A good name is rather to be chosen than great riches." Shapiro's effectiveness as a lawyer has been his friendship with lawyers and judges and others in positions of power. He's an obliging sort, the kind who, if you ask for a favor, will provide it if he can. I remember having asked him to come to my nonprofit trial lawyer's school to give young trial lawyers a short course on how to deal with the media in high-profile cases. After the Simpson case he should have been the world's expert. He could talk about his good days and his mistakes, and he did. He came to Wyoming and gave of his time without fee, and he talked to the young lawyers with a great deal of energy and wisdom. And Shapiro's shortcomings, if we can call them that, seemed quite normal. That he had attempted to distance himself from the "race card"—a strategy that he had more or less invented—and that he got cross-wise with some of the other members of this Dream Team was simply the case of a lawyer trying to preserve his good name—his asset. One can become overly sensitive in the high glare. One can lose perspective when one is constantly under the lights. Shapiro may, indeed, have been eaten up by the very media that spawned him. The media is a dangerous mother. It loves to devour its offspring.

We are too quick to criticize whoever is out there and to adopt the so-called conventional wisdom offered up by the pundits and the talking heads. Some writers claimed that Shapiro, yes, Cochran, too, had never successfully defended a murder case before the Simpson case. Shapiro, they said, was a deal maker, a plea-bargainer. But no one dared say he had no trial experience. His experience became evident during the cross-examination of a witness. And you can't make deals if you are ineffective as a trial attorney, any more than you can fight a duel without a pistol. Watch the impotent lawyer walk into the prosecutor's office to make a deal for his client. You can see him huddled there, all tight and choked up, the prosecutor sitting back, his feet propped on the desk, the smirk on his face. The prosecutor's thinking, "This guy couldn't find his way into the courtroom even if I led him by the hand." You can't make deals with a prosecutor if you can't back up your talk. And Shapiro not only could try a case, he could also win over both prosecutors and judges with a charm and style I was never able to cultivate myself.

As for Johnnie Cochran, well, maybe he had or maybe he

hadn't successfully defended a murder case before O.J. One writer who himself probably hadn't tried a murder case in quite some time said, "Prior to the Simpson case, however, although he may have done so, I had never heard of Cochran ever winning a murder case before a jury." He went on to argue that the only case Cochran had tried that even received "minimal" coverage "was when he defended a Black Panther named Elmer 'Geronimo' Pratt in 1972 for having murdered a white schoolteacher on a Santa Monica tennis court." Cochran was said to have lost the case and his client was sentenced to life imprisonment. Yet twenty-five years later Pratt won his appeal and was released from prison. So who never won a case? I say we criticize too quickly from positions that are always plenty safe.

Although I have tried a good many media cases, most of my trials, particularly in the first twenty years of my career, were fought in small courtrooms without a newspaper reporter within fifty miles. You don't become a skilled trial lawyer by handling only media cases. You become a skilled trial lawyer laboring year after year for the poor and the helpless, often without fee. You fight in dingy courtrooms before venomous judges and against surly prosecutors, the kind who stand in the courtroom on run-over heels and who would just as soon whip your ass in the alley as in front of a jury. And you try your cases in virtual anonymity, cases with tougher evidence laid on your clients than in the Simpson case, and with no help, no funds, no expert witnesses, no glamour, and you try those kinds of cases year after year. Then one day you find you have mastered some of the fundamental skills required of a successful trial lawyer, and some writer attacks you, saying, "I never heard of any cases the guy ever tried." But the great trial lawyers in this country work those intense fourteen-hour days in little towns in Oregon, in the forgotten hamlets in Alabama, and in the wretched neighborhoods of Chicago and Cleveland. We never hear of most of these. But these lawyers know how to try a case. And they usually know a lot more about it than the carriage-trade lawyers who claim they are "litigators" and who turn off a decent jury of twelve the first time they drive up to the courthouse in their Jaguars and swagger into the courtroom with those little doodads flopping on their shiny loafers, wearing their thousand-dollar pin-striped suits. If you want to be defended, find a lawyer who has lived a career trying to extract citizens from holding pens and who has labored in the courtroom, mostly in anonymous, pathetic cases. He may have baggy pants and scuffed shoes, and his coat may be frayed at the elbows, but he knows how to talk to people, and he cares about his clients.

I listened with amusement to the pundits claiming that Shapiro and Cochran didn't have enough experience in murder cases to try the Simpson case. I have never tried two cases that were alike. Although I have tried many a murder case, I have never found that the trial of one is very helpful in the trial of another. To boast that someone has tried a hundred murder cases doesn't mean he can win a single murder case. He may have lost them all. Yet the lawyer who has tried a whole spectrum of lesser criminal cases may have developed trial skills that permit him to win whatever case he tries.

When O.J. did call me, I was sitting in my study looking out at the Tetons. At my bird feeder on the deck the evening grosbeaks were competing with the pine grosbeaks while the yellow-bellied nuthatches were being run off by a small red mountain squirrel. And when the squirrel's back was turned, the birds quickly grabbed sunflower seeds before he was on them again. The birds and squirrels, I suspect, are a lot smarter than men. They don't fight wars in which whole flocks of innocents are killed. They don't cut the throats of their mates. They just play their games at the feeder, and when it's over, everybody gets something to eat. As I watched them, the phone rang and Cathy Randa, O.J.'s secretary, said O.J. wanted to talk to me, and she patched him through.

"Read your books," he said. That voice. "You're my hero." I am *his* hero? My God, how can this be? Does he put himself to sleep at night fantasizing that he's Gerry Spence making his closing argument to a jury in a murder case?

I didn't know what to say. I think I said something like, "It must be hard for you, O.J."—something like that. I must have told him I was sorry he was penned up and that I wished it wasn't that way for him.

He said, "I want to tell you how much I admire you for what you do, and all." What was I supposed to say?

"Thank you," I said.

"And I just wanted you to know that I am innocent. Absolutely innocent. There is nothing about what they say that's true." The deep rich pudding of a voice. "I loved Nicole. I wouldn't do anything to the mother of my children. You got to believe that." And then he went on about how he had never done anything to harm her. They'd had their beefs like other married people, but he loved her, they were trying to get back together. Things like that.

And that was about it. He didn't ask me to defend him. He didn't ask me to come see him. He didn't tell me anything about his case. He just called me up and laid his story on me, and it sounded right. And he sounded a lot better than I would have under the same circumstances. If it had been me, I wouldn't have been able to say a word. If I had been charged with killing my wife, Imaging, I wouldn't have been able to lift my head off of the cement. I wouldn't know where to turn. I wouldn't know whom to call. I wouldn't know what to say. I would be reduced to a couple hundred pounds of blubbery impotence. Meat on the floor. But then, I never did carry a football over the goal line, except, of course, when I was O.J., just before I fell asleep.

CHAPTER 2

THE OFFER

THEN ONE DAY in July 1994 Bob Shapiro called me in Jackson Hole. I'd first met him fifteen years before in Aspen, Colorado, where I'd been giving a lecture and demonstration of trial technique to the criminal defense bar of California, and afterward Shapiro had invited me and a group of his friends to his condominium for drinks. By then I didn't drink, and hadn't for a long time. I'd already drunk enough that if I never took another, it wouldn't affect my lifetime average much. Strange thing: You can sit all night and never run out of the names of great trial lawyers who soak their brains in the grog—something to do with the stress of the trade. A trial lawyer's self-medication against the pain. But Shapiro was too smart for that: didn't drink enough to mention, and never did to my knowledge. Sort of made a man suspicious of him.

When he called, Shapiro started out just as O.J. had, saying how much he admired me, and that I had always been his mentor—and that he wanted my advice. He hinted that he was thinking about inviting me into the case and asked if I could come out to L.A.

Me? Come out to talk about the case, maybe represent the Juice? I felt exhilarated, something the way O.J. must have felt when he got nominated for the Heisman Trophy. This case was becoming the Super Bowl of criminal law, and to be invited! And by this fellow Shapiro, whose face had already graced the cover of magazines.

I'd been around. I'd tried some big cases. Shapiro knew about them, and O.J., too. A lot of lawyers had tried big cases, but most of mine had been for noncelebrities, such as Karen Silkwood, Randy Weaver, the old-time gunslinger of a sheriff from Rock Springs who fast-drew against his deputy and shot him between the eyes just before a statewide grand jury was going to call the deputy to testify against him. And I represented the Mexican kid who shot his white wife, also between the eyes, and in front of nine witnesses, a kid I represented through three jury trials. Cases like that. No fee. I always had a murder case or two going because a trial lawyer needs to, and usually I had to take them without a fee because most people who commit murders can't afford to commit them.

But in later years I'd gotten to the place where I could pick and choose my cases—a great luxury for a trial lawyer. Most criminal lawyers have to take whatever case comes along. They have to pay the rent, they have to feed the kids. Besides, it's their duty to defend the accused, guilty or innocent. And when a case comes in the door, you're afraid it will be the last case you'll ever see. But by the time of the Simpson and Goldman murders, I'd been at this for over forty years, and if you stay at it long enough, and work hard enough, you can maybe get to the place where you can choose your cases.

"How do you pick your cases, Mr. Spence?" the kids always ask at the law schools when I lecture.

"I pick 'em as I pick my friends. I pick 'em because I care about them. I pick cases that have something to say—that stand for something. I pick cases that can change society." It all sounds very self-righteous, and it is, and I am, a lot of the time. You get like that to make up for all the sins you've committed along the way. But there was no overriding social issue in this case. No right of the poor that could be defended, no burning issue that could become a beacon lighting a new way to justice. Stripped of its celebrity, this case was a common, mundane murder case, bloody all right, horrid, and in its violence pornographic to the extreme, but a run-of-the-mill murder case nonetheless, without any redeeming social value, as they say. If I were to live by my self-proclaimed values, I would take the case of Willie charged with killing the clerk in a hold-up at the 7-Eleven before I would take the O.J. Simpson case. I don't know how many times I'd turned down the rich and the famous before. I sometimes gloated about it to myself: They didn't have enough money to hire me. But I would defend Randy Weaver, a pauper, for nothing. There was a special pleasure in it, a sort of late-blooming purity. I didn't work for money anymore, I liked to tell myself. I worked for myself, for my sense of worth, to fulfill my agenda in life. Along the way, I told myself, you have to pay for the space you occupy on the face of this earth—and even though I sometimes fell short, that's how, in these later years, I tried to think about the cases I took.

I often saw my life as my old Grandpa Spence's milk pail full of milk. I could see him limping up the hill on his old arthritic legs, careful not to spill a drop. Out of that pail came the butter for Grandma's biscuits and the cream for Grandpa's oatmeal, and the skim milk was left outside to clabber and then was fed to the chickens. Not a drop was wasted. In my later years life seemed that way to me. To waste life for money and money alone was like spilling one's milk.

Of course, I had represented Imelda Marcos for big money, but I could rationalize that one: The United States government was using our judicial system to play international politics. After the Marcoses were hauled off to Hawaii by our government against their will, and after Ferdinand had died, Rudolph Giuliani, now the mayor of New York but at that time the U.S. attorney, had guaranteed the State Department in writing that he'd convict Imelda. I kept wondering how it would be if the Philippine government had kidnapped Nancy Reagan and prosecuted her in Manila for the alleged crimes of her dead husband, even if she did own three thousand pairs of shoes. Besides, if you're mostly going to represent the poor in criminal cases without a fee, you have to drag in a big-fee case once in a while to stay afloat.

But the O.J. case: Well, wasn't a trial lawyer who had labored most of his life away in the sticks of Wyoming entitled to the one big case in his lifetime? Couldn't I take one case just for me? And so when Shapiro called I was flying high. I ran downstairs to tell Imaging, "Shapiro wants me to come to L.A. and talk about representing O.J."

She was silent.

"Did you hear me?" I asked.

"Yes," she said. "I heard you. Is he innocent?"

"How do I know?" I said. "I haven't talked to him. But he's still entitled to a defense."

"Right," she said. "But not *your* defense." Celebrity means nothing to Imaging. To her, big cases are just cases. I should either be in them or not. To her it was that simple.

"This is the biggest case in the history of American jurisprudence," I said, with my usual overstatement.

"So?"

"So aren't I entitled to the biggest case in the history of American jurisprudence?"

"Well, maybe."

"What do you mean, 'maybe'?"

"If you are going to talk to Bob Shapiro, you better look like a lawyer," she said. She was referring to my unlawyerly television uniform: the buckskin jackets (which, after all, she had made) and black turtleneck. "He won't be impressed if you don't look like a lawyer."

"He knows how I look."

"You better look like a lawyer," she said again.

So I went down to the town square in Jackson to the old general store that was closing—one of the national chains was taking over—and they had Western suit jackets on sale. Fifty percent off. I bought a nice dark green one—it looked black to me—and a couple of pairs of slacks, and I shined up my boots, put on a blue shirt with a button-down collar, and donned one of those can't-miss multicolored ties that goes with anything, and I looked like a lawyer—sort of.

"You need a haircut," she said.

I drew the line there. A man can go only so far.

I got to L.A. on Friday, July 15, 1994, and I was met at the airport by one of those stretch limos—the most uncomfortable, ridiculous car ever created. I got up front with the driver. Better seat. Not so lonesome. The driver had been instructed to take me to the home of a Michael Klein in Beverly Hills. Shapiro said he wanted secrecy. Didn't want my introduction into the case to become a news event: The Country Lawyer Joins the Dream Team. I punched the doorbell.

The door opened and there stood Bob Shapiro, wearing designer jeans with those rips and frays in them—these days you have to pay a pretty penny to look poor—and a denim shirt open to the waist. A gold chain hung around his neck and the hair grew on his chest like a lawn of black grass. Jesus Christ, I thought, I go to all this trouble to dress up to impress this guy and what do I get? He hugged me. People hug a lot in Hollywood. The house was empty of people but full of expensive, modern fittings. He commandeered one of those big overstuffed couches in the Klein living room. The meeting was about to begin. Shapiro curled up at one end of the couch, and I took the other. He was barefoot, and I noticed his toenails were coated with clear polish. I was glad I was wearing boots. My nails probably needed ordinary trimming.

"I just got back from the gym," Shapiro said. "Just went three rounds with a middleweight." He mentioned a name I didn't recognize, and he raised one of his bushy eyebrows at me, as if he were John L. Lewis of the old United Mine Workers.

"I'm impressed," I said. I meant it.

He ducked and bobbed his head a little. "I'm in my fifties, and I can still hold my own. Top shape."

"Well," I said, "I always contended that a trial was like a boxing match. It's just the two of you in there, one on each side, and the best man usually comes out. You need to be in top shape."

He got right to it. "How would you defend this case, Gerry?"

"I don't know," I said. "I've talked to O.J. a couple of times, but he just tells me the same story each time. Never have tried to talk to him about the facts. Only know what I've read in the paper."

"I got the best people in the business," he said. "I got Dershowitz and Bailey. But I need another good trial man."

"Why?" I asked. "O.J. has you, doesn't he?"

"This is a big case," he said. "Too big for one man."

He asked me how many murder cases I had tried, and I told him twenty or thirty. Might have exaggerated a little. A man has a right to speak well of himself.

"Heard you never lost a criminal case."

"Well, that's right," I said. "But I remember when Frontier Airlines was bragging that it had never had a passenger death in its history. I stopped riding Frontier because I figured its time was about up."

Shapiro laughed.

"O.J. is a pain in the ass," he said. "Needs coddling all the time. Needs a baby-sitter. We have a psychiatrist up there with him. Can't leave him alone. Whoever I get will have to baby-sit him."

"I'm not a baby-sitter," I said. But I knew what Shapiro meant. People charged with crimes, guilty or innocent, can lose it in those vile concrete traps—especially a man like O.J., who always had whatever he wanted whenever he wanted it. And Shapiro understood that to keep one's client from diving into some deep psychotic hole is an important part of a lawyer's job. A client half crazed from fear can be of little help to his case on or off the witness stand. Despite his blasé front, I thought Shapiro cared about the man. A guy that can go three rounds with a big-name middleweight cannot come off like a sniveling pantywaist all concerned and teary-eyed for the accused.

"I've been thinking about getting Johnnie Cochran," he said. "What do you think of Johnnie Cochran?"

What was I supposed to say? I said, "I saw Johnnie on television, and I thought he was very articulate. Besides, as I understand it, this case may be a race case."

"A race case?" Shapiro said. "You got it right, man. This is the mother of all race cases."

CHAPTER 3

THE BIRTH OF THE RACE CARD

I KNEW IT was a race case from the moment I heard about it. As soon as Shapiro called, before I went out to see him, I phoned a trial lawyer friend of mine who had spent his life in inner-city cases where race is a daily issue. "What kind of a jury would you want for O.J.?" I asked, not wanting to go to L.A. and face a similar question from Shapiro without an answer.

"I'll tell you something, Gerry," he said. "This is a black man who they say killed a white woman. That scares the hell out of the black community because Afro-American history is different from ours. Blacks know that when a black man gets mixed up with a white woman there's trouble. In the old South—I can remember it when I was a boy—a black man might cross the street just to avoid meeting a white woman on the sidewalk. Those were the bad times, Gerry, and black people haven't forgotten. They remember the thousands of lynchings that resulted from the claimed rapes of white women. Mess with a white woman and white man's justice will string you up—that's the general consensus among black people."

"And what about white jurors?" I asked.

"From the defense's standpoint you can't depend on white jurors. Some white women, the younger ones, are more tolerant.

The older ones still carry around that fear that fathers instilled in them about being raped by some sex-crazed black man. And white men—well, I wouldn't want a white man on my jury. At least not one with a small penis." He laughed.

I hadn't had very much experience in trying race cases, and there was only one black kid in the whole town of Sheridan, Wyoming, when I grew up, plus a couple of blacks in Jackson Hole. But I'd had some blacks on my juries around the country, and I thought that in some ways we spoke the same language, one that ordinary people understood. I thought I could talk to African-Americans a lot better than a lot of white lawyers I knew who couldn't even talk to their own kind.

Now, on the couch with me in Michael Klein's living room, Shapiro kept wanting to talk about Johnnie Cochran. "This guy is good," he said. "This guy knows how to talk to blacks. Ever talk to a jury of black people, Gerry?"

"Yeah, more than once," I said. "I've always liked black juries. They're easy to talk to. Had a case in Louisana. I thought the blacks on the jury would hate the government. Decided to pack the jury with blacks. Got all blacks but two. I got fooled, not by the blacks, but by myself. I didn't realize the blacks would despise my white client more than they despised the government. The two whites hung the jury for me."

"That right?" he said, as if my story didn't surprise him in the least. "Well, Johnnie Cochran *can* talk to blacks."

Then, to try to save myself, I said, "And I had several blacks on my Chicago jury in my case against McDonald's. The foreman was black. The heavy hitter on the jury was a black woman—sat in the back and always nodded good signs to me. Loved me. Got fifty-two million dollars."

Didn't impress Shapiro. "That was a civil case, Gerry," he said.

"Yeah, I know," I argued, "but I had blacks on my jury in the Marcos case in New York, and I felt like the black woman up front was my best friend. Don't know how I would have gotten through the case without her. She had those kind eyes, and I could see she hurt along with me when the judge was gutting me. I think she saved me."

That didn't impress Shapiro, either. "That wasn't a murder case. But Cochran can get along with those black jurors. And we will have a lot of them in downtown L.A."

"Well, you better ask Johnnie to come aboard," I said. I was feeling disappointed.

Then he said it again. "You've always been my mentor, Gerry. How would you work with the other lawyers? I got the team," he said again. "The best."

"Well, I might just as well tell you how it is with me. I think you got too many trial lawyers already. If I'm in the case, I'd have to call the shots. I mean, trying a case is like painting a picture. If you give the brush to one painter and then another and then another, and they are all painting on the same canvas, you end up with a mess."

Shapiro was silent.

"Now, I operate in a collegial way with my own lawyers. We brainstorm. We work together. We worry together. We create together. One thing I'm good at—that's being able to sort the good ideas from the bad ones. I can take the best ideas of any group and use them—and take credit for it, too." Shapiro didn't even smile.

I knew I was writing my own one-way ticket back to Jackson Hole. Bob Shapiro was not going to let me be the master painter. He was going to be the art director, and the lawyers he chose were going to paint his picture. Well, I thought, I can understand that. If the tables had been turned, I wouldn't let some lawyer from Lord knows where, especially one from L.A., come in and tell me what to do in my case. I started to get up.

"Hey," he said, changing the mood. "We got this case won already. You don't have to paint any pretty pictures. We got this

Fuhrman, the cop that found the glove at O.J.'s. He's a fucking racist. Got the business on him."

"How did you do that?"

Shapiro didn't answer my question. "We got this guy cold," he said. "He planted the glove at O.J.'s house. This guy, Fuhrman, hates blacks. He talks about 'killing niggers.' He tried to get retirement from the L.A. police force for mental disability from having to 'fight niggers all the time.' And," he said very confidentially with a high little chortle, "the story is coming out in *The New Yorker*. It is coming out man! This case is over. Wait till Johnnie Cochran gets ahold of it."

"That's fine," I said. And I started to get up again to go. "Wait a minute," he said. "I want you to talk to O.J." We went into the adjoining room to a speakerphone.

"O.J., I got Spence here. Say hello to O.J., Gerry."

I said hello and asked how he was doing, and without any prompting, O.J. immediately launched into the same story he had already told me a couple of times before. Shapiro had heard it endlessly and wasn't listening. When we were finally off the phone, Shapiro said, "That's the way he is. He has one story. Like a broken record." But that's how innocent men sound, I thought.

During the trial I was asked many times about my invitation to join the Dream Team. The hosts on the talk shows wanted to know why I hadn't taken the case. Some were magnanimous in their claims that Gerry Spence was too honorable to ever defend someone who was as obviously guilty as O.J. Simpson. But early on I had taken the position that the man was probably innocent. I wanted to believe that; it was my nature to believe it. And I spoke out for the presumption of innocence we all enjoy as citizens in this great land. I kept warning the people that we couldn't try this man in the media. The media was receiving only the spoon-fed fare of the prosecution. We shouldn't let ourselves be used by the D.A. and the police.

"How would you feel if one day you woke up to find that your mind had been messed with—*your mind?* You woke up to find that your brains had been molded by the hands of the state so that an innocent man could be condemned? How would that feel? That's why we have to give the presumption of innocence to every person charged with a crime," I argued.

And the prosecutors on those talk shows always argued back: "The presumption of innocence is just a legal matter. It doesn't require you to really believe someone is innocent. It only requires you to apply the legal presumption when you test the state's case to determine if the state has proved its case beyond a reasonable doubt."

No, I argued back. "No. You can't believe one thing in your heart and come to an opposite conclusion. You cannot believe in your heart that the accused is guilty and give him the presumption of innocence. The head always supports the heart. Always." The arguments went on like that.

And when I was cornered and asked again why I hadn't joined the Dream Team, I used the metaphor of the ship's captain. If you have a ship in a storm, you can't have a lot of captains each trying to steer the ship in opposite directions. It takes a captain as well as a crew. I needed to be the captain. In plain language, if I was going to be responsible for O.J. Simpson's fate, I had to have the power to chart the course. It wasn't that I was too good or too moral to represent him. Sometimes people were disappointed to hear that.

When I got home, I told Imaging about the trip. "Shapiro is probably going to hire Johnnie Cochran," I said.

"I saw him on TV," she said. "I like him." She knew I was hurting.

"I didn't make the Super Bowl, honey."

She came over and put her arms around me. "Remember what your mother used to tell you," she said. "Which way the wind doth blow, that way is best."

. . .

I was riding along with my old friend Garvin Isaacs, that great trial lawyer from Oklahoma city, who has tried about every kind of case, civil or criminal, that ever came along. He is one of those men who suffer a deep burning anger against the pretty boys in power, the corporations, the rich—"the bullies," I call them—those who want to take advantage of people who have less power then they. You can see it in his eyes when he starts talking in that double-jointed Okie drawl of his. If Garvin is after you for hurting the little guy, you better get out of his way. It was several years after the case was over—May 23, 1997, to be exact—and Garvin and I were driving on Highway 40 headed for Amarillo, Texas. Garvin was at the wheel and we were talking about the O.J. case. Both the civil and the criminal trials were now history. I told Garvin about how I had gone to L.A. for my interview by Bob Shapiro, and how, looking back, Imaging had been right, and my mother as well. Once more I had been saved from taking a case that I would not have wanted to win, a case that, had I taken it, I would have tried to win. People don't seem to understand that even if the defendant is guilty, an honest trial lawyer has to try to win the case. All the time people come up to me and ask the question—you can see it coming a mile off—"Have you ever taken a case when you knew your client was guilty?"

Here's my stock answer: "If I say no, you'll think I'm a liar. If I say yes, you will think I'm a scoundrel. Which do you wish me to be, a liar or a scoundrel?" But if the person is sincere and wants to understand how the system works, I'm willing to take the argument on.

"Let's suppose we both know the defendant is guilty and we have the power of justice in our hands. Should we simply take the man out and hang him?" I ask.

"Well, no," the person answers.

"What should we do, then? Give him a trial?"

"Yes, of course."

"We should give him a trial and *then* hang him, right?" I ask.
No answer.

"If we give him a trial, should it be a fair trial?"

"Well, yes, of course."

"If it should be a fair trial, should we provide him with an attorney?"

"Yes," the person answers.

"But the attorney knows that his client is guilty. Knowing of his client's guilt, should the attorney try to lose the case? That is, knowing he is guilty, would it be permissible for the attorney to intentionally throw the case?"

"Well, no. That would be dishonest."

"Suppose then that the attorney, knowing his client is guilty, uses his best efforts to make sure that the prosecution proves the state's case against his client with honest and proper evidence. Should he do that?"

"Yes, of course. That's his job."

"And after he's done his job, suppose the jury finds there is a reasonable doubt, and the jury acquits a guilty man. What then?"

No answer.

"Should we blame the defense attorney for doing his job? Or should we blame the prosecutor for failing in his?"

Had I taken the O.J. case, perhaps I would have won it. Surely if I had won it I would have won it differently than the way in which the Dream Team prevailed. But in retrospect I was grateful that I had been saved from the case—by fate, by Shapiro, but not by choice.

I was reading aloud to Garvin from Jeffrey Toobin's excellent account of the Simpson case, *The Run of His Life*. Toobin, the legal correspondent for *The New Yorker*, reported how Shapiro really didn't want more high-profile lawyers, but O.J.'s friends wanted another big-time trial lawyer in the case. Toobin wrote that Shapiro was "incredulous that Simpson wanted Gerry Spence as his lawyer. . . . Out of a sense of obligation to his client, Shapiro went so far as to invite Spence to California for consultations about the case. . . . And, again as Shapiro surely predicted, Spence had no desire to play second fiddle to anyone. 'I have to be captain of the ship,' he told Shapiro."

"Garvin," I hollered, slamming Toobin's book down, "for the first time I realize what happened out in California that day I met with Bob Shapiro. He invited me out to California to quiet O.J. down. O.J. wanted *me*. Shapiro *had* to invite me out. That's why he put me on the phone with O.J. while I was there—to prove to O.J. he had fulfilled his promise to look me over."

"Right," Garvin said.

"He never intended to hire me in the first place."

"Right."

"Thank God he kept me out of the case," I said. "I'll have to call Bob Shapiro tomorrow and thank him."

"Right," Garvin said.

"And listen to this . . ." I picked Toobin's book back up. " 'Shapiro and the others prevailed upon Simpson to put aside his infatuation with Spence, and Cochran was hired officially on Monday, July 18.' "

"I'll be damned," Garvin said.

CHAPTER 4

RACE CARD FEVER

So EVERYBODY SEEMS to know now, and those in the know knew then, that from the beginning the Dream Team planned to play the race card. Endless angry words have been written about the contemptible strategy. The talk shows still capitalize on it today: the outrage, the failure of the justice system to have dignified such a defense in a court of law, the ceaseless criticism of Judge Ito, who permitted the defense, the relentless excoriation of the predominantly black jury that bought that unworthy defense. Indeed, Bob Shapiro has been pilloried without end for having authored it, and then for having denied that he had anything to do with it. One day, right there in court and in front of the jury, I saw Shapiro wearing the blue ribbon that Chief Willie Williams wanted folks to wear signifying their support of the LAPD. But that was late in the trial, and by then Shapiro was fighting his own battle. He was no longer the captain of the ship. There'd been a mutiny and Shapiro was trying to hang on to the deck in the storm.

Before the case was over, both sides had played the race card for all it was worth—the prosecution hardly less subtly than the defense. Both sides wrapped themselves in the American flag and denied they were playing into the race issue. But race *was* the issue, from the beginning, and those who never understood it, who never respected its power, paid the price in the jury's verdict, and those who denied that race was the issue could never hope to understand the verdict.

People pointed their finger at the defense and cried foul: "The defense played the race card." Marcia Clark railed about it in court. She claimed the defense had leaked the Fuhrman issue to the media "in a very *hideous* and damaging way. They have attempted to speak of Mark Fuhrman with the most vicious of allegations concerning racism, one of the most inflammatory charges that could possibly be made. [my italics]" I thought her adjectives remarkable. But before the case could conclude, an even more phenomenal set of epithets, fueled by Clark's bottomless scorn, would be turned against Fuhrman himself. But for the moment she was attacking Johnnie Cochran. "The defendant is playing a race card while denying they're playing a race card," she cried, "a very subtle game, but a very dangerous one for the People, because the officer who found the key piece of damaging evidence they have attempted to discredit in the most *hideous* of ways." That word again. [and again my italics]

The race card. The defense was playing the race card, and it was dirty business. I heard it up and down the halls of the courthouse during the recesses. "What do you make of the race card, Gerry?" A dozen media people came up to me and asked the question, and they asked it of each other. "What do you make of it?" they kept wanting to know, as if they were in shock. Some had those blank, inquiring faces. Some seemed angry, some bored. But that's how conventional wisdom is born—a roomful of reporters and TV anchorpersons interviewing each other in the hallway at recesses, forming their consensus. Then the talking people rush back and tell it to the listening people in those short sound bites, and the listening people in Apache, Oklahoma, and Newark, New Jersey, hear what the people in the halls of the courthouse have come up with—the damnable race card has been played—and suddenly we have a national consensus.

Few in the media want to hang out on a limb by themselves. That's why the consensus is necessary. If the reporter from one newspaper reports his story with a spin that's too far off from the spin of the others, his boss wonders why his reporter didn't get it right. But if there's an informal consensus of sorts, everyone is safe. So the nearly all-white media formed the consensus that the defense, playing to that predominantly black jury, had dared throw race in their faces. And after the consensus had been formed—and it didn't take long, maybe ten or fifteen minutes in the hall during a couple of recesses—some of the media people would come up to me and ask questions like, "If you had taken this case, Gerry, would you have resorted to a sleazy tactic like that?" But they didn't have time to hear my answer. It took more than six seconds.

I remember sitting that July afternoon with Shapiro on the couch, I in my new coat and he in his threadbare jeans. I was wondering how the defense intended to prove that the bloody glove had been planted by the cops in Rockingham. The proof, of course, was that the cop who claimed he discovered the glove was a racist. Yes, racist cops can plant gloves. But you don't have to be a racist to plant a glove. On the other hand, the fact that the cop is a racist doesn't mean that he planted the glove. That's true, but it's more likely that the glove would be planted against a black man by a racist like Fuhrman than by, say, a black Methodist minister. The arguments go on like that.

Who the players are is often a relevant issue for the jury to consider in sorting out the truth. In the O.J. case, the prosecution wanted the jury to know *who* the defendant was. According to the prosecution, he was a wife beater. That was his history. Therefore, we were to conclude he was more likely to have killed his wife than if he were one who brought her pizza and beer in bed every night. We want to know *who* the witnesses are in every case, what their backgrounds are. If the witness is a convicted felon, we want to know it. The convicted felon, we believe, is more likely to lie than the ordinary citizen. And *who* is the cop who found this suspicious glove lying there so fortuitously in the yard of this black defendant? If the cop who found the glove is an out-and-out rotten-cored racist, we want to know. The jury has the job of assessing the credibility of all the witnesses. The information as to *who* the witness is, his pertinent history, is relevant to that inquiry.

At the time Bob Shapiro was putting his finger on Fuhrman as a racist and suggesting that he had planted the glove at the Rockingham estate, the blood and DNA evidence that created such a convincing case against Simpson had not yet been presented by the state. What did Shapiro know about Fuhrman? It was all in his personnel records. In the late seventies Fuhrman had sought to leave the force. He was tired of dealing with the "low-class" people he had to face and fight every day. He claimed he had to be "violent just to exist." His lawyers sought a disability pension for the man, and brought an action against the City of Los Angeles Fire and Police Pension System, asserting that the stress of his work as a cop was so great that "I have the urge to kill people that upset me." He was talking about blacks. He explained to an examining psychiatrist, Dr. Ronald R. Koegler, that he could no longer stay in the marines because he got tired of "these Mexicans and niggers, volunteers and they would tell me they weren't going to do something." Evaluating Fuhrman, Koegler wrote, "However, his overall production is unbalanced at this point because of the greater proportion of time spent trying to make the 'big arrest.'"

Indeed, Fuhrman had a violent past. He bragged about the choke holds he used to subdue suspects, and he said he would break their hands, their arms, their faces, even their legs if necessary. Shapiro claimed the evidence revealed that Fuhrman was the kind who woke up and told his wife, "I'm going to kill some niggers this morning." So what does an honest defense attorney do with this evidence? Bury it in a file somewhere? He does the same thing that the prosecution does with its evidence that Simpson was into habitual domestic violence. Both sides throw everything they have into the pot and let the jury sort it out.

Put it another way: If Shapiro had an all-white jury and presented evidence of Fuhrman's racism, would it be the same race card as when he presented the same evidence to a black jury? I know very honorable defense attorneys who claim it would have been malpractice for the defense not to present the race issue revealed in Fuhrman's file. In a trial, you take the witnesses as you find them. The defense didn't make a racist of Fuhrman any more than the prosecution made a wife beater out of Simpson. Facts are facts. When the defense revealed Fuhrman's racist propensities in support of its theory that Fuhrman planted the glove, the defense, to some, played the race card. When the prosecution presented the facts about Simpson's inclination toward domestic violence in support of its theory that he murdered his wife, the prosecution, to some, played into the prejudice and loathing we hold against men who abuse women. It depends, as it were, upon whose ox is being gored.

But there was more: Joseph Britton was a black man whom Fuhrman had shot during Britton's robbery of a man at an automatic teller machine. Britton claimed in his later suit that Fuhrman not only used racial epithets in the course of the arrest but had dropped a knife at the plaintiff's feet to justify the shooting. Britton insisted Fuhrman shot him without cause. Fuhrman himself admitted that "some of [Britton's] wounds came from my weapon." But Fuhrman claimed that a few feet south of where Britton lay the cops found a large butcher knife. Britton allegedly had been holding the knife while hiding in the bushes, the reason, I suppose, the cops shot him full of holes. I have trouble visualizing an ATM robber running around brandishing a large butcher knife. Be that as it may, Britton hired himself a lawyer and sued Fuhrman. The first trial against Fuhrman ended in a hung jury. When the Simpson case took the headlines, the city settled the Britton case, presumably to keep this damaging evidence from the media. So what does a defense attorney do with this information?

The defense begins to put things together this way: You just happen to have a black client charged with murdering his wife, who just happens to be white. And you also just happen to have a racist cop, who just happens to find a bloody glove that just happens to match the other bloody glove at the murder scene. The racist cop was alone when he supposedly found the glove just lying there in plain sight. The racist cop has been charged previously with planting evidence. So what do you do with all of this? Do you say forget it, man, I'm not playing that race card?

Yet I never thought Simpson's guilt or innocence turned on whether Fuhrman did or didn't plant the glove. Fuhrman, a cop looking for the big arrest, could have planted the glove—and Simpson still could have been guilty. The blood evidence alone seemed to attest to his guilt. Yet I always thought it strange that the matching glove just happened to show up at the right place at the right time. Life usually isn't like that. And I'd been around long enough to know that some cops plant evidence. It's not because they are inherently evil; it's because they want to win. They reason, "What harm is a little lie compared to a bloody murder? If we have to spike the evidence a little, what harm if we get another criminal off the streets? They kill and we get shit for dropping a knife or a glove someplace. We're doing the citizens a favor. And all the thanks we get are investigations brought against us by our own department and lawsuits brought against us by a bunch of shyster lawyers looking for a quick buck."

Fuhrman may have been a cop who wanted to make the big arrest. What cop wouldn't? What lawyer isn't drawn to the big case? What judge shuns the chance to sit in a celebrity trial? If we enjoy no glory of our own, it's easy to criticize people who have a chance at it. We don't admit it, but it's true—we all want it.

Then on July 18, 1994, *The New Yorker* published Jeffrey Toobin's article, "An Incendiary Defense," in which the world was told that Simpson's defense team intended to float "a new and provocative theory. Those conversations [with leading members of the defense team] revealed that they plan to portray [Mark Fuhrman] as a rogue cop who, rather than solving the crime, framed an innocent man."

Fuhrman's racism, now widely publicized through *The New Yorker* and the ripple effect of the media, had become the axle around which the whole defense seemed to rotate. Then suddenly the defense was faced with the blood evidence. The DNA. Still, Simpson's possible guilt didn't necessarily mean that the glove wasn't planted by Fuhrman. The investigating officers like to argue that two or a dozen or fourteen other officers (the number has varied from time to time and from witness to witness) were at Bundy *before* Fuhrman arrived, and not one cop saw two gloves at the scene. But how do you explain the unlikely scenario that the killer lost not one, but *both* gloves—one at Bundy and the other at Rockingham. That a whole army of cops saw only one glove at the scene before Fuhrman arrived doesn't mean much. The second glove could have been in the bushes or elsewhere out of plain sight. Officers may or may not have been looking at the scene for specific evidence. I doubt that anyone said to any officer, "Hey, Officer, be sure and note whether there are one or two gloves here. We need to record this fact very carefully because it's going to be claimed down the line that Fuhrman stole one and planted it at Rockingham." People aren't counting gloves. People are looking at the horror of butchered bodies, the gore, the blood all over. People are fascinated with blood and bodies, not gloves.

Before the blood evidence had smacked Shapiro in the face, how could any defense attorney, confronted by the unvarying insistence of his client's innocence, conclude that his client was guilty and, therefore, the possibility of a planted glove should simply be forgotten? At that point in the case Shapiro could hardly be criticized for his exuberance when, on the day *The New Yorker* article appeared, just three days after my visit with Shapiro, he called F. Lee Bailey and said, "It's over. I won the case."

This case was so loosely investigated, so scattered, the evidence so played with and manipulated, that one could put any spin on the case that might strike one's fancy. Who saw what when is one of the mysteries of this case. Three years after the crime, Mark Fuhrman, in his book, *Murder in Brentwood,* recalled that up in O.J.'s bathroom he and his partner, Brad Roberts, found an open knife box bearing the Swiss Army logo—one designed to hold one of those larger knives. "Where is the box?" Fuhrman asked. "Where is the knife that went into that box?" Fuhrman suggested that the stab wounds more closely matched those that could have been made by a large Swiss Army knife than the weapon described by the prosecution. In fact, he argued that none of the stab wounds were as deep as the 6⅝-inch blade on the German stiletto, the type of knife the prosecution theorized was used in the stabbing. How, Fuhrman asked, could such a blade be used in a violent stabbing attack without leaving at least one six-inch wound out of nearly thirty?

In his book Fuhrman claimed to have found blood smears on the light switch and various other locations upstairs, and his book presented his original notes in which he recorded the finding of a bloody fingerprint on the gate at Bundy that no one else saw and that was later apparently washed away. He says that Brad Roberts found freshly washed clothes in the washing machine that were described by Roberts "then and now" as black sweats. So why didn't anyone else see any of this? Why didn't the officers, who had already completed their searches, find the knife that Simpson purchased at Ross Cutlery and that was later retrieved by Gerald Uelmen, the law professor on the defense team, from inside a vanity cabinet in Simpson's bedroom, and which purportedly ended up in the secret envelope that Uelmen delivered to the judge? What was there to see, and who could or couldn't have seen it? Was the LAPD a covey of incompetents, or was Fuhrman lying? In the end, either way one takes Fuhrman—as a crooked racist who planted the glove or as an honest racist who didn't, but who found a lot of other evidence that never saw the light of day in the prosecution's case—Fuhrman begins to cause the bell of reasonable doubt to at least tinkle a little.

I met Fuhrman when I was invited by his attorney, Robert Tourtelot, to dinner one night at Tourtelot's home. When I arrived with my friend John Gibson of NBC, there, to my surprise, stood Fuhrman, a couple inches taller than I, and I'm over six foot two. He was lean, muscular, and, I thought, handsome. He had just given his testimony in court and his exposure as a perjurer concerning the "N-word" had not yet been developed in Bailey's cross-examination. At that point I thought he had survived Bailey's well-shouted cross pretty well. Despite Bailey's unrelenting frontal attack, he had remained calm, like a matador who watches the bull charge—*ver llegar,* as the Spanish say. I thought he had Bailey under control. I admired his demeanor on the stand. This was the kind of officer, if you were in a tight spot—and he was in a tight spot up there on the witness stand—who would keep his head and come through. He was friendly, polite, at times funny. He seemed like an Eagle Scout with a sense of humor. It was hard for me then to see him as a man who was going to get up and "kill some niggers this morning."

What I didn't realize when I heard Fuhrman's testimony that day was that he had lied, and lied intentionally, this placid, cool killer of the truth. If he would lie on the witness stand, if he was brimming with hate, if he could look at Bailey with those calm eyes—like a skunk examining a garter snake he's about to swallow—if he could subdue Bailey and hide the stench of his racism behind the deodorant of the oleaginous cop, ought not the jury be told about it? If he was quite willing to lie under oath on the witness stand, namely to proclaim to the whole world that in the last ten years he never used the so-called N-word—a word so horrid we are all afraid to even whisper it—ought not the jury know who he was? If he would lie about the N-word, wouldn't he plant a glove? Wouldn't he lie about whatever he needed to lie about to make the big arrest, and of a black man to boot?

During the trial Marcia Clark argued, and most of the talking heads supported her, that Fuhrman's racism was irrelevant. Irrelevant to what? The question was, did he or did he not plant the glove? The prosecution screamed that there was no evidence that he planted the glove and that therefore evidence of his racism was irrelevant. But that sets us to tail chasing. Suppose there had been a window washer next door who said he happened to be up on a second-story scaffolding and looked down in time to see this cop drop something back there by the air conditioner that the cop removed, say, from his lunchpail. Would this evidence make the racism of Fuhrman any more or less relevant in this case? If Fuhrman had testified that he shaves with Burma Shave every morning and the defense wanted to introduce evidence that Burma Shave hasn't been manufactured for twenty years, such evidence would be inadmissible against Fuhrman to prove he's a liar because the rule is that you cannot impeach a witness on a wholly irrelevant issue because sometimes honest people lie about irrelevant matters. But it seems to me that Fuhrman's racism, in an obvious race case, clearly bore some relevance to Fuhrman's credibility as a witness.

The wild furor of the media and of the pure white community over Judge Ito's ruling that allowed evidence of Fuhrman's racism to be introduced, itself became a kind of reverse racism. That Judge Ito was taken in by Johnnie Cochran and had made a despicable ruling became the standard wisdom of the nation. The judge was a poor judge, people said. The people said it because the pundits said it. The pundits said it because that view reflected their consensus gathered up in the hallway of the courthouse. The judge let the defense, those evil, amoral shysters, play the race card! Something's terribly wrong with the justice system in America. Charles Grodin said so twenty times a week. Geraldo Rivera said so as well. You can hear it today from the lips of schoolchildren. *Racism.*

In retrospect we tend to forget that this was a race case from the beginning. When Simpson left his first wife, a black woman, and took a blond white woman in her stead, the race card was played. Involuntarily or not, he took on a racial issue as part of his daily life. Everywhere he walked in public with this beautiful blonde, the race issue was advertised and reinvigorated. The bigots stared and mumbled under their breaths. White men made their nasty little remarks about the black male, whom they viewed as unfair sexual competition. Black women glared. I am not criticizing interracial marriages. People ought to be able to marry anyone they damn please, black, white, or chartreuse. Men can marry mates who shave every morning so far as I'm concerned. The law, the preachers, the racists, the women haters and men haters, the bigots—none of them ought to be able to tell us whom we should marry. Marriage is our business.

But when we marry anybody other than the girl or boy next door in a purely conventional relationship, we have to expect a social response. We still live in an often unabashedly racist country, a country that staggered under the whip of slavery for nearly 250 years. The scars of one of history's most venal holocausts still mar the hide of our nation. When O.J. married Nicole, it provided the open bigots, the secret bigots, the unintentional bigots, the subconscious bigots—I have now covered millions of citizens in this country—the fuel to ignite even the most latent racist feelings that still endured across the land.

Many black people are undeniably racists as well. Shouldn't they have equal rights? In the end, they have more cause than whites to be racist. My ancestors came to this country as free dirt farmers. Theirs came over in slave ships. And when the embittered portion of the white community cried out that the race card had been played by Johnnie Cochran, well, if he was guilty of it, he wasn't alone.

The nation has just begun to emerge from these racist woods, "so dark and deep." And at times I fear we have sneaked back into these less than "lovely" woods, and this business of political correctness may have silenced the wrong people, namely us. No one dares mumble an errant thought about racism unless it has stood the test of political correctness. No longer can we speak out, even wrongly, even as racists, and receive back the response of those we hurt and thereby learn hard lessons. We hurt them silently instead, insidiously. We gather together in secret groups to mouth racist comments. Then we deny it all on television. Carefully we choose our public words. We say one thing and think another. We have become liars of the worst order, we racists who never speak the truth about our racist feelings. Others may have such feelings. But self-righteously we proclaim that we do not. Nor, we pretend, does this great country of ours harbor racist sentiments. Yet this is a racist nation, and although we proclaim our disgust and dismay, and speak out against our latent biases, in the end, we are what we do, and, I would contend, we are what we publicly dare not say.

I haven't forgotten the words of my lawyer friend who reminded me that, in America, for over two centuries, when a black man was suspected of taking a white woman, the traditional response of the dominant white power structure has been to "lynch the nigger." Throughout American history this theme has been persistent. In the Lincoln-Douglas debates less than 150 years ago, the putrid message was spoken aloud from the public podium. "If you Black Republicans think that the negro ought to be on a social equality with your wives and daughters while you drive the team, you have a perfect right to do so," hollered Stephen Douglas, running for the presidency of the United States. "Those of you who believe that the negro is your equal . . . of course will vote for Mr. Lincoln."

When in 1860 the Republicans placed a constitutional amendment on the ballot to enfranchise blacks, other Democratic orators cited, "If you want to vote 'cheek by jowl' with a large 'buck nigger,' " if you want to support "a party that says 'a nigger is better than an Irishman,' " if you are "ready to divide your patrimony with the negro . . . vote for the Republican candidate." The church usually joined in. "If you are tame enough to submit," declared South Carolina's Baptist clergyman James Furman, "an abolition preacher will be at hand to consummate the marriage of your daughters to black husbands."

Our racial history has been persistently vile and ugly. Although we are recovering, we have not yet recovered. To rid ourselves of racism is like one trying to rid himself of the herpes virus: He can treat it when it breaks out. He can go on for months without notice of it. But the virus lurks nonetheless, and at an unexpected moment it will suddenly appear as an ugly cold sore on the lip.

Yet when O.J. Simpson was charged with the murder of his wife, few white people gave any consideration as to how the charge against a black hero would play in the black community, both in L.A. and across the land. Whites still considered O.J. the corporate son, one of their own, despite his black skin. But black history is different than white. Whites remember Washington and Jefferson as the sacred fathers of the nation. Most African-Americans remember Washington as the owner of three hundred slaves who rotted in squalid huts and labored their lives away for his profit, and Jefferson as the theoretical abolitionist, who proclaimed that all men are created equal while he bred black children on his plantation like farm animals. We forget. We want to forget. Yet African-Americans can no more forget their holocaust than Jewish people can forget theirs.

Whites view the Supreme Court of the United States as that venerable body that protects their guaranteed rights as citizens. Yet many blacks remember that a slave-holding chief Justice Roger Taney, appointed by the slave-holding President Andrew Jackson to succeed the slave-holding Chief Justice John Marshall, would one day decree, from the highest court of the land, that a black man, Dred Scott, was merely property, like a sack of potatoes or a garden hoe.

African-American history is, indeed, different, and the state's complaint filed against a black icon who had achieved success in that unattainable, far-off white world, a hero charged with the murder of a white woman, awakened once again over three hundred years of obdurate horror. To the black community it was a return of the same old nightmare. As paranoid as one might argue the misconception to be, a majority of blacks nevertheless believed that once more the collective white posse had gathered—and that the mob was going to lynch O.J. Simpson. I say the race card in the Simpson case was played when the first slave ship docked in Jamestown in 1619.

I remember sitting in the NBC studio in L.A. early one morning waiting to appear on the *Today* show. A black cameraman and I were the sole occupants of the studio at a little past 3:00 A.M. The day before, Carl Douglas of the defense team had concluded his cross-examination of Ron Shipp, a former LAPD officer and a longtime friend of Simpson's. Shipp had testified concerning a conversation in which Simpson had allegedly told Shipp that he had dreamed of murdering Nicole—that's why he was afraid to take the polygraph test. Indeed, if our dreams are admissible against us, all but the permanently comatose would eventually go down as criminals. Douglas's cross-examination was hostile and mean. According to Douglas, Shipp was trying to make himself famous, to enhance a stalled acting career. Douglas asserted that Shipp was lying because Simpson was already in bed when Shipp's conversation with Simpson supposedly took place. He continued to lay the whip on Shipp, attempting to portray him as a drunk and a lecher. Douglas's cross, I thought makes the lawyer look like a hateful hatchet man. I had said something like that on one of the talk shows the night before—that this was the kind of cross-examination I would hold up to young lawyers as the epitome of poor lawyering. One does not attack an ostensibly nice, quiet man by trying to make him out to be a womanizer and a fool, even if he might be one. Certainly these things were irrelevant, and to pursue them came across as bullying. None of us like bullies—juries included. The dynamic is simple: If juries don't like the attorney, they are likely not to like his client, either.

At the NBC studios that morning I was being hooked up to a mike and an earpiece was being poked in my ear. "What did you think of Douglas's cross-examination of Shipp?" I asked the cameraman, who happened to be black.

"I thought it was wonderful," he said.

"Are you serious?"

"Absolutely."

"I thought he was an insufferable bully," I said.

"I didn't see it that way," the cameraman said. "That Shipp had no business turning on his friend like that."

"You thought Shipp had a beating coming from Douglas?" I asked.

"You bet. There isn't a black mother in America who wouldn't be proud to have Douglas as her son," the cameraman said. As he saw it, a brother had turned on a brother. Racism? Whose racism? At that moment I began to clearly understand the whites and blacks, each viewing the case through innocent eyes, saw a different case.

And as for Christopher Darden, it's not politically correct to suggest that he was the prosecution's choice because he was black—in other words, the state's race card. There were over nine hundred deputy D.A.'s in Los Angeles, and Marcia Clark nominated Darden, who was ultimately approved by Garcetti? I asked the cameraman what he thought of Darden.

"He's the state's nigger." The cameraman was a decent man, a black man whose experience as an African-American dictated a different view of the players in the case, a view few of the white pundits, the white media, the white legal community, the white power structure, ever understood. Darden understood it but denied it. Clark never understood it. Instead she complained that Johnnie Cochran "went around telling reporters that we'd hired a token black man. Even after the dirty tricks I'd seen him pull during the voir dire, I would still have believed Johnnie had more class than that." But no one has yet to explain what rare, unmatchable qualities Darden possessed that qualified him to try the case of the century, except to offset the black Johnnie Cochran on the other side. Yet no one but a black man, a Cochran, dared say so publicly.

Some of the writers who covered the case liked to present themselves as unsullied by racism as any newborn. Yet they did not shy back from their own racism, not one whit, when they complained that the state blundered by failing to file the case in the whiter Santa Monica. There, they cry, the state could have avoided the black jury that tried O.J. "Dumb," one writer wrote, "for the D.A. to file the case downtown where he was sure to draw a predominantly black jury." Other pundits echoed this proposition, which soon became the conventional wisdom of the case. White commentators were really saying, "If we could have gotten an all-white jury, we could have convicted Simpson." The furtive argument they never dared make was the racist argument that a white jury would be less prejudiced against the white police and more prejudiced against the black defendant and his black lead lawyer. The hidden assumptions were also that a white jury would be brighter—that blacks are ignorant, prejudiced, vindictive, and racist themselves. Indeed, how could one argue that this was not a race case from the beginning?

I have admired few things undertaken by District Attorney Gil Garcetti, but that he did not take the case to Santa Monica in order to get a whiter jury seems laudable. Some of his critics imply that he was a political animal, that he obviously thought he might lose the black vote by filing in the white courthouse. Others suggested that if he filed in Santa Monica and a white jury returned a guilty verdict against a black man there would be a replay of the Rodney King riots, and that Garcetti wanted to avoid being blamed for the melée. Still others argued that he wanted to be downtown where he could "micromanage" the case and exploit its mammoth publicity to his political advantage. And finally, others, less cruel, said he simply made a mindless blunder. But even the prosecution is entitled to the presumption of innocence.

The case, by its nature, was so racial from the beginning that the purest of pure nonracists, Robert Shapiro himself, thought he should have a black man to talk to a black jury. Indeed, he chose Johnnie Cochran over me, presumably for just that reason. And the purest of pure nonracists on the prosecution side made a similar decision based on race and tapped Chris Darden. Even Darden, the black man who hated racism, said, "I looked around the room and realized how white they looked. All these white people and me. How would that look to the homies in South Central: one brother surrounded by all this whiteness, sticking out like a scratch on a new Mercedes? Damn, I thought, I really am going to pay hell for this." Fuhrman, whose racist views became obvious in the end, had his own comments about Darden's racism: "If a racist is someone obsessed with race, whose perception is clouded by the color of a person's skin, and who sees himself as a member of a racial group first and a human being second, then Chris Darden could be called a racist."

And one wonders about the racism of a man who displays his contempt for his innocent brothers and sisters of lighter skin. In his book, *In Contempt,* Darden wrote, "When you look at me, you don't see the remnants of slavery—light skin, thin lips, pinched nose. You see an African face. I am proud of that."

When it came time to deal with the race issue, few wanted to face it or comment on it publicly. No one except Johnnie Cochran, in his arguments, and the jury, in its verdict—and that, in the eyes of the white community, made them the racists. Robert Shapiro, in the end, tried to cover himself from the racist fallout by donning that blue ribbon on his lapel to show that the wearer thought the cops—I suppose even the racist cops—were pristine public servants. And Shapiro took to the media right after the Fuhrman fiasco had blown up in the courtroom: "My preference," he told the mob of cameras, "was that race was not an issue in this case and should not be an issue in this case, and I'm sorry from my personal point of view that it has become an issue in this case." At another time Shapiro said, "Not only did we play the race card, we dealt it from the bottom of the deck." But the deck had been in Shapiro's hands from the beginning. Many accused Shapiro of attempting to ingratiate himself with the white society of West Los Angeles. Yet Johnnie Cochran was ingratiating himself with the black jury and the black community, while Chris Darden was worried about being banished by "the brothers," and Marcia Clark through it all thought she could handle black women, although black women in the state's focus group thought she was "a bitch." So what we finally smell here, more or less, is the same old racial stench that has polluted the air of this country for over two centuries. It just found its way out of the sewer once more in the Simpson case.

Perhaps Johnnie Cochran said it best in open court: "I just want to say something about this 'race card,' " he began. "I've been trying cases for a very long time, both civil and criminal throughout this country, and anybody who doesn't believe that when you have a case like this, when you have a case of murder, that race [doesn't] play a part in everything . . . these jurors know it. Everybody knows it. . . . Race plays a part in everything in America."

Hosts on television shows devoted to the Simpson case have a favorite question they like to ask their guests: Why, they ask, has the Simpson case permeated the hearts of every man, woman, and child of every class, of every race, in America? Why are we obsessed with this case? Why do we sit and argue, and line up for hours to call in to the talk shows? Why have Geraldo Rivera and Charles Grodin and Larry King and the endless parade of others taken to this case like addicts to a pail of crack? The obvious reasons—the ones we can talk about easily—include the celebrity status of Simpson, the Hollywood atmosphere of the stars, the decadence, the blood, the horror. All of that makes for powerful drama, an American tragedy greater than anything that Theodore Dreiser could ever have imagined, the kind that America loves:

another fallen hero, another exposure of the very traits we are most afraid of in ourselves, the exploding violence, the players being led around by their genitalia. We can see the suffering, and it is not we who are suffering. We can see the violence, and it is theirs, not ours, thank God. We can see the decadence, and it is theirs in reality. Ours is only in our pornographic dreams.

Yet people do not want to admit to themselves or to each other that the underlying hook of this case is racism. Americans are no longer permitted to have public racial feelings. We have them, but they are suppressed. America is populated with closet racists, and most do not even know they are in the closet. Yet the sentiments are there as real and as potent as any other feeling, and when they are repressed long enough, they are released in unpredictable ways. Sometimes they explode in freeway shootings. Sometimes they slip out the mouths of famous athletes during an unguarded moment on the golf course. But the need to talk about race, to protest, to strike out, to hate in one form or another, persists, and, like endlessly expanding gasses in the alimentary tract, it must find its release.

The O.J. Simpson case provides the instrument of relief. It tells us a good deal more about ourselves than about Simpson. We need not talk about our feelings of racism. We can cry about how Cochran injected the race card into the case and how Judge Ito let him do it. We need not recognize our own racial feelings. We can rage over the failure of the justice system. We need not proclaim our superiority; we can, instead, point our fingers at the black jurors and call them witless and fools to have been taken in. The Simpson case became the new, acceptable weapon by which the race war can be fought again on a politically correct battlefield, fought out in the open, but under the cover of our endless verbiage about the evidence in the case, the law, the lawyers, the witnesses, the jurors, and the judge. The case exposes the corroded hearts of the people who have claimed their hearts are pure. It exposes our hearts. Alas, the case reveals that we, the bigots who cry foul, are at last the most unforgivable racists of all. We are all racist. Blacks and whites. All of us.

God damn it.

CHAPTER 5

BIG GIRL

THE O.J. SIMPSON case installed voyeurism as America's leading daytime sport. Collectively, America could not stop itself from
reveling in the pain, the disgrace, the shame of it all. We are all
voyeurs in these late days of civilization, hooked up mindlessly, as
we are, to our screens. The networks, of course, were heavily invested in the case, including NBC, which had hired me to consult
and to comment on-air. When I showed up for my first day, I joined
the horde who had crowded into that trailer town across from the
courtroom in downtown L.A. It reminded me of the gold rush days
in Wyoming when a tent town was thrown up at Atlantic City near
South Pass and ten thousand scraggly miners charged in to strike
it rich. In L.A. it was the gold rush of the media, the exposure that
made unknowns as common as old shoes, that took ordinary faces,
even homely faces, and pushed them into our faces on the screen
and made them celebrities overnight. Think of it: You can have a
camera aimed at you, and you can look into the lens, and you can
talk to the lens, and you are suddenly looking right into the faces
of a million, maybe even ten million Americans. They are sitting
in the kitchen eating Cheerios, they are pulling on their shorts, or
they are primping or sitting on the toilet, gawking absently though
the open bathroom door at the TV screen, and you are talking to

them. Some just hear the voice. Most don't really listen. They are thinking about the boss they hate, or the pain they feel in the lower back, or how they would like to make it with Mary Lou next door. But if you have an agenda, you then have a brief chance to dump it out there to the people, a few chopped-up words at a time.

So I went to the courtroom to report and comment for NBC. I wasn't their favorite commentator. I didn't know how to speak in those precisely measured sound bites. As Imaging said, I tended to run off at the mouth too much. I was a storyteller. I remember that after I tried the Randy Weaver case, Tom Brokaw came to Ruby Ridge in Idaho, where all of the killing had taken place. Brokaw and I were walking along—the cameramen running backward in front of us, you've seen them, these men looking silly running backward—and Brokaw says something like, "This Randy Weaver must be a pretty dangerous fellow, guns and all. Didn't the feds have a right to be afraid of him?"

"Well, Tom," I say, "do you see that hole over there?"

Brokaw looks. "What hole?" he asks.

"That hole right there. Can't you see it?" He stops and looks where I'm pointing. Before he can say there's no hole there, I say, "Now, Tom, you see that rabbit in the hole?"

He's starting to catch on. He nods.

"That little bunny wouldn't hurt a flea. Not you, not me. But if you reach down into his hole and try to grab him by the ears and pull him out, he will bite you."

"Right," Brokaw says.

"And that's the way it was with Randy Weaver. Leave that rabbit alone and nothin' happens, to you, the feds, to anybody."

"I see," Brokaw says, with that slightly sardonic inflection that always means more than it says.

And that's the way it was with me on television. I wasn't made to utter those crisp, well-worded sentences. I like to tell stories, to think in pictures, to have a good time with the images, and that cuts into precious time the networks can sell to Toyota and Prudential. So I never made it big as an expert for the evening news. NBC preferred my friend Ira Reiner, the white-haired former Los Angeles D.A., in my judgment, the dean of the TV experts, a man who looked right and talked right and sounded right and, in fact, was and is right. He knew how to talk to Brokaw. He could make sense out of something in a few terse sentences, while I would be wanting to talk about everything from bucking horses to house wrens just to make a simple point. I mean, you have to give the TV people a break. If you're selling potatoes, you don't have much patience with someone who wants to spill half a ton on the ground while you're trying to load the truck.

I remember my first day in Judge Ito's courtroom. First you had to go through security. They checked everyone out pretty well, metal detector and all. Then you had to show your courtroom pass to the marshals at the courtroom door. Mine was a media pass issued to NBC. And when I entered the courtroom my first day, there he was—Bob Shapiro. He came rushing over, all smiles and friendly, the arm around the shoulder. O.J. saw me as well, and he stood up from counsel table and waved and hollered my name, and suddenly I was a big shot with a media badge, all the people staring, nodding, my buckskin jacket with the fringes that Imaging made for me casting me as someone who just blew in from the sticks. We all have to market who we are or want people to think we are. The jacket, the black Levis, the boots, and the black turtleneck were my uniform. I found out that if I didn't wear it, people felt let down. "Where's your buckskin jacket, Gerry?" they invariably asked. And you could see the disappointment. "I met Gerry Spence today, but he didn't have his jacket on." What would you think if you met the pope and he was wearing a baby-blue sport coat?

"Come on in," Shapiro said. "I want to take you back to meet Judge Ito." The bushy eyebrow that you could chin yourself on. I liked Shapiro, still do. He liked me.

I was about to say that would be an honor when this big nofoolin', all-business female marshal interrupted us. She was a decent sort who was there to do a tough job. But some of the media people had already given her a bad time, and because she wasn't wearing the latest frills and was obviously in pretty good physical shape, they had pinned a moniker on her: When she was out of earshot they called her Big Girl.

"You will have to leave," the marshal told me. She had a gun, short hair, and the kind of half-snarl that went with the territory. How would *you* look after wrestling a couple hundred crazies from the media a half-dozen times a day?

"Why do I have to leave?" I asked. "I have a pass." I motioned to my NBC badge. On any ordinary day it would have been good enough to get you into the Vatican.

"You have to leave because you have violated the rules."

"I've only been here thirty seconds. How many rules have I violated?"

"You have been talking to counsel in this case, and there is a rule against a member of the media talking to any attorney in this case inside this courtroom." She was nearly as tall as I, as blond as I used to be, and she wore flat-heeled shoes that were shined, and I didn't think I ought to cross her.

"What are you talking about?" Shapiro interjected. "This is Gerry Spence. He is the best trial lawyer in America, and I am taking him back to meet the judge." He pushed by her and I followed him. I looked back at her, and raised my eyebrows and shrugged apologetically as if to say, "What can I do?"

Inside Judge Ito's small chambers, Shapiro immediately introduced me to His Honor. The judge was very gracious, said that he had seen me on TV and had read a book or two of mine, and a couple of other nice things, and he offered me a chair. I sat down. I told the judge that this was a great opportunity for all America to see the judicial system at work, that we were educating America on the law and lawyers and the functioning of the courts, and that most Americans had never been inside a courtroom in an important trial.

"You can be the teacher for the whole country on the law," I said. "Just think of it!"

"Well, I hadn't thought of it in those terms," he said. He was friendly, open, interested. I usually don't have the luxury of appearing before judges who have retained much of their humanness.

"Yes, and this is our opportunity to let America see how a real court of justice works and to renew the people's faith in the justice system," I added, being a little preachy because I didn't know what else to say.

Then Shapiro led me out, as if my audience before the pope had concluded, and as I walked past Johnnie Cochran, he motioned me over and reached for my hand. Shapiro had hurried to the other side of the room to talk to somebody else.

"Glad to see you around," Johnnie said. "I may need you before this thing is over." He gestured with a hostile nod of his head in Shapiro's direction.

"How you doin', Johnnie?" I asked.

"Doing just fine," he said. "We got a hung jury right now. Now I'm going for the acquittal." One thing Johnnie was famous for—he knew how to read jurors.

When I came to the tough female marshal, who was still standing near the door, I stopped to apologize.

"Sorry I caused so much trouble," I said. "I didn't realize I was so good at it. Broke all the rules without even hardly trying." I was trying to be nice. Gave her a little smile.

She glared back.

"I will promise you one thing," I went on, getting closer to her. She backed away half a step. "I will be a really good man. I will not break any rules without consulting you first. I am going to make you extremely proud of me."

Still glaring.

"And we are going to become famously friendly before this trial is over." And when she still didn't say anything, I took my leave and found my seat at the end of the jury box next to Sally Stewart of *USA Today*. I had to excuse myself as I slipped past half a dozen genuine reporters who turned their knees to the side so I could pass by. I nodded to them and they nodded back, and I felt very proud, being as how I was now finally a member of something: the media. I had a badge. I had fellow members. There were no monthly dues. And everybody was very friendly. I couldn't have been happier.

I sat down next to Sally, giving her my best smile. She had that big head of blond hair and those large eyes. Reminded me of one of the girls I fell in love with at Laramie High who ran off with that guy who got wounded in the war and married him when he came home and moved to a ranch out by Pinedale and lived, so far as I know, happily ever after. Sally was one of those bright, good-natured women. Full of jokes and sass.

"What did you say to Big Girl?" she asked.

"Who?" I had no idea who Sally meant.

She nodded toward the female marshal. "What did you say to Big Girl?" Sally had her pencil poised like a rattler about to strike.

"Oh," I said, "I didn't say anything of importance. Nothing to write home about."

"Come on, Gerry, give it to me," Sally insisted.

"Nothin', really," I said. "Nothin' at all."

"Now, I know better. I was watching the two of you. I could tell. You told her something and I want you to tell me." She gave me a little nudge in the ribs with her elbow.

"No, Sally, I assure you it was nothing."

"I demand that you tell me," she said like a mother whose child had brought home an F in "Deportment" on his report card.

I waited. Then I said, "Sally, are you ready for this?"

"Yes," she said, her eyes as big as silver dollars.

"Sally, this is utterly confidential," I said.

"Yes, utterly. You are speaking to the grave."

"You promise?"

"I promise."

"All right," I said. "I told Big Girl to . . ." and then I whispered the salacious verbage in her ear.

"To *do what?*" Sally shouted.

"Shhh," I said back.

"My God!" she cried out loud. "You really didn't say *that!*"

"You promised not to tell."

"I won't tell a soul." She was stunned. "My God," Sally said. "It's a wonder she didn't arrest you!"

Before the day was over, I had suddenly become very popular among my fellow club members in the courthouse gang. More than one person came up to me and said, "That was really funny what you told Big Girl to do. How did you have the nerve to say such a thing?" Then someone else would come up and say, "Did you really tell Big Girl to do *that?*" They wouldn't say the words, either.

Some of the people in the media had been a little upset with her because she was tough and humorless. To them she was very authoritative, even mean, like a cop about to beat the life out of you for going five miles an hour over the speed limit. But she had a job to do, and she was doing it pretty well—too well for some who wanted to run the place.

That night I got a call from Shapiro. "I hear you had a little talk with Big Girl this morning."

"You did?" I played dumb.

He was laughing. "I hear you told her where to get off."

"I didn't tell her where to get off," I said.

"I hear you told her to . . ." and I won't repeat his words for fear my dead mother is reading this over my shoulder.

"You know I'm not that kind of a person. Besides, only a fool would tell Big Girl to do that to him."

In a month or two an article appeared in *Penthouse* magazine with my alleged salacious verbiage printed out as bold and nasty as you please, which taught me never again to trust the media. I'm sure Sally was silent as a tomb about what I said, except she may have told her best friend under a blood oath of secrecy. But that's how secrets get turned loose on the world.

And that isn't the end of the story.

Sometime down the line, maybe three or four weeks later, I was standing out in the hallway during a recess. Shapiro came up to me. Friendly as usual, the good hand, and me wanting to reach out to pull his eyebrows. He looked mad.

"You know what that son of a bitch over there said to Judge Ito a little while ago in chambers?" He was pointing to Johnnie Cochran.

"What?" I said.

"He told the judge that he should throw you out of the courtroom for what you said to Big Girl."

"Really?" I said.

"Yes," he said. "Really." Then he hurried on to talk to another member of the media. He knew most of them by their first names, and he wasn't even a member of the club.

Pretty soon Chris Darden came along. I stopped him. "Chris," I said, "I hear you folks had a little discussion in chambers concerning me."

"Right, Gerry," he said. He was smiling.

"I hear somebody told Judge Ito he should throw me out of the courtroom for what I supposedly said to Big Girl."

"That's right," he said. Still grinning.

"Who was it who said the judge should throw me out?" I asked.

"Shapiro," he said.

CHAPTER 6

THE NEW TABLOID PEOPLE

I FELT LIKE Elmer Gantry preaching against sin and sinning, and mostly enjoying the sin. I was a trial lawyer, not trying a case, but instead sitting in the courtroom shoulder to shoulder with the most celebrated journalists in America, watching, always watching, taking notes, composing sage comments, a full-fledged member of the media. But my first allegiance was to the bar and to the process of justice. And the justice system and the media are sometimes at odds in odd places. We need justice and we need the media to expose injustices. But we do not need the media to deprive us of our constitutional right to a fair trial. Those who speak in "constitution" rather than English describe it as a classical conflict between the First and the Sixth Amendment. The media, like a father who can both protect and abuse, is able, and often eager, to run over the rights of a defendant to sell its stories and to thereby sell its wares. But the media is also a child—the child of the corporations—and the media serves them first and well, and if along the way it serves justice, that is usually an unintended gift. As a member of the media I was in conflict.

This is the tabloid age, and we are the tabloid people. It was different in the days of our founders. The media then included the likes of Patrick Henry, the great revolutionary orator who cried,

"Give me liberty or give me death," and Thomas Paine, who was writing his best-seller, the pamphlet "Common Sense," which molded a nation's revolutionary psyche against George III. But we have become a people no longer concerned with freedom or grace or style or decorum or good manners. Intellectual thought mostly bores us. Our lips get tired reading the funnies. Our brains have withered like stale grapes on limp stems, soaked in Budweiser, which all too often has become our daily due: This Bud's for you. Our love of innocent romance, of simple justice, is the remembrance of bitter old men. Our creative juices flow onto the pornographer's pages. Our religions are the religions of loving God and hating man, hating the hungry children of the nation and the world, the poor and the homeless. Our heroes are as empty as paper sacks. They traipse across the stage dragging behind them insatiable libidos that get sprayed over little boys, baby-sitters, and other men's wives. Our ambitions are not for life, but for dead money. Money is beauty. Money is intelligence. Money is worth. Dead money is everything worth living for.

Most of our leaders are the sick, the hollow, and the petty, whose noses have been worn smooth and turned a permanent brown from a lifetime of toadying, and whose pockets are stiff from the dirt of payoffs. Senators are the cheapest commodity on the political market. You can buy one for practically nothing—the price of a used Mercedes, maybe less. Stuff the money in his campaign can. Make it legal.

In this tabloid age we are the children of the media. We have been nursed on blood and gore and sex. The media is also our incestuous father who wishes to bugger his child. Come to me, baby. Come, sit on Daddy's knee and let me tell you a story. And after the barren story is told, after the blood, the bleak and breathless sex, the father wants something from the child. The father wants the child to give it up—in this case, the child's money. Buy my burgers. Buy my swill. Buy my junk, my cars, my sprays that will cover the stench of the decaying soul, that will cover the ugly and make you beautiful. Let me gorge you with barrels of fat and cut it off of your bones with frozen garbage, diets, and drugs. You want to be beautiful? You want to be successful? You want to go to heaven? Stuff your chest with silicone and lipo the yellow fat from your thighs and praise God, and, yes, send your money to the TV Chapel on Channel 47.

Sometimes I preach along like that. But now I was sitting in the courtroom, myself a member of the media, taking part in this whole decadent thing. I had been hired, I thought, to help throw the cloak of dignity, of expertise, over this maudlin thing, this murder case that the media had turned into pure pornography. There she lay in her thin dress, the candles still burning in the bathroom, the warm tub waiting. Waiting. She was the older woman, blond, of course, who knew how to make a man crazy, who had driven the great Heisman Trophy winner, her black husband, crazy. And he, the young lover, was lying, bled out, beside her. Some saw it that way. The place was tracked up with blood, muddy with blood. Her body was punctured with countess knife wounds as if the killer had copulated with her one last time, the stabbing, stabbing, stabbing, stabbing, the in-and-out of the longest, most steely weapon of all. Oh, it was so marvelous, and America, the child of the media, sitting on the media's lap, on Daddy's lap, was lapping it up. And now I was part of it.

I rationalized that I could make some sense out of this thing. I could keep the media straight. I could do a service to the American people, slip a little truth to them before they even knew it while the media sold insurance to frightened old people at outrageous rates and marketed pain pills and cold remedies. A person can rationalize anything.

I remember the time I first encountered rationalization in my public life, this process that permits us to do what we want, and to live with ourselves in the face of the guilt that might otherwise descend upon us in its dark, nasty little cloud and make our lives wretched.

I was a young prosecutor in Riverton, Wyoming, that quiet, innocent little town where I learned to try cases. But the country had its whorehouses. After I was elected county and prosecuting attorney—at the age of twenty-five, my ears still wet with the sweet dew of the unfallen—I thought I should close down the whorehouses. Not that I was against a woman making an honest living down there in the Little Yellow House, which was what they called that miserable pleasure palace, that yellow shack down by the railroad depot in Riverton. I rationalized on behalf of the girls: You can sell anything in America—your soul to the company store, your heart and your body to the corporate master—but if you sell your body to a randy sheepherder who comes stumbling down from the hills on a Saturday night, all honked up on whiskey and looking for fun, you are a bad person, and you should go to jail. My rationalization even took me to the conclusion that you had to admire an honest whore more than a banker. The girls worked for their money and gave a little pleasure along the way. The banker, after he had screwed the poor people out of their last penny, foreclosed his mortgages and threw the widows out on the street.

But I knew if I didn't close the whorehouses they would say I was on the take. And the law is the law, I also rationalized. Prostitution had been against the law since the state's territorial days, and I was supposed to enforce the law. So I did, my final rationalization being that it was better to be on the side of the law, even if it was irrational, than on the side of the whores, even if they were trying to make an honest dollar. Politicians are the species' experts at rationalization, and I was a politician. I closed the Little Yellow House and the houses in the towns of Hudson and Shoshoni. Then suddenly the churchwomen were up in arms, attacking me with their own rationalizations.

One of the churchwomen, rationalizing the virtue of the Little Yellow House and speaking for the rest, stood up in a public town meeting and said something like, "I am against prostitution. It is the work of the Devil. But our first duty is to our young girls in

Riverton. If we do not have the Little Yellow House, when those drunk cowboys and sheepherders come to town they will have no place to go, no place to release the heat of their loins, and they will be raping our innocent daughters. Raping them, I say! And if Mr. Spence, that young firebrand"—she was pointing at me— "wants to close our Little Yellow House, I personally will lay the responsibility of the rape of our daughters at his feet." The floor shook when she sat down. I thought she and many of the others supported prostitution for other reasons, the least of which was the pathological, joyous fascination of the overly pious with the very sins they preach against. But I wasn't going to have the Ladies Aid telling me what to do, especially not at twenty-five!

The ability to rationalize is the single most evil talent lurking alongside the virtues of the human species. No other creature on the face of the earth can rationalize—probably none other in the universe. We can rationalize killing millions of people with a single bomb in support of an economic system. We can rationalize the destruction of this gorgeous planet to wrap crap in plastic. We can rationalize blowing holes through the ozone in order to spray our hair in the morning. We can rationalize killing people in gas chambers while we demand that our citizens cease killing. And now, in Los Angeles I was rationalizing my part in this whole shameful, mindless, carnival sideshow: I could help America see the straight of it, the truth about the justice system. Oh, my rationalizations were grand and heady, and I was ready.

The O.J. Simpson case had become the bastard child of the media. Take the television out of the courtroom, put the case in proper perspective, an obscene murder case that most sensitive people wouldn't want to know much about—I mean, what can you learn from the grisly slashing of the throats of two people—and all you have is another not very creative kind of killing. But we, the tabloid people, loved the case. Adored it. I daresay that if Jesus had come strolling over the brine and walked up to the front door of the courthouse in downtown Los Angeles, most of the people standing out there would have rather had a front-row seat in the courtroom and Johnnie Cochran's autograph than the blessing of the Son of God.

I could see it clearly: the man standing there in his flowing robes, the gleaming aura around his head.

"Hi there. Come to see the O.J. trial?" asks the guy with the potbelly pushing out against his Nike T-shirt, the guy wearing the Nike baseball cap with the Nike logo and the Nike running shoes.

"I have come for you, my son," the man in the flowing robes says.

"Me? You got a ticket?"

"I have a ticket to Paradise, my son. Follow me."

"How did ya get it? Ya know somebody?"

"I know the Father. If you seek eternal life, follow me."

"What are you talking about, man? The trial's in there. Hey, come back. I'll give ya fifty bucks for your pass. A hundred and a half . . ."

Circuses have tents and elephants and monkeys and clowns. The O.J. case came freighted with the same baggage. It had the media trailers, the television tree houses built up high where you had to climb stairs like those on a fire escape to get to the camera platform. They had sideshows, the TV people chasing anyone who might have a story to sell, the street vendors selling O.J. T-shirts, and barkers trying to sell Jesus Christ. The participants, the media made clowns. The judge was cloned and became the Dancing Itos on Jay Leno, while other comedians turned the lawyers, the cops, and even themselves into gargoyle puppets that danced and pranced across the stage to the horror and delight of us all.

I was guilty of it, too. Once I was coming down from the court-room in the elevator and Marcia Clark stepped in just as the doors closed. She stared squarely at me a moment and then turned her head in disgust.

"Aren't you going to speak to me, Marcia?" I asked.

"I will never speak to you again as long as I live," she said, turning her head away, her chin up.

"How come?"

She didn't answer. And when the elevator stopped, she stepped out and huffed off down the hall.

When I got back to the hotel, I said to Imaging, "I saw Marcia Clark today. She said she was never going to speak to me again. Wonder what I could have done to her?"

"Have you read the *L.A. Times* today?" Imaging asked.

"No," I said.

"Well, you ought to read the paper." She handed it to me. I glanced through the article, looking for my name. There it was, the Gerry Spence quote: "Marcia Clark was prancing around in the courtroom like a high school baton twirler."

"Well, I was supposed to tell the truth, wasn't I?" I asked.

"We women don't speak to men who tell the truth," Imaging replied.

CHAPTER 7

THE NEEDLE

MARCIA CLARK, TOO, was an expert at rationalizing. She could look a man in the eye and argue until the shoe leather burned off his soles, that the death penalty was justice. To kill the heinous, the evil, the muck and puck of the human race was God's work, by God. Kill the fuckers, was her attitude. But should we kill O.J.?

Anyone can rationalize killing. Kill the skinny black kid named Derek who shot the clerk at the 7-Eleven during a holdup. How about his wheel, Willie, who was waiting outside, the motor running, and when Derek came busting out of the store he could tell something sure as hell went wrong: "Get the fuck outta here, man! The mothafucka went down, man!" and the prosecution says they both should get the needle. The needle is just fine. What is everybody so upset about? The needle is humane; we are humane. The needle is a whole lot more painless than when the clerk at the 7-Eleven underwent three emergency operations and died anyway ten days later. None of those bleeding hearts out there were crying when they hauled the clerk off and stuck him in a cheap plot at the back part of the cemetery where they bury the penniless.

The prosecution can paint those kinds of pictures for us, and our anger wells up, and we get confused about what is anger and what is justice. Anger and justice often get in each other's way. It makes me angry to see the clerk stretched out there with the tubes in his nose and his eyes glazed, and I want to kill the bastards who were trying to take fifty bucks out of the till to buy crack. Kill Derek, and kill Willie, too. Stop the senseless killing. Marcia Clark and Christopher Darden and the nine hundred plus prosecutors in the D.A.'s office holler that sort of liturgy every day. Kill to stop the killing. A merciful death is more than they deserve. We are here for the victims.

The bleeding hearts didn't show up at the cemetery when they lowered the clerk into the hole. The prosecutors say that. The bleeding hearts didn't show up at the hospital when Derek and Willie were born, either. I say that. The bleeding hearts didn't see who picked those babies up, babies as innocent as the white babies next to them. The bleeding hearts didn't see who hauled Derek or Willie home to that nasty hole with garbage dumped all over the floor and with nine other fatherless urchins, mostly hungry, and all of them dirty and snotty-nosed and wild, their mother doped-out on crack laying with some mule who gave her a moment's peace from the pipe . . .

Justice and anger get mixed up. Justice is lost in the dark places, in the projects, in the people trapped in those crumbling hellholes. But the bleeding hearts were not there. And Marcia Clark? She and the other nine hundred in the D.A.'s office adored, more or less, the death penalty. That was their justice, the ultimate justice. That was also their weapon.

But should we kill O.J.? That is another story. Clark said, "It [the death penalty] just wasn't an option. No jury—not even one composed of white, middle-aged Republican males—was going to sentence O.J. Simpson to death." That was because the death penalty is reserved for a different class. If you are black, if you have no money, if you live in ugly places, and if you kill, we will kill back. When we kill you that will teach you. But if you have been kissed in certain ways—that is, if you were kissed by Hollywood and given celebrity, or if you were kissed by God and given the genes of a great runner, or if you were kissed with the Heisman, and then Hertz kissed you, too, and the money gods kissed you—then you will not be killed, even if, as Darden confessed, "[I]n thirteen years I'd never seen such a brutal murder."

One of the marvelous things about the death penalty is that you can use it to rationalize about what justice is and know nothing about justice. Justice is killing Willie. But justice is not killing O.J., even if his murders were those brutal, bloody murders. We couldn't even guess how many other murders before O.J. the D.A. had sought to avenge with the needle. But it would be immoral to kill O.J., Marcia Clark said.

Listen, and we shall discover a new definition of justice: *Justice is the rationalization of those who have the power to rationalize.* This is Marcia Clark speaking out of her well of deep morality on the point.

> There was an even more compelling reason for not asking for the death penalty in this case. I didn't feel—and I don't believe that any of my colleagues from the brass on down felt—that it was warranted. Apart from the incidents of battery, Simpson did not have a prior criminal history. Over the course of his life he had not shown the kind of callous disregard for society's rules that you look for in a hardened criminal. O.J. Simpson was not an incorrigible, nor was he a danger to society at large. Under those circumstances *it would have been immoral to seek his death.* [my italics]

Clark writes this and expects us to believe it. "Simpson did not have a prior criminal record . . . he was not an incorrigible . . . and he was not a danger to society at large." This is the chief prosecutor in perhaps the most famous criminal case in America's history rationalizing why the prosecution did not ask for the death penalty. It was a matter of morality, for Christ's sake. We aren't supposed to remember the well-publicized statistic that, on average, *34 percent of prisoners sentenced to death had no prior felony record*. We are supposed to ignore the well-known fact that over a third of those on death row never had been convicted of a major crime, not even, say, selling an ounce of pot, or stealing a radio out of a pawn shop. And 92 percent of prisoners sentenced to death had never been convicted of a prior homicide. So Willie gets it and O.J. doesn't because it would be immoral to ask for the death sentence against a man who had no prior criminal record?

And so we begin to see it clearly: The first thing to think about when the death penalty is considered is *who* is going to make the life-or-death decision about whether it will be invoked? The Marcia Clarks of the world, the young, the unwise, the tough, those who know all about morality, the people looking to sell books? Let's leave the decision in the hands of the D.A.'s of the country who want to be governor. How about trusting the screaming politicians who want to be reelected? It is immoral to stick the needle in O.J.'s arm for the most brutal murder to come along in thirteen years, but not immoral to get rid of the Willies of the world who can't defend themselves. At last, is it not truly immoral to leave the threshold decision on the death penalty in the hands of the likes of Marcia Clark, who argues that a celeb who beats the hell out of his wife for years and finally stabs her and her companion to death, cuts their throats down to the bone, stabs them not once but over forty times, is really a pretty good fellow when it comes right down to it?

I agree with Marcia Clark: It would have been immoral to ask for the death penalty against O.J. It is equally immoral to ask for it against Willie and all of the others. If the death penalty is an instrument of ultimate justice, when it should or should not be invoked ought not be left to junior D.A.'s and politicians.

The death penalty is immoral for a lot of other reasons as well, but there is one that jumps out at me when I read Clark's words: "I was born Marcia Rachel Kleks, daughter of an Israeli immigrant. . . . I spent my babyhood in the Bay Area. At the age of three or four I decided to become an actress." She took ballet and her mother played the piano. Her father was a chemist with the FDA. She lived in a place touted as "a sort of Shangri-la laid out along a string of lagoons." She learned how to sail. And then she went on to college and acting school and all the rest. I see her in the cradle at the hospital. I see a kid like Willie in the cradle next to hers there in the same hospital nursery. My mind won't stop working that way.

Then along comes this loving mother and father and pick up this darling little girl and take her home. And Willie, as darling as she, gets picked up the same day. And we already know where he goes. Then thirty-some years later we have a Marcia Clark or someone else like her prosecuting Willie, asking for the death penalty. Kill Willie. It is his fault. Look at me—I made it. It was tough, I tell you. When they bused me to junior high, there I was in "knee socks and pleated skirts, with long, straight brown hair, sitting next to babes wearing ass-hugging skirts, black fishnets, a pound of makeup, and hair teased into humongous lacquered swells." It was tough. They smoked in the bathroom. And now Marcia decides what is just and what is not, what is moral and what is not. Marcia Clark speaks for us. Willie, of course, doesn't speak for us, nor Willie's mother, nor any of Willie's people. The Willies of the world are the ones who get killed. But those who have been kissed right can live. And Marcia Clark, of course, was kissed right. And so was O.J. And therefore she knows it would be immoral for the kissed-rights to ask for the death of the kissed-rights.

It's easy to get confused about what is moral and immoral and whether a crime is one of those particularly heinous crimes that would allow a prosecutor like Marcia Clark to ask for the death penalty. You might not ask for the death penalty if the crime were just a plain, ordinary sort of killing. But even Marcia Clark knew this was a heinous crime. She knew it from the start. She just forgot. She writes:

Everything was standard [in the complaint filed against O.J.], except for one thing. David [Conn, Clark's immediate boss] and I had carefully worded a clause invoking "special circumstances." As I've explained, this means that the crime was *particularly heinous*—in this case a double murder. Invoking the clause allowed us to consider the death penalty. [my italics]

We are led from death to life by Marcia Clark just like that—however the whim at the time strikes her. One day Simpson is facing a potential death penalty case for "a particularly heinous crime," and the next day it would be immoral to ask for it, this the same person speaking. I stagger at the lack of logic, the inconsistency. But politics and strategies are not logical or consistent. And they are not just. But death, the tool of the strategists and politicians, is final.

The death penalty is also a wondrous weapon that can save the prosecutor an abundance of trouble and the taxpayers a powerful lot of money. If you are the D.A. you can ask for the death penalty where it ought not be sought in the first place—say, where a husband and wife get into it and someone gets killed—and when the prosecutor asks for the death penalty, the accused—let's say the wife, who might have a pretty good defense—is so frightened, and her lawyer, poor and without much to fight with, is so scared, that they decide to give up an honest defense and take the prosecutor's deal: life imprisonment. What if the lawyer fails in court and the jury kills his client? Happens all the time. The lawyer can sit there in the cell with the accused, shivering there in her short-sleeved orange suit and her paper slippers, and the lawyer can cite a dozen cases where the defendant refused to plead guilty and ended up on death row. And after all those nights dreaming about the warden rolling in the gurney, and seeing the dripping needle, and seeing your kids out there crying and your old mother dying from wretched sorrow, the woman says, "All right, I'll take the deal."

The death penalty is a marvelous instrument of justice. Put it in the hand of the prosecutors—*any* prosecutor, decent, evil, fair, blindly ambitious, sane or not—put it in the hand of *any* prosecutor like you put a pistol in the hand of any man who stands over the fallen. He has the power of justice in his hands.

Clark's decision on the death penalty was not founded on morality at all, but upon the *politics* of the case. If the prosecutors asked for the death penalty they might not get a conviction, Clark admitted. In a death case the jury has to be "death certified," which means every juror has to be willing, in principle, to vote for death. What you'll likely get when you try a case before a death-certified jury, Clark wrote "is a panel of tough talkers who, when push comes to verdict, can't bring themselves to convict. Why? Because it has only just dawned on them that their actions may result in a person's death." What she is saying is that this *was* a "particularly heinous" crime—a double murder. We were therefore entitled to go for the death penalty. But if we went for death we might lose it. So the decision as to whether at trial you go for the death penalty or not depends upon not justice, not the law, not what is moral or immoral, but whether asking for the death penalty will lessen your chances of winning. The *politics* of the case, not justice, make the decision. And that, among other reasons, is why the death penalty, in the hands of the prosecutors of this country, is itself immoral.

If winning and not morality was the issue, Clark had a much better chance of winning with a death-certified jury. When the jury panel is composed of predominantly African-Americans, it is a lot harder to find African-Americans who will agree to kill their own than white people, many of whom, death certified, are all too ready to kill blacks. Those who will kill are usually more prone to convict.

But still I agree with Marcia Clark. It would have been immoral to ask for the death penalty in O.J.'s case or in any case, and so, in the end, I have no criticism of her decision. I only criticize *how* she arrived at the decision. On moral grounds? Willie's buried out there in the back part of the cemetery, too. Tell Willie's mother the decision to kill her son was moral but to ask for the death penalty against O.J. was not.

I remember when, in my own state of Wyoming, I, as a special prosecutor, asked for the death penalty in a case. The defendant was guilty, all right. Killed four people, an old country lawyer, his wife, their fifteen-year-old son, and my star witness. The killer was Mark Hopkinson. After he was charged by the grand jury with murder, Hopkinson hired some thugs to "do" our witness, as that ilk likes to say. Our witness, a tall, gangly kid named Jeff Green— looked like an adolescent Ichabod Crane—knew the whole story on Hopkinson, how he had hired another ranch kid to blow up the lawyer and his family. Used dynamite the kid's father had stored on his ranch to blow out the beaver dams that plugged up the creek. The thugs, hired by Hopkinson to "do" Green, took him to the prairie, burned out his eyes while he was still alive, burned his body with cigarettes—a "T" for traitor on his chest—burned his genitals, and then shot him and left him on the prairie for us to find. His death was to serve as a warning to any other witness in the little town of Fort Bridger who might get the idea to testify against Hopkinson. You don't have to go to New York to run into Mafia tactics. But a Wyoming jury rendered the death penalty.

I had taken the case at the request of the district judge and the victims' family. I took the case because no one else around was as able as I to do the work. The local prosecutor had been intimidated by the defendant—his family threatened—and I was a younger kick-ass trial lawyer, brave (I told myself), and nobody was going to intimidate me, not even Hopkinson and his gang of thugs. Besides, the lawyer Hopkinson had killed was Vince Vehar, one of my old friends, and his brown-eyed wife, Beverly, and their young son, John, a high school football star. So I was only doing what the state, the judge, the surviving family, and the people in Fort Bridger wanted. I worked pro bono, except the judge ended up giving me, as my fee, the judge's antique chair. Always admired the chair. You don't take money to do work like that, I thought. You do it because it has to be done.

When it came time for Hopkinson's trial, I asked the jury for the death penalty. I thought I had to ask for it because the crimes were "particularly heinous." But you think when you take on a death penalty case that you are only following the law. It's that rationalization thing again. It was the legislature's fault, not mine. I didn't make the law. If that death-certified jury brings in the death penalty, well, it's the jury's fault. The jurors can decide the case any way they want. They have the power. The power was out of my hands, I rationalized. Any one of the jurors could keep the defendant out of the gas chamber, because the verdict had to be unanimous, and any one of the jurors had the power to say no and save his life.

And if the jury was convinced by my argument and comes in with the death penalty, then the courts have the power to set the verdict aside. The Supreme Court of Wyoming had the power. The federal courts had the power. And that case was up and down the judicial ladder so many times the rungs were finally worn out—for nearly ten years the appeals went on, including another jury trial in which another jury rendered the death penalty all over again against Hopkinson. And then there were appeals from that verdict. And I thought, well, surely it isn't my fault anymore. You rationalize, and the juries rationalize, too. Each of the jurors says, "I didn't do the killing. Hopkinson was responsible. Besides, all the other jurors on the case voted for the death penalty, too. It wasn't my fault." And the judges rationalize, too. It wasn't their responsibility. The jury heard the evidence. The judges only have to look at the black-and-white transcript, and it looked all right, and the law is the law. They didn't make the law; they only apply and interpret it. Then one day ten years later while they are preparing to kill the condemned, the plea for clemency lands on the governor's desk.

I got back into the fray. I wrote the governor, a longtime friend of mine. Wrote him a many-paged letter asking that he commute Hopkinson's death sentence to life imprisonment without parole. This killing has to stop. This rationalizing and blaming, this pretty passing of the buck, has to stop. But the governor said something like, "Well, I don't have the right to substitute my judgment for that of two juries and endless judges, all of whom have reviewed the facts and the law. I am just the governor. It's not my fault. And besides, it was the defendant who brought it all upon himself."

The problem is that no one need take responsibility for the killing in any death penalty case, not even the executioner. He was only ordered to do it by the judge, who was ordered to do it by the jury, and on back to where it all began, and then back and around again. It is very easy to kill if you don't have to take personal responsibility for the killing. We demand that the defendant take responsibility for what he did. I think that's right. People should be responsible for what they do. But the justice system bears no responsibility for what it does—that is, no individual in the justice system does. There is always someone to whom the buck gets passed. Worse, it often leaves the life-or-death decision of whether the death penalty will be sought in the hands of stony-souled prosecutors, and the self-righteous, ambitious politicians and book writers who decide who lives and who dies depending on what's good for them. The justice system sets up a death machine that begins with the prosecutor and ends with the governor, and no one from beginning to end bears any responsibility—not the prosecutors, not the jurors, not the judges, not the governor, not the executioner.

And then we have someone like Marcia Clark espousing what is moral and what is not in asking for the death penalty. It is immoral, she says, to ask for it against the moneyed, the famous, and the powerful, but not immoral to ask for it against the Willies of the world. And that, my friends, ends up being the mother of all immorality.

The executioner stuck the needle in Mark Hopkinson's arm

and they buried him out there someplace. Old Vince Vehar and his brown-eye Beverly and their son John and Jeff Green, all of them are buried out there someplace as well. But that didn't end the anguish. Hopkinson's old mother, a good woman who was innocent, bears the punishment and these many years later still suffers. His brother, a hardworking family man, has suffered as well. In avenging murder we hurt the wrong people. We hurt the innocent. We hurt ourselves, because, at last, we have become the killers.

CHAPTER 8

THE MEDIA MONSTER

SINCE I HAD become one of them, I became interested in the so-called talking heads. The most unlikely heads were chosen— heads that weren't particularly interesting to look at: people with cocked eyes and glazed eyes, people who seemed more blind than seeing; people with cracking voices, whining voices, dead voices, voices flat as floors; people who couldn't speak the English language, the illiterate, the mumblers, and those who thought syntax was a mouthwash. I wondered why we were chosen. But the worst among us were those who knew nothing at all and who, without the first pink of embarrassment, professed to know everything. These were the ones who knew nothing because they had never done anything, and having done nothing and having been nowhere were like ants crawling around in a saucer whose view of the land-scape was hard, barren, and lifeless.

The worst were those experts—most of them, in fact—who had never tried a murder case, who had never had to look a terrified client in the face and fight for his life, who had never seen the inside of a jail except through a Grisham novel, and who had never left their fingerprints on the doorknob of a courtroom door. Cer-tain professors were quoted daily as trial experts. Professor Such-and-Such from this or that law school made the front page of the nation's leading papers telling the world the strategies he would have employed in the case on any given day. These morticians of the profession whose only relationship to the judicial process was to do postmortems on Supreme Court decisions, to postulate and presuppose and presume in their dark, safe little closets, and to lie prostrate at the feet of the dean whenever he whistled, now became the nation's gurus on the O.J. Simpson case. And America, of course, believed them. If we cannot believe our professors— those sanitary souls who, if they were teaching surgery, would never have held a scalpel in their hand—who can we believe? Besides, what they say is in print. And if it is in print it must be true.

And the talking heads all wanted to compete with each other. The minute they got on television they lost all of their manners. They wouldn't think of interrupting each other at a faculty meeting, but once the camera was on them they fought like piranhas after the kill. They ripped at one another, tore at one another's dignity, and chewed at the flesh of one another's being. You could watch some of the programs and come away with only noise and static. But the producers loved it, especially the ratings. People loved to see the pathetic dueling. It was the Roman Colosseum all over again, except the gladiators were long-winded klutzes who mostly made noise and swung harmlessly at the air. See the Christians eaten by the lions, or some alleged defense attorney being chewed up by some vicious woman prosecutor with red hair. What a spectacle.

And some of the talking heads tried the case from beginning to end before the first word of evidence was introduced. My old friend Vincent Bugliosi, that tough and talented prosecutor of Charles Manson, said it best: They had a "sweet tooth for silliness." But my friend himself had no problem with announcing from the start that O.J. was guilty. He said so in *Playboy*. It was as obvious to Vince as the pubic hair on the centerfold. And although he may have been right, it seems to me it is wrong to be right at the wrong time. I doubt that Vince had heard or seen any evidence

in the case other than that which was available in the media before
the trial had begun. He was trying the case from the leaks and the
stuff we all had gleaned from the preliminary hearing. He hadn't
heard the defense yet. He didn't know anything about the credibility of the witnesses. Maybe he meant it when he wrote, "I take no
pride in having been the first public personality to come out publicly against Simpson." I wouldn't take any pride in it, either. But
Vince was right, as he usually is about such things. Besides, most
people who are charged, guilty or innocent, end up being convicted, so the odds are with you that you'll be right if you come out
publicly for their guilt whether you know the first thing about the
facts in the case or not. In any event, Vince was the first, and being
first has a lot of importance these days, when in this world of talking heads, everyone is jostling for front time in the center ring of
the Barnum & Bailey of the law.

What about the presumption of innocence? Vince seems to
hate the presumption of innocence. He says it is a legal argument
that nobody should believe, which sounds as if he is arguing that
if a man is charged he must be guilty. Vince writes in one of his
widely acclaimed books, *Outrage:* "Conviction rates show that it is
ridiculous to presume that when the average defendant is arrested,
charged with a crime, and brought to trial, he is usually innocent."
He then says that someday some guy standing before the judge is
going to ask the seed question: "Your Honor, if I am legally presumed to be innocent, why have I been arrested for this crime,
why has a criminal complaint been filed against me, and why am I
now here in court being tried?" The answer, of course, is that staring into the presumption of innocence, the police are forced to
arrest only those against whom they likely have sufficient evidence
to overcome the presumption. I revere the protection of the presumption of innocence. Ever try to explain to somebody why you
were late coming home on a Saturday night? Ever try to prove your
innocence to your boss, your spouse, the neighbor down the
street? Without the presumption of innocence, we could all be

locked up whenever it struck the fancy of the stomping brown-shirts, and we wouldn't get out until the hangmen got tired or the state got bored with housing and feeding those who incessantly plead their innocence.

So how, I ask, are we going to learn anything about the justice system from the talking heads when our nation's leading prosecutor thinks the presumption of innocence is something that ought to be tossed in the shitcan? Bugliosi's argument tells you one thing: You should be very grateful that there are defense attorneys out there—those villains, those flesh-eating shysters, who live off of the scum of the earth but who, perhaps accidentally, are still doing something in the courtroom, even in the most frightful of cases, that tends to preserve our freedom.

Vince presumed O.J. guilty from the beginning, and of course he was probably right. If, therefore, we were going to come to any conclusions concerning the justice system based on the O.J. case as revealed by Vince's judging strategies, we might abolish trials altogether and leave the whole messy business to the talking heads. Or we might just leave it all to the police, trust them, presume that the thugs they bring in are guilty, and save us, the taxpayers, a lot of money. And while we are at it, we might just as well kill them, as they do most of them in China. Saves a lot of time and a lot of money. There the accused is often arrested in the morning. By ten o'clock the trial is over. By noon the appeals have been satisfied, and by nightfall the accused is dragged before a firing squad and executed. The Chinese don't make a big fuss over human life. They seek to be a practical people, and their justice system is wonderfully efficient—and cheap. A laudable system, we might conclude, until, of course, the police come after one of us.

But we were talking about the media. The problem with the media is that it does not report the case, it *creates* the case. The media stirs up all the ingredients for this blood pudding, dumps in the nuts, throws the concoction in the oven to bake, and out comes this blown-up monstrosity with the naked and the dead inside, and when it's all over everyone thinks the case stands for the justice system itself—that it is representative of all the judges, prosecutors, and defense attorneys across the land.

In the O.J. case, by the end of the preliminary hearing the media had us all gasping and gurgling with some kind of perverse passion, with its images of the dead bodies floating in their own blood at the front door, the frightening dagger that had been purchased at Ross Cutlery, the howling Akita—you could hear the dog's long death knell echoing across the empty streets—and who could forget the Bronco chase on television? We watched, enthralled, as O.J. was headed down the road, reportedly to commit suicide, and we cheered him on, "Go, O.J., go!" the cops behind creating a reverse color guard, while across the land—in unknown shacks and lonely bedrooms and filthy alleys—hundreds of anonymous wretches, for sick and deep reasons of their own, slashed their wrists and put the gun in their mouths and no one gave a damn.

No sooner had the case become this media monster than the tabloids joined in. At the beginning of the murder investigation, Commander David Gascon of the LAPD made a little-publicized plea to the media asking that reporters not attempt to interview the witnesses during the days to come, since doing so would interfere with the police. It might "delay and negatively impact the course of this investigation. I need to stress that. It's critically important." But justice is not the ruling law to the media; ratings, sales, and advertising dollars are. Although the tabloids were often the first to reveal a new fact and were often more accurate than the so-called legitimate press, and despite the plea of the LAPD, the tabloids rushed out and bought witnesses like sides of beef, like pork bellies, like any other commodity offered for sale in this money society.

On June 12, 1994, a key witness, one Jill Shively, had decided to drive to San Vicente Boulevard to pick up some food at a salad bar. It was about 10:45 on the night of the murder. Heading east on San Vicente, she put her foot to the gas, attempting to make a changing light. A large white vehicle headed north on Bundy sped into the intersection in front of her, against the light. She slammed on the brakes, and the white vehicle did likewise, running partially over the raised median on San Vicente. Another car, a gray Nissan going west on San Vicente, also came to a sudden stop to avoid hitting the white vehicle.

For a brief moment the three automobiles were stopped within a few feet of one another. Then the driver in the white car began honking his horn. "Move your damn car!" he was hollering at the driver in the gray car. "Move it!" At that moment Shively noticed that the driver of the white vehicle was a familiar-looking black man, and as she heard him screaming she recognized the voice and realized it was O.J. Simpson. She got a look at the license plate jut before the driver in the car peeled off up Bundy. It was 3CZW788.

The next morning Jill Shively's mother asked whether she had heard that Nicole Simpson had been murdered the night before.

"That's weird," Jill Shively said. "O.J. nearly ran me down last night." She called the police, and detectives interviewed her on June 14. Four days later she was subpoenaed to appear before the grand jury on June 21. On June 19 her name was leaked as a witness, and the reporters, the hounds of the media, went howling after her. On Monday, June 20, she gave an interview to *Hard Copy* in exchange for some money that she badly needed—$5,000. Compared to the $4 million plus that Marcia Clark would eventually receive as a book advance, it was a pittance.

If, as a defense attorney, I paid a witness $5,000 for her testimony, the prosecutor would have me locked up in ten minutes for obstruction of justice. But to the prosecutors and the judges, the media are like the leopards in the night. The prosecutors and the judges fear the media as baboons fear leopards. Like baboons, the prosecutors kill the smaller monkeys. The prosecutors kill those they have cornered, kill them with their words, kill them with their arguments for death. The judges, too, kill the smaller monkeys, kill them with their judgments, their rulings, kill them with their death decrees. Like baboons, the prosecutors and the judges hang together in herds, and they kill together. In herds they will sometimes even take on the larger monkeys and kill them, too. A prosecutor and a judge have more power than any single citizen in the nation, more power, in fact, than the president of the United States, whom they can order into court to face his own political death at the hands of whoever wishes to claim they have seen the inside of his drawers. But the prosecutors and the judges are afraid of the leopards in the night, and they will run and hide from the leopards and, when cornered, placate them. The leopards are untouchable. Ah, the inexorable, merciless power of the media.

I remember when one of *Hard Copy*'s producers, an old friend of mine, called me after the Shively issue heated up and became still another media event. She had been threatened. She wanted to know what the prosecutors could do to the show, to the network, to the producers, to her. She confirmed that the show had paid Shively the $5,000 for her appearance, and now she wanted to know if it was illegal. No, it wasn't illegal. The media could act with impunity. She hadn't understood yet that the media is untouchable, that the prosecutors and the judges could only howl and scatter and make a big ruckus.

And so a key witness in the Simpson case became disqualified, allegedly because she had been seduced by the media; at least, she was now judged unchaste in the mind of Marcia Clark. Jill Shively could have placed O.J. in his white Bronco on his way home from the scene at the approximate time of the murders. She was the closest thing the prosecution had to an eyewitness. Numerous officers urged Clark to call her to testify, including Fuhrman. Why not use her? She had called the police and given her interview to the officers *before* she made the deal with *Hard Copy*. And, as Fuhrman argued in his book, Clark had not hesitated to use the testimony of the owner and salesclerk from Ross Cutlery, where

Simpson had bought the stiletto knife, even though both had also sold their stories.

Bugliosi said he would have used Jill Shively's testimony. He was right again. She had made a positive identification of Simpson and had given an accurate license plate report. Her testimony placed Simpson near the crime scene and contradicted Simpson's various alibis that, instead of cutting the throats of innocent victims, he was chipping golf balls or sleeping or taking a shower. But her testimony didn't match Marcia Clark's time line exactly, and if anyone, including the facts, didn't agree with Ms. Clark, well, forget it. The consensus was, and is today, that Clark had locked herself into a too-precise time frame and, being headstrong, wouldn't open it up to meet the facts as they developed. After all, the Akita had no reason to lie.

The media—charged with protecting our rights as free Americans, entrusted with serving as the watchdog of the system, empowered to expose injustice and corruption—used its freedom instead to make a mockery of the justice system. If the decision comes down to whether someone gets a fair trial or whether the media gets a story that serves to render a fair trial impossible, the result is predictable. I remember when Judge Ito issued his plea that the media not interview Nicole's friend Faye Resnick following the publication of her scandalous but, I think, mostly accurate depiction of the Simpson's lives. The book was released during jury selection and before the jury was sequestered, a time the book could do the most damage to the defendant, a fact that surely had not escaped its publisher. Resnick was scheduled for interviews with CNN's Larry King and others. The judge, begging the leopards for mercy, pleading for a little time, a little restraint while the court was attempting to select an impartial jury, wrote a letter to the major networks asking them to cancel pending interviews of Resnick until jury selection had been completed. Tom Johnson, the top guy at CNN, a decent and responsible man, called me for advice. I told him I thought that he should cancel the interview.

The media has a duty to the judicial system. If the judge thought the interview would affect the right of the defendant to have a fair trial, Johnson would bring honor to his network by complying, and he would be setting an example for the rest of the industry as well. It would be a clear statement that CNN not only recognized its own First Amendment rights, but that it also recognized that the defendant's Sixth Amendment right to a fair trial was vitally important to the citizens of this country.

Tom Johnson and Larry King canceled the interview. Connie Chung of CBS did not. But Judge Ito's letter requesting that the media refrain from promoting the Resnick book had the predictable effect of promoting the book. *Nicole Brown Simpson: The Private Diary of a Life Interrupted* exploded on the *New York Times* best-seller list, leaving Pope John Paul's *Crossing the Threshold of Hope* in its wake. One thing: The leopards in the night are not choosy. They will eat the innocent and guilty alike. Blood is blood.

The Resnick book exposed Simpson as a merciless wife beater, a womanizer, a woman hater, a bad father, and, in sum, a fiend of the worst order. The book, snubbed by the intelligentsia, nevertheless was read by the intelligentsia, who would no more admit that they had read the book than that they might have had a copy of *Hustler* stashed under the mattress. Although hundreds of thousands of copies were sold and the book was on the *New York Times* best-seller list for weeks, no one would admit that he or she had read that little epistle of smut. Marcia Clark wouldn't listen to Jill Shively, a very good eyewitness to the whereabouts of Simpson on the night of the murder, but she had Chris Darden flush Faye Resnick out of her alleged hiding place in Vermont to induce her and her publisher to come to L.A. to talk to Clark. The inducement turned out to be yet another promotion for the book. Suddenly, Clark later wrote, Resnick was no longer a "trembling, fetal creature" but a "burnished vamp" who bore right down on her with hugs and kisses. Although Resnick had been in rehab for her coke and Valium habit and had presumably made over a million on her book, this did not stop the prosecution from adopting the Resnick take on the Simpsons almost line by line. One thinks how poor Jill Shively was turned aside as a witness purportedly for having clutched her pittance of $5,000 to her bosom, while the millions scooped in by Resnick and the $4 million plus taken in by Marcia Clark herself rendered neither of these women, per se, vamps of disbelief.

Now, both Clark and Darden insisted they believed Resnick was telling the truth about Simpson's abuse of Nicole. Clark claimed in her book, *Without a Doubt,* and I have no reason to doubt it, that "Faye's information supplied the connective material to turn our collection of isolated police reports about Nicole's deeply troubled marriage into a coherent history. It gave us a badly needed boost."

Most of those who claimed to be in the know (but who would never admit that they had read the Resnick book themselves) said the book was just muggy tabloid stuff, humid junk, the "bitch" cashing in on her dead friend. This was porn, a druggie spinning her tales of sexual peccadilloes, including the "Brentwood hello," which turned out to be the supposed propensity of Nicole and her friends to provide fellatio to any nearby stranger at the drop of his shorts. Despite the fact that the book sold all those copies, the Bible panting to keep up, I have yet to meet a single person who will admit that he has read it.

I admit it. I read the book and thought it had that ring of truth to it, and obviously Marcia Clark thought so, too, and she seemed to like Resnick, despite her complaint that Resnick flirted "outrageously" with Darden. As I watched the trial unfold, I realized that Faye Resnick more than anyone else had written the script for the prosecution's case. On the other side, the defense's lines were set in boldface type in Jeff Toobin's *New Yorker* article on how the defense would be playing the race card, the Fuhrman glove-planting angle. And so we see, as we shall see over and over again, that the media—more than the prosecutors, more than the detectives, more than the defense attorneys, and, finally, more than the court itself—shaped the course, the content, the character, and, at last, the conclusion of the O.J. Simpson murder case.

By the time the trial began, most of America knew the essential facts from leaks to the media arranged fortuitously by both the prosecution and the defense. Whenever anything trivial or otherwise occurred, either in or out of court, the lawyers raced to the cameras to make their revelations. The public became more familiar with the lawyers' faces than those of current movie stars. Nothing went unnoticed: the lawyers' attire, their bodies; the alleged size of F. Lee Bailey's penis; Clark's hairstyle, her breastworks, her marriage and divorces; Cochran's ex-wife's claims against him for whatever he'd done that was ungentlemanly and penurious; Judge Ito's wife's clashes with Fuhrman; the sex lives of the living, the dead, and the dying. If you could come up with something that hadn't yet been published, you could make a fortune. And many did. And many will.

Where were the gag orders that could have mitigated this media riot? Both Tom Lange and Phil Vannatter, detectives on the LAPD, claim they pleaded with District Attorneys Gil Garcetti and Marcia Clark to push Judge Ito for a gag order on all of the parties in the case. The prosecution had already lost Jill Shively, who might well have sealed the case for the prosecution. And Simpson's lawyers were putting their own spin on witnesses and evidence that hadn't yet seen the light of day in a courtroom. Clark seemed to have no interest in a gag order. Nor did Garcetti. And the defense lawyers—what would they do without the cameras? No one wanted to be gagged, not even the judge. This was *their* show. This was their time in TV paradise. Live a thousand lives, even ten thousand, and you'd never get this much exposure again. I remember saying a number of times on *Larry King Live* that the judge should gag the lawyers. I was told that Judge Ito sometimes watched the show. Sometimes I had the feeling that he took into account some of our comments on matters pending before him—but a gag order? Not on your life.

This case was tried in the media and became the biggest money-producing news event of all time. Its ratings exceeded even those delivered to the networks by the Gulf War. *Rivera Live* would not give the case up, not even for a day. *Inside Edition* and *Hard Copy*, along with *A Current Affair*, burst prominently onto the scene and made multimillions of dollars on the case. Larry King had his favorite panel, of which I was a member. We talked on and around and speculated shamelessly inside and out of the case for endless days. I hosted King's show six or seven times, and the topic was always O.J. And after the trial I was given a show of my own on CNBC as a sort of filler on the weekends.

By then I was getting pretty fed up with the Simpson case and was resisting my producers, who were urging me to continue on with my comments about the case: Ratings, baby, that's what it's all about—ratings! Finally I could bear the shame of it no longer, and I told my audience that this was the last night I would be talking about the O.J. trial. There were more important things going on in America, like the more than 20 percent of the kids in the country who were living below the poverty level, many of whom were going to bed hungry at night. The producers were horrified that I would abandon the one subject that guaranteed ratings. But milking the last squirt from that infamous udder could go on for only so long before I lost all self-respect. I needed to retain a little. Just a little.

Once, after the case had been over for months, I was invited to be on the *Charles Grodin* show. Faye Resnick was also a guest, and I said on the air something like this to Charles: "My God, Charles, have we no shame? How is it that we still hang on to this damn case, ostensibly for one thing—ratings?"

Grodin was taken aback. Ratings? He never did things on his show just for ratings. And what about me, he asked? Here I was promoting my autobiography, *The Making of a Country Lawyer,* the story of my early years as a Wyoming boy and a young lawyer, on *his* show—talk about commercial motives! Wasn't the sooty pot calling the kettle black? He had me. Of course I wanted people to read my book—otherwise I wouldn't have written it. And we want people to watch our shows. If we lived alone on a desert island, there would be no books, no shows, no paintings. Most do not create and perform for themselves alone. We want to communicate, to be heard, to make a difference. And for that we need an audience. But I thought that there were many issues around our troubled world more important at the time than the O.J. Simpson case that Americans might be interested in.

Yet after all of the ballyhoo on the case was logged into history, the case, magnified, distorted, and distended as it was by the media, became the media's begotten monster. Loosed on the public, it trampled into the home of every American, to the exceeding joy of its parent, and to the fascination and obsession of the American people it endlessly engaged.

We are entitled to wonder how the media affected the minds of the men and women who were charged with the responsibility of delivering justice, both to the accused and to the people. Marcia Clark claimed America became addicted to the media. "The media fed the addiction, covering every twitch in the case as a 'stunning new development.' By the time we got through those preliminary hearings, nothing was ordinary. Nothing was *allowed* to be ordinary. It was all reported at the same hysterical, accelerating pitch." But *who* got addicted?

One can see Marcia Clark rolling along in her car, taping her thoughts (as was suggested by her therapist). The tapes became running extracts in her book. Notwithstanding one's cynicism, one can see her sitting with the publisher and her agent as they attempted to make the book deal. "I have the tapes of my thoughts— taped them in the car as the case was progressing, faithfully, accurately."

"Where are they?"

"Here."

In my mind's eye I see she has them in a neat little shoe box with big rubber bands around it. The publisher wants to hear a couple. Some end up in the book—edited, of course. But the question remains: Does one think about a potential $4 million plus book deal when the tape recorder is running? Does one think about a $4 million plus book deal as the strategies for the trial are being laid out? Women are the big book readers these days. We all know they are more literate than men, who are too busy building muscles down at the gym and following their testosterone-driven impulses around town to have time to read much. Did Clark shape the prosecution—a domestic violence case—to appeal to women, who have a wide and vital interest in the issue? Some critics in the LAPD thought the case should have been couched as a plain and simple murder case. And, as I will explain later, I agree. When Clark made her moves in court, was she aware of her persona, the precious asset she had in her story, even if she lost, and the appeal she might engender with the book-buying public—particularly women?

I doubt that Marcia Clark's decisions in this case had anything to do with book writing and the $4 million plus most of us covet. I give her the presumption of innocence I demand on behalf of the accused. I think she is a hardworking, dedicated, well-meaning woman. Yet the fact that I raise the question of her motives only means that millions of others can and have raised it as well. The opportunity for media influence to enter the case, and the *appearance* that it might have, worries me. I think Clark was facing a mammoth descending avalanche of media from which there was no escape. Had this not been a media extravaganza, the facts were ordinary enough that Clark could have dealt with them and probably could have won the case as easily as any of the other murder cases she had tried. Had she been facing lawyers on the other side who were not addicted to the same media lure as she, had she kicked the addiction, had the judge been oblivious to it, this case could have been tried and disposed of in a couple of months at most. I know I could have tried the prosecution's case in two or three weeks, and if there was a single most important reason for the prosecution's loss, it was that the case dragged on like the eternal murmurings of the delirious. Had everyone in the case put a gag on themselves, or had the judge gagged the lawyers and himself as well, had everybody been concerned only with their jobs, and had the media not become the forum where the trial was actually conducted, most of these hard questions would not have arisen.

The probable billions generated in the O.J. gold rush spurred a frantic fever to cash in and to keep the case going. Few were immune from the lure of the gold, including all of the attorneys, many of the witnesses, and even some of the jurors. The gold rush fever created an atmosphere in which justice could never prevail. When the chief prosecutor is worried about how she looks on camera—the circles under her eyes, the length of her skirt, the way she walks, her hairdo—how can she be focused on the trial? I am not critical of one's interest in how one looks or how other people perceive me. But I become concerned when an attorney spends any of her limited energy on such issues when she is already on the edge of sheer exhaustion, as Marcia Clark admitted she was.

"The debate inevitably descended to the length of my skirts," Clark later wrote. "Drive-time radio jocks wore themselves out complaining that my hems were 'too short.' . . . When I'm on my own time I wear my skirts any damned length I please. And that is usually about three inches above the knee. It's not an attempt at seduction." Then she made this generous concession: When she is in front of a jury she wears "hems slightly above the knee." That wasn't the way I saw it.

It wasn't only Clark's knees the public saw too much of—it was her persona as well. "I was overexposed," she admitted. She claimed she got about the same exposure in seven days as five years' worth of *Seinfeld* episodes. "Like it or not," she wrote, "I was a celebrity." I think she liked it very much—most of the time. Even today she hasn't disappeared into obscurity. The last I saw, she was being interviewed by Barbara Walters on *20/20* and lately hosting *Rivera Live,* and she was looking into the camera with those soft, loving eyes that can, as fast as a cobra blinks, strike out at you to kill.

But so what? No one can criticize this woman for writing books or getting rich or becoming a celebrity. This is America. The only question I raise is what this exposure does to our heads, our minds, our judgment, our decision making, when we are charged with critical responsibilities in the case. How does the media influence the strategies we choose? Whether we ask for the death penalty? Whether we make our case a domestic violence case or one of simple murder? And what effect do the talking heads and the talking shows and the talking comedians and all of the other endless talking have on the decisions that are made in the privacy of the attorneys' offices, or behind the closed doors of the judge's chambers?

I can hear what Marcia Clark might say in her inimitable style: "Fuck you talking heads." That's the way she talked to talking heads. One must admire her for this as well. But, as we shall see before the last pages of this book are turned, this very talented woman made some critical mistakes, as did her partner Darden, whose own fortune was also made in the case—through his book, the more than a million dollar advance, his royalties, his professorship, his appearances on the networks, his fame. He became more famous than the president of General Motors. Who the hell is he? He became more famous than the big guy over at the United Nations—what the hell is his name? And the question remains, what part did the media have in the judgments the prosecution made, some of which were foolish to the extreme? What power did the media wield over Chris Darden? I felt bad for the man. He was and is a decent person, the most honest lawyer in the courtroom, I thought. His parents and his family were exposed in the *National*

Enquirer in shoddy, painful ways, and he was in constant turmoil not only over the racial issues in the case but about his being portrayed to his own people as an Uncle Tom. How do you try a case in the presence of such constant overexposure?

I think of Cochran and Shapiro, who probably got more for their books than from their fees in the case. These are highly sophisticated men. Weren't they aware that what they said, and how they said it, could eventually become one of their most salable assets? Did they make the deals for their books or their shows before the case was over? I doubt it. But again, that one can even ask the question points to the problem.

I think of the pressures on them as well. They used the media, sometimes skillfully; Shapiro was a confessed expert at it. By the time the trial was over, Shapiro was divorced from his longtime friend and the godfather of his children, F. Lee Bailey, over charges made, one against the other, that one of them was leaking confidential defense materials to the tabloids. And Cochran and Shapiro, both clamoring into the mikes and the lenses, would become permanently estranged as well, over their media-driven disagreement concerning the playing of the race card.

But the media used the lawyers on both sides as well. A word in court brought on a dump truck load outside of court. The case was constantly fought on those two battlefronts, the media and the courtroom. It should have been fought only in the latter. The canons of ethics demand it. Justice demands it. But the players on both sides had little choice. Either they used the media themselves or the other side used it and devoured them. Eat or be eaten.

Nor did the sequestering of the jury help. No one believed then, nor do we believe today, that the jury was unaware of the cascade of swill, the unsubstantiated crap they were forbidden to hear or see. But the jurors heard and the lawyers knew they heard. And that merely propelled both sides into a further media frenzy— more leaks, more statements, more posturing, more unseemly strategies both in and out of court, and the media, in turn, pumped them further, jacking the players into more and more perform- ances and positions from which there was no return. But always what was said and what was done was said and done to be swal- lowed, regurgitated, and excreted by the media.

How can the justice system deliver justice when the judge him- self has a television set in chambers, when he's watching the media watch him through his own television cameras that peer down from the roof of the courtroom, his monitor on the bench taking in every movement of the media gallery itself? Once the marshal came over and told me to either leave or spit my gum out—judge's orders, for Christ's sake. Were we back in the first grade, with the judge cracking down on gum-chewing kids? I stuffed it under my seat. How can the justice system work when the chief prosecutor is being tailed by the *National Enquirer* wherever she goes? The whole scene had gone mad from top to bottom and side to side, and the crazier it got the happier the media was and the more America became obsessed with the case, embittered and disillu- sioned by it, sickened by it, addicted to it.

To the players, the media always came first, not justice. I think of Paula Barbieri appearing in nothing at all in *Playboy* but being less than cooperative with the lawyers in a murder case. In *With- out a Doubt,* Marcia Clark mentioned the deposition Barbieri later gave in the civil trial, in which she testified that she had left a "Dear John" message on Simpson's machine the afternoon before the murders. Clark claimed the message was clearly the emotional trigger for the murder. She lamented, "We certainly could have used it at the criminal trial. Thanks loads, Paula." I think of Faye Resnick appearing in the same scant folds of skin, selling whatever the media wanted to buy for whatever price she could get. I think of how the judge recessed jury selection so that he and the lawyers could read Resnick's book in order to assess its damage on the psyches of the potential jurors. He told the jurors not to read any- thing that had just come out, which was tantamount to an invita- tion to read *everything* that had just come out. In this case, more than any other in the history of jurisprudence, the evidence, the testimony, and, at last, justice became mere commodities that were laid out on the table by everyone for sale to anyone.

Judge Ito was said to read five newspapers a day. That would take more time than it took to read the attorneys' briefs, though granted, the judge could probably make more sense out of the reporters' takes on the motions and arguments before the court than he could from the motions he had to read and the arguments he had to listen to. The judge admitted he was aware of twenty-five different television shows, and during jury selection he even gave an unprecedented interview to Tricia Toyota of KCBS television in Los Angeles—and thereafter, having polluted the jury pool himself, he was required to dismiss jurors who had seen it.

One thinks of the Goldman family's appearances and the Browns'. They had a right to talk. They needed to talk. But they stirred up the frenzy, and some say they, too, profited. They had their own agenda beyond being grieving parents and sisters, and they beat their drums until we were all deafened by it. The participants spent as much time reading their press, watching the shows, and attempting to control the media as they spent on the case— probably more if the truth were known. The media loved it. The people loved it. The more the lawyers whined, the more the media displayed them whining. The more they hollered, the bigger headlines they suffered. Ratings went out of sight. The networks cashed in beyond our ever knowing, and their programming will never be the same again.

The mistakes made in this case were born of ego, of greed, of confusion, of failure to hear and to listen, but mostly of the participants' refusal to step out of the center ring of this circus of all circuses. These mistakes would never have been made had the lawyers on both sides been working in the ordinary course of business without the media hounding them, without the glare and the breathless glamour seducing them, without their adversaries using the camera as a weapon against them and vice versa. These lawyers, these witnesses, these police, this judge, were only human beings. These were no superpeople. These were not even super-lawyers. These were ordinary people and ordinary lawyers and an ordinary judge who were caught up in an extraordinary swell. They were converted, by the magic of the media, into superstars, super-villains, superfools, though they were none of the above. But their stardom did not provide them with anything they needed to cope with the implacable pressures of the glare. They were still the quite ordinary people they had always been, not the Dream Team, not the centerfolds in magazines, not the front-page heroes of women's causes or the new icons of the black movement. They could not be sucked up, like Jonah, into the belly of the media whale and still carry on an unblinking, competent life in and out of the court-room. They got wet in the whale's belly. They got soaked in the whale's belly. They got digested. And the losers were the system, the people, and justice, and justice to come.

CHAPTER 9

PEOPLE v. *JOHN WAYNE*

IF I WERE writing the stage directions for *O.J.*, the play, they would read something like this:

> *NIGHT: EXTERIOR SHOT: Nicole's condo on Bundy. The killer, in black, hulking, powerful, flashing knife in hand, stalks. Suddenly he grabs the beautiful blonde from behind. He jerks her head back, slashing deeply at her throat before she can scream. Now a young man, handsome, unsuspecting, unarmed, comes onto the stage and the villain strikes out at him. The victim cries out, "Hey! Hey! Hey!" but the lunges of the murderer are sudden and deep and it is soon over.*

The director can change the order that the victims appear on the stage—it makes no difference. They are both murdered with such dispatch, such unleashed fury. The villain leaves no throat uncut, no time for screaming. It is quick. Terrible. Then the villain runs as we watch the victims bleed out on the stage. Then lights slowly dim, and all is dark. And before the curtains are drawn, a dog begins to howl.

Who created this drama? The real-life players, of course: the villain, the victims. We could start the drama at another place if we chose, the small blond girl running out in toddling steps into her father's arms, and across the town, in a poorer place, a black child, with his angel face, his eyes large and innocent, his crooked legs running like a prairie antelope. Or we could start the drama when the villain and the victim meet and become lovers. The lawyers write the script. They become the directors of the play and eventually its stars. They can begin the play wherever they wish, present the drama as they envision it. But no such play was ever produced at the O.J. trial.

Instead, another producer came onto the scene. The new producer that took over was, of course, the Media. This producer was mad. But this new play had no theme, no story line. This new producer, the Media, created its own stars, held them up, glorified them, put them on the covers of the great magazines, put them in the glare of the lights, and then destroyed them, as Medea, the great mad, tragic heroine of Euripides, did her own children. Onstage the media, this producer, ordered a proctologic examination of the living and the dead while we watched, fascinated, and often gagged. The media took minimal personalities and made them into heroes or fools. It took the judge and set him to dancing. The producer was quite mad. This script, written by the media, became the case it created for the lawyers to try. And we were the audience glued to this explosion of insanity, we the people of the world, which, of course, included the jurors who would be chosen to try the case.

Any sane director who came onto the scene would have hollered, "Cut! Cut! We are trying to portray a simple double murder, not some raging, hysterical scene lifted out of Euripides." The sane director would have run the thousand players off the stage. He would have taken the script-gone-mad and ripped it to shreds. He would have ordered in new writers. "Write me a new script," he would have cried, "one that has a beginning, a middle, and an end. One that has a climax. One that has heroes and villains. One that is consistent from beginning to end, one that a sane audience can make sense of and care about. Make me a script where the audience will walk away angry at the villain. One where the villain will at last be brought to justice, and the audience left satisfied." If this extravaganza of sheer pandemonium, as produced by the media, were left unedited and no credible script authored in its stead, the prosecution's case would surely be lost.

But what if the media not only produced this rabid spectacle, but it also took over as the director? What if the lawyers abdicated their role as directors and the media, instead, laid out the strategies of the attorneys and plotted their roles? More than that, what if the media somehow crinkled the minds of the audience before the play ever opened? What then? And what if, all the while, the D.A. and his team of twenty-five or more lawyers stood by and, instead of running the insanity off the stage, tried in desperate, feeble ways to manipulate the media like a child screeching at its parent while the parent was writing his insane play?

The prosecution must have known, as we all knew, that the jury pool had already been infected. The prosecution knew what kind of audience it had. We cannot often choose our audience; we can only author an honest script. Was there a potential juror in the world who had not heard of the case? Was there a potential juror who did not have an opinion as to Simpson's guilt or innocence? Show me such a juror, and I will show you an idiot or some poor soul who had been in a coma for six months preceding the commencement of the trial. Finding the juror with a pristine mind and an unsullied viewpoint was like searching for a petunia in a Wyoming blizzard.

By the time of jury selection, the case had already been tried not once but a thousand times in the media. Vince Bugliosi, as we remember, had gleaned enough evidence from the media alone that he had no difficulty in concluding that Simpson was guilty, guilty as charged, guilty to his evil quick, and anyone who didn't agree with Vince was non compos mentis.

I know, of course, that judges and prosecutors like to argue that the defendant is not entitled to a jury composed of persons who have never heard of the case. Moreover, the prosecution routinely argues that the defendant is not even entitled to a jury composed of citizens who have no opinion concerning his guilt or innocence. Instead, most prosecutors and many judges claim the defendant is entitled only to a jury of folks who assure the court they can set aside whatever opinions that burden them and give the defendant "a fair trial."

How precisely, primly foolish are such judges. You could have twelve Nazis sitting on a jury trying a Jew, and all those brownshirts would have to say to the judge before they shoved the defendant into the oven would be that they could set aside their hatred of Jews and come up with a fair verdict. You could have twelve confessed racists sitting on the jury trying a black man, and all they would have to say (which they often have) would be that they could set aside their racism and come up with a fair verdict before they hanged him. Why not put twelve women on a jury who have been raped to try a man charged with rape? Over and over in the cases I try, I encounter some Zeus of the law up there on the bench who has long ago given up thinking for himself, since the law now thinks for him. Accordingly, he asks this silly question of the prospective juror:

"Well, Mr. Jones, even though you have heard and read certain things about this case, could you set aside your opinion and give the defendant a fair trial?"

"Yes, of course," the juror says dutifully.

"Would it take evidence from the defendant to cause you to set aside your opinion?"

"Oh, no," the juror says, understanding fully that any other answer might lead to his disqualification.

The judge is the father figure, the law, in the courtroom. He expects the juror to say he can wipe away his opinions and set aside his prejudices. But prejudices by definition are an inbred part of us. We can no more set them aside than we can sever ourselves from our heads or divorce ourselves from our souls or barricade ourselves against the memory of our experiences. We *are* our prejudices, our experiences, our opinions. If we do not have them, we either have not lived or are too dense to have acquired them. When a judge asks us if we can set these opinions aside, he is asking us if we can set ourselves aside from ourselves, separate ourselves from who we are and yet still be who we are. It is judicial nonsense with a deadly serious result. It deprives the defendant of a fair jury. And any thinking judge knows it.

The notion that, despite the endless media cloudbursts that have rained upon the juror, he has formed no opinion—or that even if he has, he can set it aside—is a legal fiction unfounded in human experience. An opinion, if it is based on mistaken fact or assumption, can, of course be changed. We occasionally change our opinions about people when we get to know them better. But more often our first opinions prevail. And too often we are too proud, too insecure, too stubborn, to change our opinions and to ever admit we were wrong. Too often, as well, "opinion" is nothing more than a euphemism for "prejudice." I have an opinion about bankers. My opinion is that they are generally robbers in pinstriped suits. I actually suffer a prejudice against bankers. I have an equally negative opinion about insurance companies. My opinion in both cases is a prejudice. Can I put these prejudices aside? Yes, of course, for as long as it takes me to decide against a banker or an insurance company were I chosen as a juror in their cases. My experience has been that those jurors who admit they are unable to set aside their opinions are frequently those who know such an admission is the surest way to be excused from jury duty.

"Can you set aside your opinion, Mr. Jones?" the judge asks.

"No, I can't set aside my opinion, Your Honor."

"What?!" the judge hollers, his eyes popping out like loose marbles.

"Sorry, Judge, my opinion is etched in stone."

"No matter what evidence is shown you, you still can't change your mind?" the judge asks, incredulous beyond belief.

"No. Never."

"What kind of a person are you, anyway?" The judge's face is red. The marshals move in, fearing the judge may have a seizure right then and there.

"Well, Judge, I am an intransigent, implacable, hardheaded, stubborn old jerk."

"Under those circumstances, and those alone, you are *excused*." The judge shakes his head in disbelief and declares a recess. No juror has ever escaped his withering voir dire. He could seat a jury of Baptist preachers and get them to swear on the Bible they can set aside their prejudices against the Devil and give him a fair trial. This kind of judge predominates in our courtrooms and, by such tactics, too often carelessly, even intentionally, deprives defendants of a fair trial. In the end, this has everything to do with the media.

In the O.J. Simpson case, every possible aspect of the case had been fully presented to the American public before jury selection began. All that was left unsaid were the boring details of the DNA evidence. Little else. The racial issues had already been exposed, defined, and defiled, and sides chosen up. The more people denied it was a race case, the more obvious it became that it was. The more people denied that they had any racial hangups about the case, the more the hangups were irrevocably embedded. The more the haughty pundits, the self-righteous, and the mavens of political correctness claimed that this case had nothing to do with black people against white people, the more the general public concluded that everyone in the media was lying. And all but a few were.

Fearing they themselves would be tagged as racists, most pundits took the position that this was not a race case, this was a plain old murder case. They said that blacks could decide this case as well and as impartially as whites, that blacks were as responsible as whites. O.J. Simpson wasn't black, anyway. His genetics to the contrary, he was a white man who had abandoned the black community. Few pundits ever dealt squarely with the racial issue, even though it became the irreducible factor in the case. Instead, the race issue was avoided, skewed whenever it emerged, and cloaked in the ever present, ever odious politically correct language. The depth of the racial strife in this country was never admitted. How could Larry King say things like "This is going to be a race case. The black people on this jury have different feelings about the justice system than the white people do"? Instead King asked questions about race, and the pundits who answered the questions, on the whole, convinced their predominantly white audiences that race was not an issue, or shouldn't be an issue, or if it were ever to become an issue, it was nasty as bad breath. The talking heads were above it. And since they were absolutely not racists, how could they conclude that anyone else had any racial feelings in the case? Besides, as we all know by now, if they did harbor any racial feelings, they could easily put them aside and give the parties a fair trial. No?

Any thinking judge—and there are actually several—knows that a prospective juror with an opinion as to the merits of the case should not sit in judgment of the case. In the celebrated trial of Aaron Burr for treason in 1807, Chief Justice John Marshall wrote, "Why do personal prejudices constitute a just cause of challenge? Solely because the individual who is under their influence is presumed to have bias on his mind which will prevent an impartial decision of the case according to the testimony. He may declare that notwithstanding these prejudices he is determined to listen to the evidence, and be governed by it; *but the law will not trust him . . . he will listen with more favor to that testimony which confirms, than to that which would change his opinion.* [my emphasis]"

The pretrial of the Simpson case, conducted nearly two hundred years after Burr's trial and produced with sickening redundancy in the media, set the stage. Sixty percent of the respondents in a poll conducted by the prosecution's jury consultant, Donald Vinson, told him that they had *already made up their minds.* People don't like to admit they have made up their minds. Such prejudging is seen as unfair, un-American, and even stupid. I should think, therefore, that the percentage of potential jurors who had made up their minds before jury selection began was even much higher than Vinson's poll suggested.

Think of it not as the O.J. case, but as your own case. You have been charged with an infamous act. It has received huge local publicity. You are innocent. You want a fair trial. You are entitled to a fair trial. The Constitution says so. Your lawyers says so. The judge, yawning, mouths the same sentiment. Yet 60 percent of your neighbors have already come to the conclusion that you are guilty. The first juror hasn't even been called to the box and a majority of the people waiting to try you have already rendered a verdict. And when they are asked if they have an opinion, they will say that they can readily set it aside and that they will be governed by the facts alone. We can already predict what is going to happen to you. You are going to go away from us, and for a long, long time. We will miss you, of course, and we'll hope the food is good at Leavenworth, but after all, you had a fair trial, with an unbiased jury, a magical jury whose members could set aside their prejudices against you. Why are you complaining?

But something profoundly different was happening in the Simpson case. The 60 percent of the public who had made up their minds hadn't concluded that Simpson was guilty. Many felt to the contrary. But of those who were actually summoned as potential jurors and who answered those ridiculously long eighty-page questionnaires, only 23 percent now admitted that they had made up their minds. What did that divergence mean? If 60 percent of the population as a whole had already made up their minds but only 23 percent of the jurors chosen from the whole population now admitted it, something was indeed awry. A jury consultant wasn't necessary to provide the answer: A lot of people wanted on that jury. And who were these people? They were people who wouldn't admit they had an opinion because their opinion, whatever it was, would likely affect their chances to be chosen. On the other hand, those who admitted they had an opinion were mostly people who wanted *off* the jury. My guess is that more people who had private-sector jobs or were in business wanted off the jury than those who worked for the government or were retired or unemployed. More blacks than whites were in the original jury pool in downtown L.A. and more blacks than whites wanted to sit on the case.

In a preponderance of headline cases, pretrial publicity manages to get defendants convicted before the first witness is sworn. In the O.J. case the tables were turned. The publicity often worked in O.J.'s favor, and for a number of reasons that extended beyond the manipulation of the media by Shapiro and company. For example, this was a case in which the LAPD was on prominent display and many black citizens living in black communities in L.A. saw the LAPD as the Los Angeles equivalent of the Gestapo. The show of the day was "The Race Case," starring Mark Fuhrman, and it had already been billed on the marquee of *The New Yorker* and *Newsweek*. The theme of the drama, racism, was echoed without cessation by the rest of the print and electronic media. Did these then predominantly black jurors have an opinion as to the credibility of the state's case before they were called as jurors? They likely did. Those who did agreed they could set it aside. Those who agreed to set their opinions aside likely attempted to do so out of honest hearts. But the media had poisoned the well. And no one, white or black, who had drunk of the water could ever recover.

Powerful dynamics were at work here, dynamics anyone could understand. Suppose that you are a white person who lives in some hypothetical town called Kingsville, in a hypothetical world that exists in a time warp removed from our chronological march through history. John Wayne is still alive. You live in this nonexistent state in which the power structure has been reversed. Your city is a predominantly black city and those who run the government are all black, except for a few token whites. You live in a white neighborhood surrounded by a black world. You are unemployed because most of the good jobs are held by members of the black majority. Nevertheless, in this hypothetical world you are an American citizen and you are told you have certain inalienable rights—whatever those are supposed to be. You are told you are equal to the blacks whose kids go to the best schools and who live in the plush neighborhoods. You are told you have the same privileges as the blacks who run the banks, but who won't cash your paycheck without a surcharge whenever you happen to get a little work. Because you have these rights, you are told you have duties as well, one of which is to respond when called as a juror.

You have heard all about the case on TV. A big case. The black media is going wild. John Wayne, your hero, has been charged with the murder of, say, his beautiful, black young wife.

When you get to the courthouse, you find that the judge is black. The D.A. is black. The deputy D.A. and the chief prosecutor are black. The investigating officers are all black. The lab technicians are black. The criminalists are black, as are the experts called by the black prosecutor. The marshals in the courtroom are black and the clerks are black. The audience in the courtroom is predominantly black. The media is black and usually takes the side of the black power structure—a few white comedians and pro golfers notwithstanding.

Moreover, let us assume that in your neighborhood in Kingsville, your personal experience is that black officers arrive each morning from their black neighborhoods from the other side of town—the good side—and push you and your white kids around. You have had experience with these black thugs in uniform, and so have your white neighbors. These black officers are known to plant evidence and, often without cause, beat up white folks unmercifully, sometimes, it seems, for the mere sport of it. They are known to commit perjury as often as is necessary to put white men in prison. You have a white brother in prison. Your son has had run-ins with these black officers for years, and they are laying for him. Of all the people on the face of the earth, you and your neighbors fear the black cops the most. They call you "cracker" and "honky" and pull you over and search your car whenever they feel like it. Just recently, you recall, they broke into the apartment of the lady on the third floor and, she claims, planted illegal substances there so that they could arrest and incarcerate her husband. Now this same group of thugs is after your hero, John Wayne.

The black cops insist they have a mountain of evidence against Wayne, as they always claim to have. They say that Wayne beat up his black wife all of the time and is guilty of a long history of domestic violence. But you know what that's all about: The black cops are trying to set up your white hero for killing a black woman. And you know that even if he is guilty of domestic violence, the black cops are using it, as they always do, to convict this white man. The fact that a man beats up on his wife, deplorable as it is, doesn't mean he killed her. That's dirty tricks all over again—the kind the black police are always using to put away another white man.

Well, the knock comes at the door, and surprise: You're summoned to jury service. They provide you with an official-looking questionnaire that asks if you have made up your mind as to the guilt or innocence of John Wayne. Of course you haven't. You will listen to the evidence. You can be fair. And you want to be on this jury. This is a famous case—the most famous in the history of Kingsville, probably the world. And you will be able to see the best lawyers and the big stars, and you—*little old you*—will be called upon to judge your hero, John Wayne. Can you imagine? But you will always stand firm on one thing: If they prove John Wayne guilty beyond a reasonable doubt, you will vote him guilty—just like that!—without any hesitation whatsoever. Don't forget, white citizens are as honest as black ones.

Before you were called to jury duty, you had heard about how the defense is accusing one of the black cops who had been at the murder scene of having planted key evidence at John Wayne's house. You wouldn't doubt it—for two reasons. First, John Wayne has always been a good citizen. He isn't the kind to kill his wife. Second, those black cops plant evidence all of the time against white people. Everybody knows that. The defense attorney, a white lawyer with a slick tongue and a cute little mustache, has made a big issue of it all over the black media, and you admire him for it. And you've also heard on TV a lot of other fishy stuff that is supposedly going on in the case. Nothing the cops would do would surprise you.

But overall the black media is making it look as if John Wayne has drawn his last six-shooter and has muttered his last, "Hello, pilgrim." As a matter of fact, the black media is turning this tragedy into a circus—dangling John Wayne before its audiences from a high wire, replaying his old movies, recounting his life in the most intimate and disgusting ways. As far as you can tell, this case has become mostly grist for the media machine from which the black media will make millions over the dead body of a black woman that your white hero has supposedly killed. You've seen injustice before. But you can sort it out, and you will, even though as you sit in the courtroom being examined as a juror, you have an opinion, based on the relentless cascade of media, that John Wayne is being set up, and further, that he is being used as a tool of the black media for their own profit.

Mostly black pundits have been talking, and then talking even more. Although the black media admits that it once admired John Wayne, and its corporations had transformed Wayne into a corporate spokesman through commercials on TV, the black media has turned on him and now concludes without saying it that this white man is nevertheless guilty. He must be—black cops don't lie merely because the accused is white. But you know better. You have been there. You know you can't trust the black media. It has betrayed you before. But that's another point.

Now the black D.A. decides that Jimmy Jones, a white man, should be appointed as an assistant prosecutor in the case. You suspect the D.A. is attempting to manipulate you and the rest of the whites on the jury panel. You are not sure you trust this cracker. Well, you will see. When at last you're in court and the lawyers question you during jury selection, you answer the questions right. You did not lie to get on the jury. You are not prejudiced. No one has ever accused you of that. You are as reasonable and honest as the next person.

"Yes," you answer the prosecutor. "I have heard about the case. But I do not believe everything I see on TV. Yes, I can put aside what I have heard about the case and try the case on the evidence."

You, the juror in our hypothetical case, will be seated. You are a good, decent citizen. But you have your own take on the events that arises out of your experiences as a white person living under the dominance of the black community. And the prosecution had better have a credible story to tell, one that gets right to the point, doesn't talk down to you, and will overcome your already robust suspicion that you will be lied to.

It's this simple: Some people love that little mutt looking up at them, wiggling his tail. Others are terrified of any dog, having been severely mauled and bitten by one as a child. One who has had such a harrowing experience as a child ought not sit as a juror on a dog-bite case, no matter how decent and honest that person is. In the end, the color of a juror's skin is irrelevant. Our experience in life, not our race, is the key. But in America, the color of our skin will have played a major role in forming our experiences. We certainly will have been bitten, one way or another, by the racist dog. And whatever our experiences, no matter how hard we may try, jurors cannot be severed from their personhood. We are our experiences.

We know that it would have all been different had O.J. Simpson been O.J. Jones. But O.J. himself was a child of the media—a star of whatever brilliance one wishes to endow him with. In the end, had the media not been so mercilessly focused on this case, the trial would have come and gone with the extraordinary attention of a celebrity murder case, but without the explosive power of some bizarre social epidemic that, like the plague, infected the entire nation. The O.J. case, in the ordinary course of business, would probably have been filed in the district where the murder occurred, which was Santa Monica, where a predominantly white jury would likely have been chosen whose collective experiences would have been quite different from those of the black jurors who occupied most of the seats in the courtroom in downtown L.A.

Although it is clear that the Fuhrman fiasco, at the behest of the defense, came tumbling out of the firmament to help save O.J., nevertheless the media became the tattoo artist that indelibly inked the racist issue onto the hides of the jurors. The more the pundits denied the existence of the race issue and excoriated the "race card," the more it was ground into the frontal lobes of the jurors. No black juror could trust the evidence, not even the DNA, not after someone accused of being a racist glove-planter was held up by the media and later hauled before them to coolly proclaim that he had not used the N-word in the last ten years.

It was inevitable that some of the media blitz, like a torrent of rain beating down on a leaky roof, would dribble down on the sequestered jury and be absorbed in predictable ways by each of the members seated to try the case. The words on the Fuhrman tapes, in which the detective laid out his cruel and ugly script of racism and torture for a screenwriter, one Laura Hart McKinny, were turned over to the public by Judge Ito, thereby launching the media into high lunacy. We remember from the tapes the matter-of-fact Fuhrman voice:

> "We grabbed a girl that lived there, one of [the suspects'] girlfriends. Grabbed her by the hair and stuck a gun to her head and used her as a barricade. Walked up and told 'em: 'I've got this girl, I'll blow her fucking brains out if you

come out with a gun.' Held her like this—threw the bitch down the stairs—deadbolted the door. 'Let's play, boys.' "

"Anyway, we basically tortured them. There was four policemen, four guys. We broke 'em. Numerous bones in each one of them. Their faces were just mush. They had pictures on the walls, there was blood all the way to the ceiling with finger marks like they were trying to crawl out of the room."

"We had 'em begging that they'd never be gang members again, begging us. So with sixty-six allegations, I had a demonstration in front of Hollenbeck station, chanting my name. . . . [The Internal Affairs investigation] lasted eighteen months. . . . I was picked out [of a photo line-up] by twelve people. So I was pretty proud of that."

"Immediately after we beat those guys we went downstairs to the garden hose in the back of the place. We washed our hands. We had blood all over our legs, everything. . . . We had to clean our badges off with water; there was blood all over 'em. Our faces had blood on them. . . . We handcuffed [the suspects] and threw them down two flights of stairs."

The word "nigger" was seemingly as in common usage by Fuhrman as bread and butter. "Those niggers, they run like rabbits." "How do you intellectualize when you punch the hell out of a nigger? He either deserves it or he doesn't." Fuhrman referred to women as "split-tails." Marcia Clark said, "Hearing these tapes just did me in. After that [I succumbed to the flu and] I was flat-out sick."

I do not agree, as *Newsweek* blandly asserted, that this case was lost "virtually the day the predominately Afro-American jury was sworn in." The severe potential for loss occurred the day *Newsweek,* along with the rest of the media, both print and electronic, told that predominately African-American jury that a racist was at work behind the scenes planting evidence against the accused. The analogy offered by Geraldo Rivera made some sense: He suggested this was like an all-Jewish jury who was called upon to decide the fate of a Jewish defendant, when the principle witness was a Nazi. Chris Darden claimed he knew there would be a defense verdict from the moment he walked into that courtroom and saw that jury. "I could see in their eyes the need to settle a score," he later wrote. But a score with whom? With Uncle Tom—as he believed the "brothers" were seeing him—or with the white community, from whom Chris Darden himself felt alienated? Or did Chris Darden see the jury through the too worried eyes of the paranoid?

Vincent Bugliosi thought the jurors were dumb and prejudiced. "What I [saw] were jurors who (1) clearly did not have too much intellectual firepower and (2) were biased in Simpson's favor, most likely from the start." He wrote that the prosecution should have put bibs on the jury and spoon-fed them to overcome their vacuousness and prejudice. On the other hand, I contend that those twelve people were as insightful, as wise, and as just, given their experiences in Los Angeles, as a jury composed of twelve clones of Bugliosi, given his experience. Juries are, as a composite intellect, incredibly smart. Trial lawyers make the mistake of tripping over their own arrogance. Most lawyers, I fear, know practically nothing. Most lawyers have never had a mop in their hands or scrubbed the toilet of a rich man. Most lawyers have never fought with all of their human energy to eke out a living for themselves and their families and then had people call them lazy. Most lawyers have never looked under the hood of a car, have never built even a bird house, and are essentially illiterate except for the endless tripe they read in law books. You could read all the many thousands of volumes contained in the law libraries of the ABA-accredited law schools and end up knowing substantially nothing.

But a jury composed of retired people who have gained wisdom, of schoolteachers, who care for and understand children; of factory workers, who comprehend machines and have experienced the vicissitudes of labor strife; of small businessmen, who fight for survival and know about banks and can also read a financial statement; of farmers, who must be everything from a mechanic to a botanist to survive—these are the people who know something about America, about life, about right and wrong, about pain and guilt, about fear and anger and love. Assembled, their collective intelligence, gleaned from their combined experiences in life, provides a fund of wisdom that would put to shame the pinched-up brain-stuff that so enthralls those who have a paper hanging on the wall announcing to the world that they are lawyers, these legal boys who think that because they have passed the multiple-choice test of the Multistate Bar Examination they are also uniquely qualified to pass judgment on the ordinary folks who sit as jurors in this country, sometimes for as little as five dollars a day.

No, this was not a dumb jury, nor one with prejudices other than those that arose out of their experiences as human beings. Had Bugliosi, still with his unique and razor sharp intellect, grown up in the black community of L.A. as a black man, and had he been selected to sit on the Simpson case, I daresay he would have voted along with the rest of the jurors in this case. He probably would have led the way. Given the facts Bugliosi gleaned from the media, *as the jurors did from the same media,* his high pronouncement in *Playboy,* even before the trial began, that Simpson was guilty was the product of his experience as a white prosecutor who grew up in a different community than most of the black people on the jury. If you asked Bugliosi if he was prejudiced by this experience, he would doubltess say to you, out of an honest heart—and he does have one—that he was not, or that if he were he could set his opinions aside. All of us are creatures of our experience. But tell me: If you are charged with a crime, do you want a jury of ordinary folks, such as sat on the Simpson jury, or a jury composed of superintellects of the likes of my friend Vince Bugliosi, or, as some of the blank-eyed professors are now pleading for, a jury of judges? God save us then!

In the end, the villain and the victims did not produce the final facts of this case. This trial became a bizarre, insane production authored by the media instead. As we shall see in later pages, this was not a case that had to be lost. This was a case that could have been won, but that took some small part of wisdom, a large part of devotion, a sense of story, and skilled storytellers. It was a case that demanded the use of common language, as well as a vow, never broken, that not once would the jury be bored nor lied to. It took the selection of a leader for the prosecution who would present nearly all of the case and whom the jury not only liked but could trust. It required honesty, not strategy. Openness, not cleverness. It was a case that required the prosecutors to become human beings themselves, humble, reasonable, dedicated human beings. Somewhere along the way the prosecution had to become credible *persons*. And, unfortunately, that is a skill that is most difficult for lawyers to acquire.

CHAPTER 10

THE LAWYERS

NOTWITHSTANDING MY COMMENTS to the contrary, I agree with many things my friend Vince Bugliosi says. Most lawyers, he says, are incompetent. And I agree. It isn't because they want to be incompetent. They study. They try. Some of them worry. Some even grieve. But most lawyers don't recognize their incompetence. That's because their incompetence begins not as lawyers, but as human beings.

What I am about to discuss is important because the O.J. case has become a major symbol of the American justice system. It stands in the minds of most Americans for both what is right and what is wrong—mostly wrong—with the nation's courts and lawyers. People who have eaten only one bad oyster but gotten deathly ill from it tend to judge all oysters based on that one wretched experience. So, too, do most people who have had little experience with the justice system judge the system by the O.J. case.

Prior to America's O.J. debacle, most people had little understanding about such things as searches and seizures under the Fourth Amendment or the right to a fair trial under the Sixth Amendment. Few had ever seen a trial from beginning to end, much less nine months of it. Few had ever watched a real cross-examination or heard an opening statement. One of our most astute young producers on television, still ignorant of a citizen's Fifth Amendment rights, told me she thought that O.J. should have been forced to testify, and that it was a terrible prosecutorial error that he wasn't called by the prosecution to take the stand and regurgitate his pathetic story. But most people had already learned that in America we do not have to testify against ourselves, that such is reserved for the terror of totalitarian states. By the time the case was over, such terms as *bench conference* and *voir dire* were in common usage in America.

"Hey, Ma, lets you and me and Dad have a bench conference," some kid was said to have hollered into the kitchen when he wanted to ask to borrow the family car for the evening.

We should be grateful for the small part of our legal education that was accurately delivered to us by the media. Nonetheless, this newly acquired education was more akin to going to medical school and observing doctors only butchering the patients, the patients in dreadful agony, while the professors snored in the cooler beside the corpses. What we as a viewing audience were treated to was often a horror, a perversion of the justice system, only occasionally sprinkled, most often accidentally, with sparkles of genius. Regrettably, most of the pundits didn't know a good cross because they'd rarely seen one. Some saw brilliance because they had been in the dark so long. So before we make our judgments in the case, let us begin where we ought to begin—by understanding who the participants in most American courtrooms are, and how they come to be there.

As we have seen, the directors of a courtroom drama are the lawyers. They also become the principal characters who, as Shakespeare put it, strut and fret their hour upon the stage. Each side presents its own story, its own script. The play is to be based on fact. It must be accurate and honest. But facts are subject to interpretation. Suppose the protagonist runs off to the village three hours before the murder. The prosecution says she ran into town to buy ammunition. The defense says she ran into town to buy groceries. She did buy ammunition. She did buy groceries. The prosecution says she bought the ammunition that was used in the gun that killed the deceased. The defense says she bought the groceries for the cookout she hosted that night and she bought the ammunition to kill the gophers that were desecrating her backyard. She did kill gophers. The neighbors saw her in the yard shooting at gophers and called the police to report that she was discharging a firearm within the city limits. The evidence is presented, on and on, and finally the arguments are made and the jury is left to sort out the truth.

The lawyers, being the directors of their respective scripts, must understand drama. But lawyers are not trained as dramatists or storytellers, nor are they encouraged to become candid, caring, and compassionate human beings. Most could not tell us the story of Goldilocks and the Three Bears in any compelling way. We would be fast asleep by the time they got to the first bowl of porridge. Their legalistic language would probably sound something like this:

Once upon a time in an unspecified and otherwise unidentified place was found, upon reasonable inquiry, a certain female child who allegedly bore the given but unlikely appellation of Goldilocks. She ambulated into and around a conifer growth one day and, unintentionally and without malice aforethought, lost her directions and was thus unable to ascertain whether she was proceding in a northerly or southerly direction. By random unanticipation the said female child came upon an insubstantial abode constructed of conifers severed from the surrounding growth, and at said time and place, the said female child, allegedly named Goldilocks, entered, without invitation, inducement, or encouragement, the said structure, which, at said time and place, therefrom the rightful and legal owners had absented themselves. Thereupon she espied three bowls of various sizes con-

taining a substance that, upon inquiry and investigation,
proved to be a concoction created out of certain boiled meal,
grains, and legumes commonly known as porridge . . .

Good trial lawyers need to be evolved persons underneath all the lawyer stuff. Most aren't. Good trial lawyers must be able to speak the ordinary language of people. Most can't. And that, as we shall see, became a serious problem in the Simpson case for both the prosecution and the defense.

I am put in mind of my old Uncle Slim, my father's older brother, who spent his life on the back of a horse. Uncle Slim and I were standing at the corral one day watching this dude saddle up. The dude had carefully lifted a fancy silver-spangled saddle onto the back of an old nag with a hanging head, the typical dude horse that plods safely along a trail with its nose to the ground and its eyes closed in virtual ambulatory sleep. Uncle Slim began to laugh his high, whiny laugh. He was pointing at the dude.

"Look at that dude," he said. "He's puttin' a thousand-dollar saddle on a ten-dollar horse. Why, ya can't get no place with a thousand-dollar saddle on a ten-dollar horse."

The story has become my parable for the description of the typical American trial lawyer. He has acquired a fancy education and has learned certain tricks and techniques. That, together with an acquired arrogance, becomes the saddle in Uncle Slim's parable. But if there is no horse underneath the saddle—a whole, well-evolved person—just as Uncle Slim avows, "Ya can't get no place," in or out of the courtroom.

By the time the young lawyer has percolated up through grade school, high school, and then college, he is pretty well domesticated, pretty well worn down as a person, pretty much weaned from the positive and the creative, pretty much suckled to the negative and mechanical. By the time he gets to law school, he is pretty much trained not to think for himself. He has become a predictable drone. He has lost his creativity. I would suggest he has been educated against feeling, against caring, against being. As I see him, he has learned that to do what one is told, to accept the myths presented to one as truth, to embrace the status quo, to look right rather than to be right, is the way to success. He has been taught that to conform without protest and to accept without question are means by which he will be rewarded in this society. One does not get to heaven on Rollerblades. One gets there hooked up to the eternal treadmill of mindless drudgery.

By the time the young person enters law school, he has learned to play those little word games that permit him to get a high score on the Law School Admissions Test (LSAT). Rarely is the student looked at to determine what he intends to do with his life. Rarely is any effort made to discover if he has the moral and personal attributes desirable in a lawyer. Rarely are questions asked on admission to determine if the applicant is honest. Does he have courage? Does he harbor any love of justice, any caring for people? Does he possess any laudable characteristics whatsoever? The fiend of Bugliosi's most famous prosecution, Charles Manson, could doubtlessly have obtained a high score on the LSAT and would likely have been welcomed with open arms into the law at Harvard or, for that matter, the University of Wyoming. But Christ, traipsing up to the same law school door in his flowing robes, and being gifted with his great storytelling ability, would probably have miserably flunked the LSAT. This proposition, as ludicrous as it sounds, is in part what is wrong with lawyers today. They are kissed on all four cheeks by computers—a computer that selects them as law students in the first place and another computer that checks them out with a similar test, the Multistate Bar Examination, before they enter practice. Lawyers today, intellectually and emotionally, look too much alike. If we have seen ten of them we have seen the near million who scramble across the land trying to somehow scratch out a living and pay off their student loans.

In law school, the students learn substantially nothing. For the most part, they are taught by professors who have spent the major portion of their lives injecting formaldehyde into their students' brains and, in the tombs of endless dusty books, burying whatever creativity, whatever life, the students might have escaped with before they came there. In law schools students learn little or nothing about trials. Unlike students pursuing social work, unlike medical students, law students likely have never seen a living client. They have never visited a jail. They have never walked into a courtroom, except, perhaps, in a misdemeanor court as part of a clinic offered in their third year that serves as little more than an apology for their tragic paucity of trial experience. What they learn is taught to them by professors who have had little, if any, practical experience and who wouldn't know how to file and perfect the simplest slip-and-fall case in a court of law.

When the student graduates from law school and passes the bar, he is equipped to do substantially nothing in the nation's quest for justice. He is more suited to labor in some dank hole in a mammoth corporate law firm and bill out his services at hundreds of dollars an hour than he is to enter a plea of not guilty on behalf of a citizen charged with a crime and to thereafter competently defend him. I would rather hire a good nurse to help me than a young lawyer fresh out of the moldy academic covers. The nurse went to nursing school not only to make a living but to do so by helping people. She went to nursing school and learned to listen to people, to hear their complaints, to care about them, to treat them, and to record, with accuracy, their course of treatment. The young lawyers, many of whom feel as if they have been cheated of their opportunity to fight for justice, can do little except what they were taught in law school—to read cases and to speak in legalese that no one can understand, nor cares to.

What are we to make of America's trial lawyers? Who are they? Why are we so disappointed in them? Where are the William Jennings Bryans and the Clarence Darrows? What we see instead are too many pampered kids with diplomas hanging on the wall who have had no life experience, who wouldn't know a shovel handle from a dildo, and who, by the time they have entered law school, have been stripped of most of what makes a human being, their openness, their compassion, their ability to feel, and who, after they get out of law school, are more equipped to cause trouble than solve problems. Never in the history of America have there been so many lawyers, and so many people who need a lawyer but can't find a competent lawyer who will care about them and fight for their justice.

You saw them in the O.J. case, those bright lawyers droning on and on in their examinations for the state about DNA. It wasn't the subject that was boring, it was the lawyers. You heard the professors arguing the law sounding like Rip Van Winkle staggering out of a sleepy hollow. And we wanted to scream out in agony, "Stop! My God, Almighty! Give me a break! Stop that incessant mumbling, that awful noise. Stop!" Little wonder Judge Ito occasionally went off the deep end. Little wonder, nailed to the bench as he was, and thus tormented day after day, that he wasn't driven completely mad. At least we could turn off the TV or walk out of the courtroom.

Alas, the trial lawyers whom you saw were not the quintessential Dream Team. Johnnie Cochran and Bob Shapiro are both bright, essentially competent lawyers who were trying to juggle many torches at once. The best of the prosecution revealed lawyers who most often were in over their heads. The lawyers on both sides of the case were trying to manipulate the press, trying to elevate themselves in the eyes of the people, and trying to pursue their own agendas, which were often in conflict with each other and their cases. All the lawyers were trying to survive, trying to gain prominence, trying to best the others with strategy, but only occasionally trying the case. They did possess, however, the minimal skills to try a case. But the Dream Team did not possess the extraordinary skills that "only money can buy," as was asserted by the *Los Angeles Times*. The prosecution did not, as some pundits saw it, present a flawless case. It was a case most any country prosecutor would hardly brag on.

The O.J. case stripped naked the underlying problem with trial lawyers trained by American law schools: They are simply not trained. By experience, by tragic trial and error, some learn to function in the courtroom. But to function in a courtroom is a far cry from being an effective advocate for a client. That the lawyers enter the courtroom, know the law, and can follow the rules, that they may even have learned to ask a question correctly and to labor through the various stages of a trial, does not mean they are trial lawyers any more than someone who knows the English language, and knows that a sonnet is composed of fourteen lines of iambic pentameter, is a poet. There is an art to the trial of a case, an art to which the lawyer is not exposed in law school. Few lawyers have mastered it. And those who have most often have somehow become the more highly evolved person. Most who have become fine trial lawyers have learned that it is all right to be afraid—that they should be afraid—and that it is all right to be real—that they must, for they are speaking to a jury of human beings who are real. Most have learned that it is all right to care about one's client, about justice—that they cannot ask jurors to care if they, the lawyers, do not care themselves. Somewhere along the way the successful lawyers have learned—to use the metaphor furnished by Uncle Slim—that it's a good horse and not a fancy saddle that gets you up the mountain and safely home again. The great lawyers, mostly unknown to the media, are out there, and they have learned what Uncle Slim taught—that "Ya can't get no place with a thousand-dollar saddle on a ten-dollar horse."

CHAPTER 11

THE IRON SHOE

IT WAS A bad jury, said Marcia Clark. Chris Darden had already made the same pronouncement. I saw the same jury. I saw people with expressive eyes, people with humor and feeling, people with notebooks handy and pencils poised, ready and able to hear the evidence. Out of respect for the court they were dressed up like churchgoers on Sunday morning. An older black man, sitting at the end of the jury nearest to me, wore a fine suit of clothes every day. He was thin and stately, and I could see his gray silk stockings and his shined shoes, much shinier than my boots. I thought he was a proud man. I would have trusted him with my case. He must have known the hurt of crime. He seemed like a peace-loving man. He would have fought for the prosecution's case if he could have believed it. I have no doubt of that.

I saw people wanting to understand, people wanting to do their duty as citizens. I saw careful people. They didn't glance over at the audience, at the grieving parents, at O.J. Simpson's elderly mother, who was wheeled into the courtroom almost every day. They were circumspect. Dignified. I watched a young, blond white woman, as pretty as Nicole herself. I was told she was married to a black man, a fireman, I believe. By her thoughtful dress and the way she held herself straight in her chair, she was obviously aware of the way she appeared. She took notes, and although I sat within a few feet of her, never once during the entire trial did she look in my direction. The still cameras were lined up behind me in the back row, the cameramen standing with their long lenses poised on monopods like sharpshooters on a firing line. Never once did I see her or any other juror look in the direction of the cameras. She was a sincere woman dedicated to her duty. When sometimes after lunch I would nod off to the low rumbling noise of the lawyers (which sounded like a vacuum cleaner suffering from terminal lung disease) I would awaken with a start, and after I discreetly inquired of Sally Stewart if I had been snoring, I would look over at this blond juror, and she would still be sitting there as attentive as a hawk watching the brooder house.

And the other jurors—they were focused on the history unfolding before them, alert, circumspect. I never saw them sleeping or laughing or giving any sign that they were not listening to the evidence. People would ask me, "How do you read the jury?" And I would say, "I can't read this jury. This jury does not want to be read." It wanted to do its job. It did not react. The press section in the courtroom reacted. The lawyers reacted, as did even the judge. But this jury was stoic. These jurors were not playing to cameras and would not communicate with the media by any oohs and ahs or raised eyebrows. They were intent on the evidence.

And after the jury had heard the testimony, took it in and masticated it carefully for nine months, they didn't have to deliberate for two more weeks to come to a decision. If they had heard some of the evidence once, they had heard some of it a hundred times. Over and over they had seen the exhibits, until they could call them up in their mind's eye by exact number. They had heard witnesses testify and they had heard other witnesses testify about what the first witnesses had testified to. These jurors knew the case intimately, as jurors do in long cases. The portion of the public that was not satisfied with the verdict criticized them for their quick return. But they had been away from their families for nine months. They took an early vote, as jurors often do. The vote was unanimous. Should they have punished themselves for another couple of days to make their verdict *look* good? Conventional wisdom among old trial lawyers holds that you can often expect a verdict right after lunch even if the jury arrives at its verdict at ten o'clock in the morning. That way the jury gets one last free meal off the state. Well, this jury had had enough free meals off of the state. Nine months of that food should be enough for anyone.

The jury I watched for many a day was the same jury that had been chosen by Marcia Clark for the People and, after its verdict, denounced by her. These jurors were the same jurors who Chris Darden looked at and saw in their eyes that they "had a score to settle." How could these lawyers, or anyone for that matter, criticize this jury? What lawyers, who sell their time for hundreds an hour, would sit for nine months with nearly no pay and work for the good of the nation, for the preservation of the justice system? Lawyers make their living from the justice system. But I daresay you couldn't have seated a jury of lawyers if you tried for the next fifty years. They would still be whimpering and moaning about how they were too busy, too important, their lives too invested in their golf games and dinner parties, to sit for one month, much less nine. And had a jury of lawyers been seated, they would probably still be out, as the old joke goes, still making nominating speeches for the foreperson.

What smart business heads would sacrifice their money-making opportunities to invest their lives for the benefit of society, separated from their families, their friends, their enterprises? You'd be lucky if you could get them to buy a package of Girl Scout cookies, much less give nearly a year of their lives, which is, after all, their money. That we might not agree with the jurors' verdict does not give us cause to offer anything but deep gratitude to these people. I would not want to go to any jail, even the jail in Judge Ito's hotel, for nine months, there to be spied upon and criticized; to be fed and clothed away from my family, my friends, my life; to be cooped up with people I did not choose to live with; and to listen to the endless mumblings of smart-ass lawyers for nearly a year—the thanks for which is some pundit's claim that I don't have much "intellectual firepower," that I am a prejudiced nincompoop who couldn't possibly have come to a decision without having re-swallowed and redigested nine months of the state's fare before announcing my verdict on the first day of deliberations.

This jury was all right with Marcia Clark at the time she chose it. She had peremptory challenges left. She could have pointed a pinkie at any one of half a dozen of the black women who ended up on the jury and said, "I don't want you," and that juror would have been replaced with another so long as she could support her decision on grounds other than race. And any first-grade lawyer could do that. Such is called a "peremptory challenge." She didn't have to have a substantial reason. All she had to do was look in the potential juror's eyes, as Darden had, and if she saw something there she didn't like, if she didn't like the way the person parted her hair, she could wave good-bye to her, and she would be gone. Lawyers pick juries. And after they pick them they usually congratulate themselves on their great perspicacity. But when they lose, the same jury suddenly, magically, is transformed into a mob of lunkheads. If they win, of course, the jurors are quite brilliant. They stand for the most admirable traits of all that is right in America. And the lawyer who chose them is, of course, the light of all legal lights.

Marcia Clark chose this jury for the People. She evaluated this jury through *her* eyes. Her criticism of the jury after the verdict tells us more about her than the twelve she chose. She wanted women. This was a women's case, she thought, a case of domestic violence. Give me a woman who has been beaten up and kicked around by her man, and she'll deliver a verdict against O.J. Simpson, the very symbol of spousal abuse. That the prosecution left peremptory challenges unexercised because the remaining candidates were even "sorrier prospects," as Clark put it, is a rationalization I do not accept. You cannot tell how "sorry" a juror is without interviewing him. People are not "sorry" on paper—that is, the jury questionnaire. "Sorry" jurors can relate to you in appropriate ways if, in return, you are not "sorry" to them.

And if, indeed, this jury was that "sorry" going in, why did we hear Chris Darden assuring Marcia Clark, as he did at the commencement of the trial, that "black people won't want to convict Simpson. But if you've got the evidence, you can overcome that. You'll make it." She found that reassuring. I find that statement true. I also remember that Darden told Gil Garcetti after Darden's Donnybrook with the glove, "Gil, it's not over yet. We'll still get him. I promise."

What if this had been a jury of twelve saints? Could those prosecutors have recognized it? We cannot understand that which we have not experienced: *personhood*. See that juror over there—the woman with the soft, tired eyes who works those dreary hours in some wretched place for low wages to support her children? She is a *person*. Could the prosecutors have appreciated her? She is afraid and vulnerable and fragile, and her back aches and she sleeps through her worry only because her weariness at last defeats her. She knows much about pain and patience and nothing about arrogance. Although she knows nothing of the art of personhood, she has learned it, as unsung saints have learned it, while those who judge her, who point their fingers at her, know little of what I speak. One can learn more about personhood from the old woman begging on the street corner than from the erudite jurists and the bookish professors. We are so quick to judge the quiet faces, the soft voices. The people with hard lines across the brow, the ones with crooked fingers. When they do not accept our cases or us, we, the lawyers who parade in front of them with our chins outstretched like strutting turkeys and a slight sneer stuck to our lips, proclaim that something is wrong with "those people." "You can see it in their eyes," some lawyer says. But I say such lawyers see only reflections of their own eyes.

Often we lawyers deal with juries as we deal with our spouses: When the marriage goes wrong it is not our fault. It wasn't Clark's fault that her choices had been wrong—wrong for her. One wonders if she could have made better choices. What jury would have been right for her? A jury of all white women who had been beaten by an array of abusive husbands? A jury of men, perhaps, who were not put off by her? How do we blame the jurors? The jurors did not write the script in her case. They did not select the domestic-violence theme. They did not direct or present the drama. They did not select the witnesses. They were not responsible for who Marcia Clark had become, how she prepared herself or presented herself. The eight black women were not responsible for how she came off to them, nor how they came off to her. Yet somehow the verdict became the fault of the jurors, not the fault of the persons who chose them in the first place and then played to them for nine god-awful months, after which they were rejected like lepers from hell.

We have already acknowledged that the prosecution could have taken the case to the whiter Santa Monica. But that would have been a racist decision. Perhaps, as was suggested, Garcetti wanted to avoid another riot should a white jury convict O.J., as happened after the first Rodney King case. Perhaps he was more a politician than a strategist or more a decent prosecutor than a win-at-any-price D.A. Whatever his reasons, we cannot criticize his decision to keep the case downtown, although many rage cease-lessly on about it as if the People (i.e., white people) had been deprived of a fair trial by his decision.

I do not agree with the pundits who make the simplistic claim that Garcetti's decision lost the case. The case could have been won downtown. Obviously the prosecution believed it at the out-set. To be sure, the pools from which the twelve and their alter-nates would have been selected may have varied in palpable ways from the ones provided in Santa Monica, but that does not mean that the case necessarily would have been won in Santa Monica and lost in downtown L.A.

I have seen nothing to suggest that the D.A. understood or dealt with any of the following simple but vital initial issues. You have a story (the case). You have an audience (the jury). You present a case that the audience can appreciate with players to whom the audience can relate, the storytellers (prosecutors). You do not win cases by letting whatever happens happen. Philip Vannatter, one of the detectives on the scene at Rockingham, had called Clark for some advice on the search warrant. She reported that she went to Rockingham "to baby-sit the cops serving the warrant," and that was how she just sort of fell into the case. She wrote, "I'd been hoping for something bigger to fill out my caseload." She wanted the case. She admits Garcetti might have seen her as an "assertive woman," maybe even a "loose cannon." But if Garcetti had doubts, he never expressed them. She was on the case. Fate, Vannatter, and Marcia Clark herself made the decision about who would star in a drama that would become perhaps the most infamous murder case in American history. Clark was thus chosen as the chief prosecutor for no apparent assignable reason, to tell a yet unknown story to an audience that had not yet been identified. That is like choosing Madonna to play the starring role in a play. "What play?" you ask.

"I don't know," comes the producer's answer. "Whatever play happens to come up, she stars in."

"You mean she might star in *Rocky*?"

"Maybe. I don't know" is still his answer. "Maybe we could make her a lady boxer. She is gonna star, that's all I gotta say."

"You mean she might star in a play designed to be performed for old ladies in some rest home?"

"I don't know," the producer answers. "Whatever. Madonna is the star."

Producers don't make decisions that way. Nor should D.A.'s. It could be argued with some efficacy that if the case was lost at the outset, it was not lost when it was filed downtown. Nor was it lost when a predominantly black jury was chosen. It was lost the moment Vannatter called Clark for advice on the search warrant, or when Clark trotted out to Rockingham "to baby-sit the cops," and thereby just happened to end up lead counsel for the People.

Still, the first decision to be made had not been made. The first decision was not *who* would try the case but *what* case was to be tried. What was the story? And before the state's chief counsel could be chosen, the second question also had to be considered: What audience would likely hear this story? Only after these first two questions had been resolved could the D.A. finally determine who among his nine hundred and some lawyers could best direct this drama and tell this story.

I think of another important case, successfully tried in Denver. In the Oklahoma City bombing case, the government determined that it would present a simple, straightforward story against Timothy McVeigh: He was a vengeful, evil man who did not care whom he killed or the suffering his victims would endure, and he was responsible for having murdered 168 human beings, including many children. The audience would be ordinary people in Denver, Colorado, a city in many respects like Oklahoma City. The lawyer chosen to tell that story to that audience would not be a chesty, powerful, loud-mouthed male prosecutor. The lawyer chosen would be a man who drove himself into the courtroom in an electric wheelchair, a human being first, a man suffering from his own disabilities who could understand the pain and the sorrow of victims, and who could speak with compassion and credibility to a jury of human beings. If that case was won at a specific point, it was when both the story and the audience were identified first, and then the best person to tell that story was selected. The important prosecutorial decisions ought not to be the product of serendipity.

Once Marcia Clark was on the case, every decision had to fit Marcia Clark. To succeed she had to choose a story that *she* could best tell, not the story that should have best been told. To succeed she had to choose an audience to whom *she* could best tell the story, not a storyteller best suited to tell the story to the audience most likely to hear the story. Marcia Clark became the iron shoe, and every foot in the case, whether it fit or not, had to be forced into it.

So serendipity became the strategiest and the producer. Serendipity chose the lawyer, and in turn, this serendipitous lawyer was given the power to write the script. And she did. Marcia Clark wrote the script. Garcetti did not. Marcia Clark was provided this "mountain of evidence." Out of this mountain of evidence she could construct several different cases. She could present the simple, understandable case of a jealous husband who killed his wife and another man. From the available evidence she could have presented the case of a man who was stalking his former wife's lover and who ended up killing them both. She could have presented a domestic violence case, one in which the accused followed a course of ever increasing hostility that finally ended in the murder of his wife. (Although this was her goal, I think she never achieved it, the story having long been lost in the murk of the scientific evidence.) Indeed, she was not even required to prove why Simpson killed his wife. His motive was admissible, but motive is not a necessary element of proof in a murder case. She could have simply proved, from the "mountain of evidence," that Simpson was the killer and that the circumstances established that he intended to kill. Clark readily admits that "in the Simpson case, the physical evidence was so amazingly strong, I felt that we could probably put him away relying on that alone."

Clark chose to construct a domestic violence case. She had the script already written—by Faye Resnick, in her book. It is not surprising that as a woman, and as a woman with her life experience, she saw this as a woman's case, one that other women would celebrate across the world. From the O.J. Simpson case, the world would learn once and for all that wife batterers are potential killers, that spousal abuse lies next to murder. This case would stand as a warning to the rest of the nation's violent males—who, in fact, are as numerous as rats in a New York sewer—and would put domestic violence on the front page for months to come. The case would be as important to the rights of women as the Scopes trial was to the right of free thought in our schools.

But for Marcia Clark to position herself alongside Faye Resnick's campaign against spousal abuse was a decision fraught with difficulty. Let us not pass this point without recognizing that domestic violence, pervasive as it is in this psychotic society, must be fought at every bush and bend. But the greater immediate issue at hand was the conviction of Simpson. How do we justify the waging of war against domestic violence at the sacrifice of justice in the Simpson case? Even the most just of causes almost always gets in the way of a lawyer and, before the case is over, tends to trip up justice as well.

When I took on the Karen Silkwood case, the National Organization for Women (NOW) wanted the public to know that they had supported the case, for which I was grateful. At the trial I had just given my final argument and was the favorite to win. The jury was deliberating. Sensing a victory for their dead heroine, NOW wanted the limelight. But when a lawyer takes on a cause, he takes on all of its warts: the prejudices against the cause, its patent and latent enemies. The cause becomes his. It can devour the case. Every case I've ever tried, without exception, has had enough of its own warts, the Silkwood case included. I demanded that NOW members back off while my jury was deliberating. They could make whatever press release they chose after the verdict, but not during the jury's deliberations. I remember shouting, "If you dare mention that you are attached in any way to my case, I will take to the press and deny I have ever heard of you. I'll claim you're gross impostors and shameless opportunists"—or words to that effect. They backed off. I did not make friends in NOW. But I didn't lose my case (or theirs) because I permitted a cause to become attached to it. Marcia Clark decided to make the Simpson case the cause célèbre for domestic violence. She admits that at the outset, "to say that I felt a sense of destiny might be overstating it. But I do remember thinking, *This is it. You were meant to do this.*"

By now the problem had been exacerbated. We have let the star, Marcia Clark, who just happened to stumble onto the stage, write the script, rather than casting the *right star* to match the *right script* for the audience at hand. But why did Marcia Clark decide to write *this* script for *this* case? We see things through our own eyes, through the lens of our own history. To Clark, men were violent—maybe not all men, but one wonders if she ever saw a man whom she didn't first measure for his violence potential. She had had a sordid history with abusive males both in the cases she had prosecuted and in her personal life. She herself suffered a rape as a teenager, and although she denies that she was at first attracted to the idea of domestic violence as the underlying theme of the trial, she admits that whenever a reminder of Nicole's physical suffering at the hands of O.J. came up she felt "headachy" and "sometimes a little sweaty." She said she would push such feelings down and keep on working on the case. In retrospect, Clark now seems to blame Scott Gordon, another crusader in the D.A.'s office against spousal abuse. She says he, together with other champions against domestic violence, argued her into their position—that domestic violence should become the cornerstone of *People* v. *Simpson.*

Tactics, too, can get in the way of appropriate decisions. Sometimes lawyers let tactics govern the drama. Tactically, if Marcia Clark made this a domestic violence case, she could argue to the judge that all of O.J.'s previous acts of violence were relevant and could be paraded before the jury in full bloody, black-and-blue color. His violent episodes were many, frightening, and ugly. Simpson, who burst into a rage whenever he didn't get his way, sometimes beat this poor woman in egregious ways. Clark likely reasoned that when she showed the jury this abuser in action the defendant would be convicted of murder.

But for the purpose of considering her strategy, let us suppose Simpson was completely innocent. I am not suggesting he was. I am saying *suppose* he was. Suppose, for the purposes of the argument, that he had in fact been chipping golf balls at the time of the murder. *Just suppose.* What jurors would believe him innocent after having heard evidence that he had beaten his wife half to death, not once but on countless cruel, terrorizing occasions? How could anyone be surprised that Simpson had finally gone all the way? And by the time the screaming and beatings had been laid out before the jury—after the jury saw the windshield beaten in, the door smashed down, the bodies thrown across the room, the horror and the fear of it all—the jury would no longer see O.J. Simpson as their hero. He would become an object of hate. If he took the stand, the jurors would never believe him. They would see him not as a great black icon with the Heisman in his hand, but as a murderer with a dagger in his hand. In her book, Clark came close to admitting the strategy: "If we identified this as a domestic violence case that ended in murder, we could argue that the incidents of abuse that led up to the crime should be admissible." Would such a strategy succeed when presented to the predominantly black female jury she was about to choose? As they say in Wyoming and elsewhere, "Would this dog hunt?"

Having decided to build her case on the cause of domestic violence, it became Clark's duty to think about the jurors who would be hearing the case, given the fact that this sometimes too tough white female would be presenting it. After Faye Resnick's book set out in vivid detail the script for a domestic violence courtroom drama, Clark doubtlessly thought that a jury composed mostly of "sisters," black or white, would join with her and bring this abuser to justice. Bearing this worthy banner, she marched into the courtroom ready to take on all of male-kind and anybody else who might cross her path. Then she walked up and began cooing in Johnnie Cochran's ear, quite oblivious to the black women on the jury who were watching.

It is not easy to see ourselves as others see us. I have no doubt that Marcia Clark was as afraid as I am every time I walk into the courtroom before a jury, with a judge looking down, the case heavy on my back. We do not appear afraid. We are too afraid to appear afraid. I have no doubt that Marcia Clark's defense against fear, similar to my own, is to become aggressive. We attack out of fear as the lion attacks out of fear, but people do not understand that. People do not cuddle up to aggressive, hostile persons, male or female. And we know what people do with those they fear—they eliminate them from their lives, if possible. In the animal world we kill snakes and mad dogs. In the civilized world we rid ourselves of fearsome things by fortifying our defenses against them, by distancing ourselves from them, by rejecting them, a form of emotional killing.

In the meantime, someone like Clark, like myself, may not be able to readily understand why we have put off these people. How can they see us as harsh and pushy, even obnoxious, when inside we feel like small, frightened children? Don't they understand that we are only the Cowardly Lion in *The Wizard of Oz*? Don't they understand that we are simply afraid, that a courtroom is a very hard place in which to survive, that we have powerful, relentless adversaries against us: those men over there with their smooth, slick ways who will kill us by destroying our case, who have the money and the big reputations, who will attack us with endless barrages of paper and media and experts, if not brilliance? And even with legions of others behind us, we are still alone in this courtroom. And still afraid. So if we seem hostile because that is how we defend, surely you, the jury, will understand. You, the jury, our sisters. But sometimes we are too tough to feel our fear, and that is because in this business we need to be tough to survive. And most often the jury does not understand why that person over there who calls himself or herself a lawyer has to come off so mean, so harsh, so unapproachable, so unlikable.

When I was a young, tough, sometimes too aggressive lawyer,

the zeal for justice hot in my veins, I sued a manufacturing company for the negligent construction of a crane, a part of which had fallen on my client, leaving him little more than a walking vegetable. I called the manufacturer's chief witness to the stand for cross-examination. As I had the company witnesses before him, I cut him up into little, pitiful pieces. It was all right to cut the company witnesses up, I thought. They had it coming. And this man was the worst of them, one of those flabby-cheeked, brown-nosed company men who, as part of their jobs, lied for the company on the stand, all smiling and sweet and nodding at the jury. He lied about the engineering on the machine that had turned Bill, my client, once a hardworking, honest crane operator with a family to support, into barely more than a turnip, a man who didn't know where he was or where he was going. My cross-examinations of the other witnesses had been devastating. Now I took what was left of the company man sitting there on the stand all pretty white-haired and pious, and I cut those pieces into further little pieces, and then, as if that weren't sufficient, I stomped on them, and ground them into the dirt with my heel. I shouted at him. I sneered at his inability to answer my questions. I paraded in front of him, pointing my finger, accusing, demanding. His old mouth opened and the words that oozed out were ridiculous. I held the words up for all to see, held them in his face and jeered. I destroyed the blinking little bastard who dared lie, who dared not own up to the truth of his company's negligence in the face of that poor man whose piteous disability was the manufacturer's lifelong gift to him.

Then the jury returned its verdict. They found against poor Bill. Gave Bill nothing. Left him to wander the streets and sleep on a grate if he could find one. I couldn't believe it. Not after that magnificent performance. How could this be? I was astounded, wounded beyond speaking. What had gone wrong? Then a juror came up to me. She had tears in her eyes. She looked up into my face, and finally all she could say was, "Mr. Spence"—she was old enough and kind enough to be my mother—"why did you make us hate you so?"

The jury had hated me? Jurors, like you and me, do not believe those whom they dislike. It is a hard lesson for lawyers to learn. Mine came at the expense of poor Bill, and I tell his story once more because the only good that can still come from his loss of justice is for other lawyers to learn the hard lesson of his case: That we, out of pure hearts, may despise the witness or the opponent does not mean that the jury shares our rancor. Good lawyers are passionate. Good lawyers may attack out of anger, out of their sense of right and wrong. But the attack may seem inappropriate and unjust and thus turn the jurors away. Good lawyers may be afraid and become hostile or too hard. "Harsh" is the word often used. And often the jurors are repelled.

Ever since Bill's case, over and over in the trials that have followed, I pass my associates a slip of paper. It bears only the letters "WGO?" which my associates know asks the question, "What's going on?" By that I am asking, how am I coming off? Am I too aggressive? Am I being too mean to the witness? Am I coming off as a smart-ass, as is the way of those of us who are sometimes insecure? I am not attempting to *act*. I am attempting to *be*—to be genuinely who I am. To be appropriate, to be aware of what is happening in the courtroom. If I am afraid, I need to be afraid, not hostile. If I feel insecure, I need to deal with it and not parade around the courtroom like a two-bit cock of the walk, my chest bursting with bogus bravado.

Marcia Clark needed help. She needed insight into who she was and how she presented herself. She needed to pass the slip around to her sometimes dozing associates. "WGO?" I doubt that she knew she was often too tough. The pundits were saying she was magnificent. She was presenting "the perfect case." But how would they know? And anyway, we all need help in this frightful, lonely business in the courtroom. The room may be full of assistants; we may have backup like the Dallas Cowboys or the twenty-nine lawyers the prosecution had assigned to the case. But in the end we, the trial lawyer, are the only one standing there, and suddenly our mouth is open and nothing comes out, or what comes out sounds like the pronouncement of Darth Vader, and we lay awake at night thinking of what we should have said that we didn't say or how we should have said it differently.

If we are Marcia Clark we have all of the smart-ass pundits second-guessing us, law jockeys who don't know the first thing about our case, who don't have our problems, and who don't give a damn, who don't have the responsibility of the trial, who are free to talk to 10 million people and tell them that we are beautiful or blowing it. I've been at this trial business a long time. You don't ever outgrow the fear. And you always have to deal with yourself. Hopefully you learn that it is all right to feel your fear and be honest about it, that it is all right, indeed blessed, to care, but at the same time be kind to your opponent.

But Marcia Clark, for whatever reason, resisted the pro bono offer of the famed jury consultant Don Vinson. In some ways I agree with her. I never use a jury consultant. Some try to create the profile of the juror most likely to stand with you, but there is no such person—not in the real world. A person who matches the profile will quickly be stricken from your list when you discover that she winces whenever *you* walk past her, or he wants to bash in your head because he is threatened by you. The ideal juror is like an automobile manufacturer who makes a seat that should fit everyone but fits no one. I say to jury consultants, if you want to choose the jury, then you try the case. You cannot pick a jury for me any more than my mother could pick my wife. You can only pick the jurors *you* like, the ones with whom *you* resonate—if, indeed, you resonate especially with anyone.

But I am too quick to criticize. Jury consultants have the ability to help us isolate the principal emotional issues that will govern the jurors' decision-making process. We make decisions out of our bellies and then rationalize them out of our heads. Judges don't like to admit it, but they do, too. Jury consultants put together what they call focus groups, made up of people representative of the likely juror types who will be on the jury panel in the case. The arguments of the respective sides are presented. Sometimes the attorney will stand before the focus group and lay out his argument on the main issues, and someone else in the same office will give the argument for the other side. Then the group is asked questions by the consultant: What did you think of this argument or that? This story or that? What did you think of the attorneys? And while the feedback is being received, the attorneys for the case observe, often via a television monitor and hidden microphones, or they watch through one-way glass.

I had been using focus groups for many years, long before they had come into vogue in the jury-consulting business. I simply didn't know that was what they were called. I talked about the emotional stuff that caught hold of me in my cases with anyone who would talk to me. "What do you feel about . . ." was always the opener. I asked my partners, my friends, my secretary, my own Imaging, who always gave me straight answers, even when I didn't want them. I talked to waitresses and schoolteachers and gas station attendants and cowboys. I talked to whoever would talk to me about the case. And after a while I learned what my case was about. With focus groups you learn something about the emotional chemistry that comes bubbling up out of the cauldrons of human pain and anger and exhilaration, which forms our opinions and dictates our decisions. And you also learn something about yourself. To most lawyers' surprise, the lawyer has the obligation to become a human being. And you learn to stop talking and listen to others—and, at last, to yourself as well.

Because of the immense media deluge that descended like an eternal gullywasher, this case was different from any Marcia Clark had tired—to the most extreme degree. The minds of the jurors in this case had been so thoroughly soaked by the media that no one's psyche in the case remained dry. Not mine. Not Clark's. Not anyone else's. The media storm was so powerful and incessant that, in effect, the mind of every potential juror had already been influenced in some way. But how? More than any other information in the case, Marcia Clark needed to know.

Don Vinson had offered to give his free service as a jury consultant to the state, which Clark had resisted. The guy didn't have a clue, she said, and only after Garcetti pressured her did she reluctantly agree to take part in the process Vinson proposed. From behind one-way glass she observed a mock jury deciding the case based on the presentation of the anticipated arguments of both the prosecution and defense. Clark was shocked by what she saw: The whites were for conviction, the blacks for acquittal. Moreover, before the group had been together but for a short while, this panel put aside a discussion of the evidence and suddenly became enthralled with the Fuhrman issue: Did he or did he not plant the glove? Already Clark was hearing one black female refer to "my man O.J." And even when this mock jury was told to assume that the blood to the left of the shoe prints at Bundy belonged to Simpson and that the skin oils on the inside of the glove matched those of Simpson, a majority of the black jurors still voted not guilty. Vinson, in questioning the black women on the panel, asked them how they felt about the issue of domestic violence. Here is where Marcia Clark, and any other thoughtful lawyer forming the dramatic structure of the case, should have listened carefully. Often the reaction of the black women was to the effect that there is always a little trouble in a marriage, that people get slapped around, *and* that the mere fact that Simpson may have threatened Nicole and stalked her, and had beaten her did not mean that he had killed her.

I made the same argument on *Larry King Live* and elsewhere when I heard how the prosecution was attempting to throw domestic violence into the case. Wife beaters are cowards, but few of them ever become murderers. Alan Dershowitz wrote that the defense was ready to prove that fewer than one out of twenty-five hundred men who slap or beat their domestic partners end up murdering them. It was unfair, it seemed to me, to argue that because Simpson was an abuser he was therefore likely to be a murderer as well. If abusers are not usually murderers, then what relevance did his acts of domestic violence have to the case? Little, I thought, except to unfairly prejudice the jury against Simpson, strip away the advantage of his celebrity, and, guilty or innocent, convict him of a murder based on evidence of his abuse rather than evidence of his killing.

Later Clark was thrown into deep shock when Vinson asked the members of the focus group what they thought of her. Several black women, almost in unison, responded, "Bitch!" "Bitch!" Garcetti saw it, and he later suggested that she might try to "lighten up a little." But a lioness doesn't whimper. A lioness doesn't listen. A lioness charges. The best Clark could do with the information Vinson provided was, as she later put it, to get "a goddamned haircut."

Between two focus groups and a telephone survey conducted by Vinson, the results were pretty clear: Black women were the greatest supporters of O.J. According to Vinson's telephone poll, black women were three times more likely to believe Simpson innocent than black men, and among black women the assumption that Simpson was guilty of domestic violence *did not* make him any more likely to have committed the murder with which he was charged. Forty percent of the black women, according to Vinson's poll, thought the use of physical force was appropriate in marriage. And black women, more than any other group, had real trouble with Marcia Clark as a human being.

Garcetti must have known this. So did Clark. Yet no one wanted to hear what Vinson was telling them. Already the jury consultant was, in effect, telling Garcetti, "Listen: You are presenting the wrong case to the wrong audience by the wrong messenger." One imagines Garcetti's predicament: If he had taken Clark off the case, he might have been tabbed a sexist. Politics and justice are never comfortable bedfellows. Perhaps Clark, knowing what she knew, should have withdrawn as counsel for the People. The trial of a murder case is no place to struggle to overcome racial prejudices that are mixed in with powerful feminist issues. Yet no one ought to blame Clark for clinging to a case that was, as she saw it, her destiny. Had I been a young prosecutor, a lion, you would have had to kill me with an ax before I would have withdrawn from that case. *But not to listen*—that is the fatal error that too many lawyers make. Too many are too smart, too sophisticated, too above it all to listen. Too many have not yet gotten the message: that the power in a trial is not in their beautifully honed brains and the air-cooled psyches; the power in a trial is vested in the jury, in ordinary human beings who, together, have more wisdom and enjoy more insight than any lawyer will ever acquire even if he should outlive Methuselah. Over and over it is the lawyers' arrogance that kills them and, ultimately, their client's case as well.

So what does a female trial attorney who is seen as "a castrating bitch" by black women do? What do you do when the jury consultant in the case tells you that domestic violence as the case's principle thrust won't fly? Well, you bow your neck and curl your lip and tell everybody to go to hell, and you seat a busload of black women on the jury and fly out your colors under the domestic violence flag. That's what you do—if you are Marcia Clark. And after you lose the case, you blame everybody in sight for the loss except yourself. Although we have been entertained with her appearances on most of the national and international television shows, I have yet to see Marcia Clark simply look into the camera and say, employing her favorite language, "Folks, I fucked up."

In the meantime, the defense, following the advise of Jo-Ellan Dimitrius, the defense's brilliant jury consultant, was selecting the same jurors that Clark was advised by Vinson to take off the jury but left on. Her retaining those jurors, whom she must have known would be most adamant against her, was like a Republican precinct worker hauling born-again Democrats to the polls to vote, convinced that on the way she could convert them the other way. Little wonder that when I walked into the courtroom at the beginning of the trial Johnnie Cochran was able to gloat that he already had at least a hung jury.

And what else do you do if you are Marcia Clark and you are determined to lose the case? You come into court, day after day, looking tough and sexy. I can describe the exact shape of the woman's knees, because for months I was sitting at knee level in the courtroom. Like a cranky old Puritan I mentioned her hems to Sally Stewart once, but she just raised her eyebrows in return. You don't talk about things like that anymore, not unless you are an old fogey or a sexist, or something equally bad. But even Chris Darden thought it worth a mention: "Now, in early July, she was up to her short skirt in the Simpson case," he said in passing. And Clark was aware of her hems as well. She referred to her usual day as "a short-skirt day" (and presumably her court dress as a "believe me" suit).

Not long ago I spoke at the Channel Club at Santa Barbara. In passing, I mentioned something about the length of Marcia Clark's hems. "Her hems? What difference does it make?" asked a petulant young woman who was severely aware of a woman's right to wear her damn hems wherever she damn pleases without someone of my ilk making a damn comment about it.

"Personally, I don't care where she wears her hems," I replied. "She could wear them around her neck if she pleased. But whatever you wear, whatever you do in a courtroom, communicates to a jury. If you are a white female trial lawyer attempting to convict a black man of the murder of his white wife and you are communicating to a jury of mostly black women who themselves are not wearing elevated hems, one has to ask what message you are conveying to them. In some ways this jury was a good deal more conservative than the hip, high-stakes lady prosecutor in the courtroom," I said.

I remember a case I tried in New Mexico some years ago. I

drove my pickup to court every day. But I had purchased one of those sport Rolex watches when I was in Hong Kong—though by the time you pay duty on it, you might just as well buy it in the States. Anyway, after the jury had returned a verdict for my client in what I thought was a clear case, I asked one of the jurors why it had taken them so long to reach their decision. The juror said that one of the other jurors had been holding out. He figured there was something wrong with a man who drove an old pickup to court but wore a Rolex in the courtroom. My watch today is a cheapie.

And what about the buckskin coats? They are just my television uniform. In court I wear a subdued sport coat of some kind, a blue button-down shirt, slacks—hope they're pressed—and boots—hope they're shined. Hope that what I wear does not distract from who I am. I claim it is not as important to *look* good as it is to *be* good. If one's dress says anything, it should say, "I am not trying to impress you with my dress. I am trying to impress you with my case."

I have said from the beginning that Marcia Clark was being too harsh. I tried to say it on television from time to time, but my fellow talking heads, thinking they were saving me (while I was trying to save her), talked over me. You don't criticize a tough female prosecutor, because she has as much right to be tough as a man—and I agree with that. And many younger white women liked her. She stood for what women should be: assertive, independent, powerful. Here was a woman who could more than hold her own with the men. Women can be as boorish and pushy and obnoxious as any man. Being noisome and disagreeable is not gender specific. But if you are a man it is risky to criticize the performance of a woman. You probably have a hangup about strong women. You are probably insecure. You probably harbor a puny, embittered little soul that is fighting to express itself. Most of the pundits blithely insisted that Marcia Clark was performing magnificently, some said flawlessly. But from the standpoint of the pundits, being politically correct was always more important than being correct. Still, everyone must have known that Clark could castrate a man in a flash. Look what she did almost by second nature to poor F. Lee Bailey, who will probably forever hide his hands from public view lest their small size reveal, as was Clark's suggestion, the size of his male appendage.

This was a woman who, in the presence of the jury, not only habitually flashed her beguilement to Johnnie Cochran, but who, at the next instant, could slash out at him with a vocabulary that sent shivers down the spine. Everything the defense did was "hideous" (her favorite word) or "inflammatory" or "cruel" or "horrible," all of which constantly caused her to be "offended" to the roots. The defense attorneys were "obnoxious" and "idiotic." Once she wrote in a note to Darden (I thought with justification) about the tabloid that was attacking his brother: "Those sleezy [*sic*] pieces of shit are fucking immoral, irresponsible, scumsucking pigs." She could run out a string of lethal expletives as rapidly and deadly as a .45 on full automatic. Then, as quickly, her eyes could turn soft, her voice loving, her being supple and gentle, and at the bench, she would whisper soft whatevers—we and the jury could only imagine—into Cochran's ear and laugh. And laugh again.

This woman took acting lessons but gave them up after she came to the conclusion she could never excel in the art. I think good lawyers are good actors. But good acting is *telling the truth*—it is revealing to the audience the truth about the person whose role the actor is playing. The truly great trial lawyer walks into court and tries, for all his worth, to be himself. He plays himself. And if he is too harsh, as Clark often was, if he swings from one emotional extreme to another, as did she; if he is too intimidating to those with lesser educations, as surely she was; and if he is too arrogant, too headstrong, too insecure to listen to others, some of which she is now able to admit, then the lawyer has to do a lot of work on himself. You have to fix the horse underneath the saddle, as Uncle Slim observed. You have to find out why you are so threatened, so hostile, so aggressive, so quick to castrate. You have to discover that it is all right to be afraid, to shiver and shake and shy back. When after long years of posturing and tough stuff in the courtroom I discovered that it was permissible to be a vulnerable person, that it was all right not to win every argument or come out on top in every little skirmish, I began to win my cases—because the jury, who listened to me, were people like that as well.

Do I think that a Mother Teresa could have won the case? Perhaps not. But perhaps Marcia Clark could have. She is bright enough, and brave enough. She is quick, and I think she has compassion. Had she given an ear to Don Vinson, she might not have packed the jury with black women. Had she given the slightest thought as to how the jury might see the case, as was obvious to all but those who were constantly blinded by the glare of political correctness, she would have understood that black people resent white people attempting to pin a murder on one of their own because a man abused his wife. Which is not to excuse domestic violence. Instead, it was as if the black community was saying one more time, "There you go again—throwing something at a brother to convict him other than honest, hard proof. That's been your M.O. for two hundred years, and we can't take it anymore."

Given the Fuhrman tapes and the other debacles of the LAPD, I am not saying that a Marcia Clark with soft hair, a quiet voice, an unassuming air, a forgiving disposition, and a gentle soul, with her skirts to her ankles—even with the support of the Mormon Tabernacle Choir—could have won. But she might not have lost. Remember, two white jurors voted for acquittal as well. She might have gotten a hung jury and the opportunity, in a later trial, to correct the many errors of the first trial. Certainly she could not have won with the domestic violence case she chose to present—not with the jury she chose, not with the Marcia Clark she chose to present, who, unconsciously or not, became the personification to this jury of yet another castrating bitch set on doing in another black man. After the last word had been spoken, this jury couldn't spare the time of day for Marcia Clark or her case. They didn't want any more of her, not an hour more, not one minute more. They had been locked up with her, like a ripening fetus, for nine months. They wanted out. Out!

By the time the parties were assembled to begin the trial, this case had become a race case as important to America as the Dred Scott decision. In that case, the venal pronouncement of the high court was that Scott was the mere property of a white man, while in this case the emotional scars of two hundred years of slavery and the racism of its aftermath were being played out in a politically correct but vicious renewal of old Civil War issues. Few understood that. Few understand it now. Marcia Clark has never understood it. She thought this was a domestic violence case. It was, instead, a simple case of murder that exploded into a symbol, for blacks and whites alike, of the nation's agonizing strife between the races.

CHAPTER 12

THE "BLAME CARD"

IF THE RACE card was played by some, the blame card was played by many. It was as if the players, stricken with the persistent disapproval of the media, lashed out in aimless fury at one another, blaming whoever was handy for the loss of the case. Except in black communities, where the verdict was celebrated, America was shocked by the verdict. Expecting the murderer to be hauled off in ignoble chains, the people instead saw him withdraw a driver from his bag and, smiling broadly, holler, "Fore!" The people were angry. Johnnie Cochran was the culprit. Robert Shapiro was the villain. These shysters played the race card, and they played it to a stupid jury that, despite the clear and unimpeachable blood evidence, bought Cochran's conspiracy snake oil. The media echoed the people, and like the howling hyenas at sunset, they began echoing each other, their yaps and yowls bouncing back and forth off the canyon walls of the white power structure.

The system, too, was blamed: We should change the system. Do away with the presumption of innocence. Eliminate peremptory challenges, which give the attorneys on each side the right to strike a limited number of jurors for any reason, valid or not—as I would strike a banker if I were representing a man charged with bank robbery, and if I were representing someone charged with

rape, I would strike a rape victim. Get rid of peremptory challenges, echoed the talking heads, most of whom were either prosecutors who wanted to sound tough and smart and convict more
and more people more easily, or people who had been elevated to
"expertisehood," as it were, by the mindless lens.

Despite the fact that the conviction rate in the country hovers
at around 90 percent, we were offered the brainy nostrum that we
must act to make it easier to convict citizens—all citizens, you and
me alike—by doing away with the unanimous verdict, even though
a less than unanimous verdict would not have changed the result
in the Simpson case, or in a majority of other cases, one iota. But
a less than unanimous verdict eliminates the one person on the
jury who may understand what the others have failed to see. It
eliminates the chance of the more careful mind, the more evolved
conscience, speaking out. It is our homage to the voice of the minority that must be heard in a democracy and that we have respected throughout the ages. But based on the Simpson case
alone, we suddenly needed to change the entire system. It was as
if we decided to rebuild the whole city of Los Angeles because
there was a wreck at Sunset and Vine.

Concurrently, the great legal scholars came out of the morgues
to join in the moaning. The neo–closet fascists sobbed like holy
martyrs, all wanting to tinker in one way or another with the jury
system and spread their own brand of racism by denouncing this
black jury. National talk show hosts were locked in perpetual holler, their faces in immutable snarl. "What is wrong with the system?" they kept demanding. "What is wrong with these lawyers?
Get rid of the lawyers." It was all too wonderful, this Simpson
verdict, providing as it did a heyday for lawyer haters and cynics
and racists and dunderheads of every stripe who, despite their public protestations to the contrary, saw the case as an opportunity
to spew out their own hatred and to shake and roll in their own
discontent, and to make minorities and the poor even more vulnerable to the already unfettered tyranny of the police.

Elsewhere young blacks were celebrating, and their celebrations were immediately misunderstood to mean that they were delighted that Nicole Simpson and Ron Goldman had had their throats cut. Instead, in this new battlefield of the races, black people were celebrating a long-awaited victory. Justice wasn't the issue; the guilt or innocence of Simpson wasn't either. The people were happy because for once a black person, guilty or innocent, had won in court. It provided hope after they had stood helplessly by for years as their husbands and sons and brothers were hauled off to the penitentiaries in shamefully disproportionate numbers. It brought hope to black people who for centuries, guilty or innocent, had been powerless to fight the system and who could not win by hiring the fancy lawyers, the Dr. Henry Lees, the Barry Schecks, or the Jo-Ellan Dimitriuses. The black community was celebrating a long-awaited victory after millions of black men had been provided only a token defense with a public defender burdened with 150 other cases, a young lawyer who didn't have time before trial to even learn his client's name or to ask him what the charge was. But when the media put its cameras on the jubilant black people, white America recoiled, and the nation's eternal racial war, still being fought according to the rules of political correctness, was exacerbated because, from the standpoint of white people, a foul had been committed. The race card had been played.

It was amazing. Here we have a prosecution that failed predictably, like a three-legged horse in a steeplechase; a prosecution conducted mainly by Marcia Clark and Chris Darden, who were so busy listening to each other's libidinous coos that they were blind to the mounting obstacles that lay in front of a conviction. And all the while the people were hollering about the race card, about Johnnie Cochran's eyewash, and demanding, because of the verdict, that we should abolish, in whole or in part, the jury system, our age-old, single most powerful weapon against tyranny.

Few suggested that Marcia Clark and Chris Darden, her alleged paramour, played the race card themselves when they engaged in an interracial affair that must have been evident to the eight black women and one black man looking on from the jury box. Are we to believe that over a nine-month trial publications such as the *Globe* and the *National Enquirer* could detect it, but that the collective intelligence of the jurors could not pick up the telltale behavior of the species in rut? Even the prosecution's domestic violence experts, Donald Dutton and Angela Brown, saw it. Darden reported that their diagnosis was, "There's some electricity between the two of you," meaning Darden and Clark. "There's some sexual tension here . . . Before this thing is over, you two are going to end up sleeping together." Whom did Clark and Darden think they were fooling? And to hear *them* charge that someone was playing a race card! What did a black woman juror think about yet another white woman taking over yet another black man in the same case? What subliminal comparisons were being made between Marcia Clark and Nicole Simpson in the minds of the black women? No one dared to make such a politically incorrect inquiry. But political correctness simply hides how people feel, it does not change their feelings. Probably the black women didn't talk about it. Even Marcia Clark understood the black backlash that resulted from white women taking the side of the prosecution. She recounts how Faye Resnick "had drawn fire from black women in the audience of a national talk show. To them, she was just one more white bitch trying to bring down O.J. Simpson."

The blame card was being dealt out like a blackjack dealer throwing a deck full of tens on hands that should have stayed pat. Everyone wanted to bust everyone—except, of course, the prosecutors, who were, in this posttrial drama, America's heroes cheated of their victory by trick and device and abominable evil, and who were fêted everywhere they went, these martyrs of justice. The people were angry—that is, the white people. The country, isolating blacks from its collective, gathered up like a screaming mob who had just discovered brass knuckles inside the gloves of the Russian thug who beat our Olympic heavyweight for the gold.

Everyone wrote their blaming books, including Mark Fuhrman and Detectives Philip Vannatter and Tom Lange. "The Blame Unlimited Series," we might call it. Fuhrman blamed the prosecution's loss on, among other things, the bumbling of Lange and Vannatter. He said he had found a bloody fingerprint on the rear gate at Bundy and reported it—*in writing*—but the fingerprint was lost and never used. He believes it was probably Simpson's, and he claims that the print would have caused even *that* jury to convict. He and his partner Brad Roberts found the empty Swiss Army knife box in the bathroom and dark sweats in the washer, neither of which ever saw the inside of an evidence envelope. Darden, too, saw an LAPD photo of Simpson's bathroom, and dark clothing was piled next to the hamper. Were those the black sweats? Had the LAPD failed once more, he asked?

Fuhrman claims that the interrogation of Simpson by Vannatter and Lange was nothing more than an amiable chat, that either they did not know how to conduct a professional interrogation of a suspect (he tells us how) or, being star-struck, they chose not to. Marcia Clark, in her usual careful language, said that Simpson was "coddled by worshipful cops, pumped up by star-fucking attorneys." Fuhrman implies that if he had been in charge, Simpson would have confessed. He is distressed by other police blunders as well, such as the tardy impounding of the Bronco, Lange's covering Nicole's body with a blanket from inside the house, Vannatter's carrying the blood sample around like marbles in a boy's pocket—there were eight major errors committed by these detectives, he says. Moreover, he suggests that Darden himself was a racist who wore a baseball cap bearing the words BLACK LAW. Clark claims Darden despised Fuhrman and protested against having to work with him. "I don't want to be in the same room with the motherfucker," he told her, which may be quite understandable on a personal level, but which also perfectly demonstrates how the emotions of an immature lawyer can get in the way of his work.

"The only difference between Darden and Johnnie Cochran,

Fuhrman charged, "is that Chris worked for the city and made less money." Finally, at Fuhrman's repeated requests, Clark ended up doing his examination in court.

Fuhrman blames Cochran, of course, for converting the case from one of murder to "a campaign of slander" against him, and he blames Clark for destroying him in her closing argument. "Did he lie . . . ?" Clark asked the jury about Fuhrman. "Yes. Is he a racist? Yes. Is he the worst LAPD has to offer? Yes. Do we wish that this person had never been hired by LAPD? Yes. . . . In fact, do we wish there were no such person on the planet? Yes." This attack against her own witness who found the infamous glove at Rockingham was not a shining way to convince a jury that Fuhrman's testimony was credible. But Clark blames Fuhrman for their loss. And Fuhrman blames Clark back, and Darden as well, and Vannatter and . . . well, the blame cards were flying in every direction.

In the meantime, Vannatter and Lange blame Clark for throwing a simple murder case into the swill of domestic violence, for her intransigence in holding to an unrealistically narrow murder time—the time of the howling of some damn dog—and they were right. This mulishness, Vannatter points out, again correctly, precluded the prosecution from introducing the testimony of Robert Heidstra, who heard a white man yell, "Hey! Hey! Hey!" and who heard the voice of a black man in response—according to Vannatter, one belonging to O.J. Simpson. And Heidstra heard a gate slam. But this was at about 10:35 to 10:40 P.M.—twenty to twenty-five minutes after the time the prosecution had nailed down as the moment of the murders. Clark's moment of murder also precluded the testimony of Jill Shively, who, at about 10:45, as we have seen, identified Simpson in the white vehicle at the intersection of San Vincente and Bundy.

Today these detectives are all over Clark like coyotes on a fallen deer for having failed to introduce the Bronco chase scene tapes, their tapes of the interrogation of Simpson, his supposed suicide note, and the evidence found in the Bronco—namely a disguise in the form of a mustache and goatee, a passport, and more than $8,000 in cash, money supposedly belonging to Simpson but found in the pockets of A.C. Cowlings, his non-accomplice accomplice. To quote Darden: You don't need a disguise or a passport to commit suicide. More than anything, the detectives blame Clark for putting up a wall between the LAPD and the D.A.'s office so that legitimate evidence found by the police did not, in the usual course of a trial, find its way to the jury. Further, they blame Clark for tarnishing the credibility of the LAPD when she should have been nurturing the police as members of the team. And they claim that Fuhrman's perjury confirmed the suspicions of black Americans that the cops do hate them and target them with fabricated evidence, a remarkably naive observation coming from these veteran officers.

In the meantime, Clark blames the cops—those miserable, incompetent cops—who "fucked up" her case. And with a good deal of skill that often seems to transform fault into mere passing comment, she blames nearly everyone else she encountered. She blames the media for her misery, for having spawned this monster called the O.J. case, but neglects to thank the rascals for having made her the silk purse of the case. She blames a long list of others for having convinced her she should go with domestic abuse as the axle of the trial. She blames a black Johnnie Cochran and the black jury for laying the racial egg and hatching it in the middle of her honorable efforts as a champion of justice: He was without ethics; he was the worst racist of all, she claims. Along the way she blames the Brown family for being less than cooperative, Paula Barbieri for being less than cooperative, the Goldman family for being too cooperative, jury consultant Don Vinson (the man "without a clue") for trying to get his face on national TV, and Judge Ito for being a spineless little nerd who had a preening ego and hankered to become a television star.

From time to time Clark even snapped in Darden's direction.

Darden, she said, showed poor judgment when he went on *Rivera Live* and criticized the sissy performance of the LAPD's officers as witnesses. The officers shouldn't let the defense push them around like that, he said. They should be more aggressive. I have never heard of a lawyer coaching his witnesses via the talk shows: Tune in to *Rivera Live* tomorrow and hear what Darden has to say to the next set of witnesses on his list. I agreed with Clark—something was wrong there. And she thought that Darden let Johnnie Cochran "jerk his chain" all the time. She was right again. And she should know—he jerked hers, too, almost at will.

This man, Darden, was the one whom, she said, sustained her—in what ways we are not told, although a fellow deputy D.A., Rockne Harmon, said on at least one talk show that one time he picked up his own note pads from the table where Darden and Clark had been sitting and accidentally got a pad belonging to one of them mixed in with his own. He recognized their handwriting. The notes presumably set out explicitly what each intended to do to the other—and it didn't have anything to do with cooking supper and washing the dishes. Whatever was said, Harmon cautioned he couldn't say the words on television—not with kids watching. But none of this was, of course, the fault of Marcia Clark. It was the fault of the muses, those nasty little libido demons that are always hanging around.

Clark blamed Darden for the glove fiasco, claiming that he was "on a testosterone high." "Don't do it," she said, referring to his contemplated demonstration with the glove before the jury.

"We've got to do it," he said back.

"Why won't you fucking listen to me? This is a trap!" She said her voice was "hoarse with tension and anger."

"This is *my* witness," he snapped. "And I say we have to put those gloves on him now, before they do!" She said she couldn't dissuade him, although she was chief counsel, and there was also the D.A. to appeal to.

It was Darden, of course, who had failed to check out the

duplicate Aris gloves that he intended to use in his demonstration before the jury. The gloves he offered as an exhibit for the demonstration were different from the gloves in evidence, but he hadn't taken the time to discover that. Now, when he insisted on the demonstration, he would have to use the actual bloody gloves. According to Marcia Clark, Darden "wanted to score a coup of his own." Instead, he shot himself in both feet. Darden could have titled his book *A Loser's Guide to Fame*. Yet, he, too, blamed nearly everyone else.

He said he couldn't believe it when he heard Cochran say on an evening news show, "All of a sudden, he [Darden] shows up here. Now why is that, after we have eight African-Americans [as jurors]? We're concerned about it. Why now?" Darden's only defense against Cochran's insinuations was to take umbrage at the obvious truth of them. Darden heard Cochran's words as a message to all blacks: "This brother is being used by the Man. This brother is an Uncle Tom." But Cochran said it again. "Christopher Darden is a fine lawyer, but I don't think he should be on this case."

Cochran was right. The prosecution's message to the black jurors was direct and arrogant, one the prosecution itself was too arrogant to hear: The message went like this: We, the People, have assigned a black man to this case to talk to you other blacks. We deny it, of course. A black man speaking to a black jury to convict a black man—that's our strategy. But anyone who suggests that this is our strategy is being politically incorrect. They will be charged as racists. But, of course, you are too dense to ever figure all of this out.

I remember again my own case against McDonald's in Chicago. Of the several black people we had on the jury, one of them turned out to be the foreman. In the middle of the trial, out of the hundreds of available franchised owners and managers who might have been called by McDonald's, the company lawyer called a black McDonald's operator to testify on behalf of the company.

When the black man took the stand, the foreman of the jury looked over at me as if to say, "Who do they think we are, a bunch of damn fools? You can't use us like that." He shrugged his shoulders. Then he closed his eyes and, as if in protest, looked as if he were sleeping.

Johnnie Cochran didn't have to tell the world on public television that Chris Darden had been chosen for reasons of race. Whether, in fact, his race had anything to do with his selection, Darden's protestations to the contrary could never convince the black people on the jury or the black community otherwise. Darden himself was painfully aware of the blacklash. Even the *Los Angeles Times* carried a story, which ran the day before Martin Luther King, Jr., Day, reporting that the blacks were viewing Darden as a sellout, the Uncle Tom caricature that so wounded him. And he had been receiving phone calls from "brothers" calling him a "fucking sellout motherfucker" charging that he was "a disgrace to [his] race," and warning, "Don't ever refer to yourself as black, 'cause you ain't."

Darden says that it was Clark who assigned him the job of questioning Fuhrman on the witness stand (which he later bailed out on). He blames Clark for this bad decision. But Darden was fully aware of the race game his own team members were playing with him. Despite the pain of such an admission, he must have begun to realize they had been playing it with him from the beginning. Now he naively asked himself a rhetorical question concerning his assignment to question Fuhrman: "Did Bill [Hodgman] and Marcia think that hearing about a once-racist cop from a black lawyer would somehow defuse the awful beliefs? I had insisted that my addition to this case had nothing to do with my race, but now I wondered if my colleagues thought they could 'sneak' Fuhrman and Vannatter through by giving them to the black guy."

Darden knew what any thoughtful person, lawyer or not, would have known: Black jurors are as intelligent as anyone else and would immediately see through the ploy. He knew black people are supersensitive to racial pandering. "Did they [Clark and Hodgman] think black jurors were so stupid that they would believe any witnesses I presented just because I was black too?" Darden asked. ". . . The only thing that having me 'sneak' these witnesses would accomplish is that the jury would decide I was being used and I would lose any credibility I had in front of them." Such was the apocalypse of his insight, one he must have possessed from the beginning.

Darden likes to blame Fuhrman for the miseries that were to ensue from his testimony, as does Clark. But these lawyers demanded that their witnesses be the kind of people they were not. If they could not pass the witness litmus test established by Clark, they were either attacked or junked. They had to be Ivory Soap pure. And they had to support the Marcia Clark revisionist history of the murder: Jill Shively had the wrong time for her encounter with Simpson at the Bundy intersection. Robert Heidstra was mistaken, too. Moreover, Shively took money for her story. And now Fuhrman had the mud of racism smeared on him. What do real lawyers do under such circumstances?

Real lawyers take their important witnesses as they find them. The jury knows people are not all sweetness and light. Real lawyers listen to their witnesses, and if enough of them tell them that the time of the murder is different from what the howling dog tells them, they put those witnesses on the stand and let them tell their honest stories. You don't try to change the facts by hiding witnesses.

What about a witness like Fuhrman? Maybe he was a racist. Probably not as bad a racist as Cochran wanted the jury to believe, but a pig is a pig, despite the amount of mud he carries around on him. Yet the overall *tenor* of Fuhrman's testimony on direct, as distinguished from what he actually said, sounded, as I heard it, something like this:

"Are you a racist?" (Such a question, of course, was never asked in court.)

"No, not on your life."

"Did you plant the glove?"

"Absolutely not. I wouldn't think of it."

"Are you as pure as the driven snow?"

Fuhrman's demeanor, calm, Zen-like, nearly saintly, told us he was as pristine and pretty as, yes, a snowflake. "You know it."

"Did you ever use the N-word?" (Clark didn't ask him this, though Bailey later did on cross. But without her asking, you already knew what his answer would be.)

"Why, no. I don't even know what that means."

These nine black jurors were watching. What had their experience with cops like Fuhrman been? He came off cool and Boy Scout–like. Why, he could have even been an astronaut. I thought he came off solid, but I wasn't listening to him through the ears of nine African-Americans, who must have taken his testimony as that of the typical lying cop who can, when cornered, sound as truthful as George Washington confessing his culpability for chopping down the cherry tree.

Bailey's cross, on its face, was as effective as kicking a wall instead of the witness. But Fuhrman was soon to get in trouble with his answer to Bailey's otherwise groping, unconnected question about Fuhrman's use of the N-word. We all know the story ad nauseam. Marcia Clark must have known the overall problem Fuhrman's testimony would create with the jury. Had she given the matter as much consideration as she gave to her latest haircut, she would have realized that Fuhrman should have been dealt with in quite a different way. She didn't have to call him in order to introduce the glove. Vannatter and Lange had both seen the glove behind Kato Kaelin's room before it was moved. But since Fuhrman was put on the stand—and I think that choice was right, given the sophistication of the jury—and given the impending impeachment testimony that waited in the wings to hoist him on the petard of his own racism, the *tenor* of his testimony should have sounded more like this:

156 / GERRY SPENCE

"Are you a racist cop?"

"I have been called a racist cop by some, maybe deservedly. I have said racist things from time to time. In front of these black people on the jury I am ashamed to admit it. But I have."

Testimony of this tenor would have borne the ring of truth. Because it is true. Once we believe that a witness has told us the truth about something, something that embarrasses him, that is painful to him, we are more likely to believe the rest of his testimony. Truth is the most powerful weapon in the courtroom—even when it hurts. Murderers with whom the prosecution has made a deal are regularly called upon by prosecutors to tell the truth. Crooks and snitches are habitually used by the prosecution to convict the accused. The worst human beings ever to disgrace this earth are regularly called by the prosecution to make the state's cases. Racists can also be established as truth-tellers before the jury. But Marcia Clark could not bring herself to honestly deal with the Fuhrman racial burr under the prosecution's squeaky-clean saddle. It was her arrogance all over again. She, Marcia Clark, didn't have to deal with it. She could fool this dumb jury and circumvent all those racist, "star-fucking" lawyers sitting over at the defense table. And so Fuhrman soon joined the numerous other scapegoats that Clark and Darden fingered as the culprits who caused them to lose this once unloseable case with its mountain of evidence.

You have a racist on your hands, and he's *your* witness. How do you treat him? Darden, who was first assigned to Fuhrman, said, "I didn't like him from the first time I saw him." I suppose Fuhrman couldn't tell. Darden had an appointment to meet Fuhrman at 1:30 in the afternoon. By 3:00 P.M. Fuhrman was still waiting. What was Darden's attitude? "And so Mark Fuhrman had to wait, until about 3 P.M., when I came into [Scott] Gordon's office and introduced myself," Darden writes. "Fuhrman didn't like to wait [who does?] and he was in a lousy mood [who wouldn't be?]. I didn't give a shit. On this case, everyone waited." That was the kind of arrogance from a black deputy D.A. that would seem to confirm the racist notions borne by Fuhrman in the first place and that tended to widen the rift between the police and the D.A.

Fuhrman has written that he was treated shoddily by Darden not just occasionally, but for weeks. Darden would sit at his desk, Fuhrman said, and read for long periods of time, never acknowledging that Fuhrman was there, waiting. How did Fuhrman feel about the way he was being treated? Here is what he said about Chris Darden in his pretty good book, *Murder in Brentwood:* "He calls his book *In Contempt,* and I agree, he is in contempt—in contempt of the people he is supposed to represent." Darden said he had intended to "go right at him [Fuhrman] in direct examination, to almost treat him as a hostile witness." Brilliant. First of all, Darden would have to establish that Fuhrman was legally hostile before he could cross-examine him as a hostile witness. You can't just tell the judge the witness is hostile. You must first demonstrate his hostility to the judge. And what kind of cooperation would a lawyer expect from his own witness if he attacks the witness in a public courtroom? What you are saying to the jury is, "I hate this witness. He is a racist. And you, the blacks on the jury, hate him, too. But I want you to believe he did not plant the glove." As we have seen, Clark later made a similar argument to the jury in her closing argument, but I have yet to hear her admit that that, too, was asking the canary to swallow the cat.

Often Darden's musings sounded whiny and self-pitying. "Marcia got good reviews as the pundits discussed the overwhelming physical evidence that she'd presented. Yet the same pundits spent almost no time talking about the substance of what I'd said. It was a sad indication of what I knew about this case. No one, it seemed, could see past race." Yet I had often said on NBC and CNN that I thought Chris Darden was the most effective lawyer for the prosecution. I saw him as open and honest. He might be amateurish and immature, but he never pretended to be anyone but who he was. If he was upset, he was upset. If he blundered, well, so be it—he was human. I thought that of the players in the courtroom he carried the most credibility. And I said so. Often.

Darden was stubborn, to be sure, and easily twitted by Cochran. He was still the juvenile lawyer who hadn't yet learned, as lawyers must learn through painful experience, that one cannot react to an opposing lawyer's jibes, or one turns one's own power over to his opponent. Cochran was playing Darden's at will when he had suggested that Darden and Clark hadn't tried a case for a long time and didn't know how to try one. The lawyers were at the bench. Darden exploded, and Judge Ito cautioned him. It had been the judge's rule that only one lawyer from each side could speak to an issue, a standard court rule in every jurisdiction, and the matter at the bench was Clark's, not Darden's. Under the rule he had no right to speak. But the judge's attempt to stop Darden was in vain. "Is he the only lawyer that knows how to try a case?" Darden demanded in anger, defying the judge.

"I'm going to hold you in contempt," the judge warned.

Darden was off, like a wild moon rocket. "I should be held in contempt. I have sat here and listened to—"

"Mr. Darden," the judge interrupted, "I'm warning you right now." Right then and there any experienced lawyer would have seen in his mind's eye the cell door at the country jail opening up to greet him.

"This cross-examination is out of order," Darden hollered. What was he going to do with Darden? What if he threw this bad boy in jail? What would the press make of that? Would the judge be charged as a racist himself? Could the case end up in an appeal, in a mistrial?

On the other hand, did Darden realize he held a certain power over the judge that a white lawyer under the same circumstances wouldn't have? No race issue would sprout up if the judge threw a white male lawyer into jail, although a judge might hesitate to send a white female laywer there—thus running the risk of being labeled a sexist!

I was in the courtroom watching intently. The judge was cool, using his head. No one ever gave him much credit for that. He excused the jury, giving Darden a little time to simmer down. Then he turned to Darden.

"Mr. Darden, let me give you a piece of advice. Take about three deep breaths, as I am going to do, and then contemplate what you are going to say next. Do you want to take a recess now for a moment?" The judge was clearly telling Darden to cool it, to realize he was on the verge of contempt, that he should consider the effect of a contempt citation on his case and act accordingly. An apology to the judge would obviously put it all to rest.

But no, Darden didn't want a recess. He was pacing, his hands on his hips, acting like he wanted to take the judge on in a fistfight.

"I will hear your comment at this point," the judge said. "I have cited you. Do you have any response?"

Again, Judge Ito was simply asking Darden to apologize, to recognize the judge's authority in the case, and to follow the rules he had laid down. But Darden had lost it. His fight was with Cochran, but he was carrying it on with the last man he should have been contesting—the judge himself.

In response to the judge's question, Darden showed his real savvy. "I would like counsel, Your Honor." This is a *prosecutor* asking the judge for an attorney in the middle of the prosecution's case? Instead of reacting, Judge Ito went even further, directly requesting that Darden apologize so that the case could proceed. He said to Darden, "When I get that response, then we move on."

But Darden's feet were in concrete. He would not move. He would not apologize. The judge gave Darden more time to confer with Clark, who seemed deaf and, herself, as stuck as a frog in quicksand. Now she backed Darden's claim that he should have a lawyer. They were in it up to their prosecutorial earflaps—in it together, by God. Stupid or not, they'd go down in tandem.

Judge Ito had lost the last of his plentiful patience. "I've offered you now three times an opportunity to end this right now.

This is very simple." All he wanted was the apology. I couldn't believe what I was watching. Any first-year law student knew better than to contest a judge like that. I was so focused on what was going on, and pulling so hard for Darden to show the sense of a pissant in a whirlwind, that without even realizing it I slammed my yellow pad down on my leg and exclaimed out loud, "Jesus Christ, Chris!"

The judge said "Mr. Spence, your comments aren't necessary," which, of course, they weren't.

Still Darden was silent. Finally the judge, growing desperate, asked Darden to take a moment and review the transcript, hoping that Darden could see the precarious position he was in. Darden and Clark had retired to the D.A.'s quarters upstairs. Even with the opportunity given him to cool down, Darden said, "I wasn't about to apologize. I had done nothing wrong." But by now Marcia Clark was on him to apologize. No. By God, he wasn't going to. The contempt would be on his bar record, she argued. After much coaxing by Clark, Darden at last came to his senses.

"Your Honor, thank you for the opportunity to review the transcript of the sidebar," he said at last, without much sincerity. "It appears that the Court is correct, that perhaps my comments may have been or are somewhat inappropriate. I apologize to the Court. I meant no disrespect."

I thought the judge in return was too generous to Darden, but Judge Ito is a generous man himself, and here is what he said in response: "Mr. Darden, I accept your apology. I apologize to you for my reaction as well. You and I have known each other for a number of years, and I know that your response was out of character, and I'll note it as such."

In a few minutes the Court called a recess. I saw Chris Darden in the hall, and he came up to me. "I suppose that's what you wanted me to say to the judge, Gerry?" he said with a big, friendly smile. He knew I liked him.

"Exactly," I replied. "I thought you'd never get it."

On the talk shows the hosts wanted to know what it was that I had said out loud in court. They wanted me to come out with the Jesus Christ expletive and make a story out of it. I simply said I was praying for Chris Darden—that's what those words meant. Nothing more.

Chris Darden was a better lawyer than the pundits wanted to give him credit for. Stubborn and sensitive, emotional but honest. Other writers have said he had little talent. I disagree. You don't have to be a great orator, or a quick-witted, sharp-tongued quipster, to be a successful trial lawyer. You don't have to be an intellectual leviathan. Mostly, you need to be honest, to be straight, and to discover your own power, which has nothing to do with the volume of your voice, the size of your testicles, or the length of your hem. You mostly have to be brave and sincere. Give that to me in a lawyer, male or female, black or white, and I'll show you someone the jury will believe. I thought Chris Darden had more of those qualities than any other lawyer in the courtroom. Trouble was he didn't know it. Trouble was he had his own racist war to fight. He was so busy fighting himself, fighting Johnnie Cochran, fighting the system, fighting those who tabbed him as the token black, fighting every ruling of the court as something grown out of racism, that he had little creative energy to apply in the case.

Darden's emotions didn't get in the way, as some said. They simply *got away*. I don't mean that a lawyer shouldn't be emotional. What are we without emotions? Machines? Machines do not have emotions, and no machine has become my role model. But emotions are the paint on the palette of communication. Darden said, "Since my early days as a lawyer, I had been advised to keep my emotions in check. Well, that wasn't me. And it never had been. I was outraged . . . ," he ranted, after which followed a litany of indignities that had infuriated him. What Darden and other young Turks do not understand is that our emotions are there to paint a picture with. You may paint an emotional picture, a van Gogh, with the paint literally heaped upon the canvas in powerful, telling, even angry strokes, or you may paint a pretty, precisely rendered canvas of graceful dancers like a Degas, but when you paint you do not throw the whole damned palette at the canvas if you want to communicate effectively. And you do not let others take your palette from you and throw the paint in your and everybody else's faces, which was what Cochran was doing with Darden every time Darden rose to Cochran's bait. But then, we were supposed to have learned that in our endless trek toward adulthood, a destination most of us never quite reach.

Darden positioned himself as the fearless, lonely black man in the case. The world was against him. The *Los Angeles Times* had pinioned him to the Uncle Tom cross. His "brothers" had forsaken and attacked him. He saw himself as despised, abandoned, and tortured by his old friend Johnnie Cochran. He felt sorry for himself. Yet he refused to realize that he, too, was one of the racist ingredients of the case and had been from the beginning. Instead, with unself-conscious sanctimoniousness, he saw his involvement not as the state's gesture to the black jurors but as "only duty: Duty to the prosecutor's office, to the families of the victims, and even to the black community." He continued to deny that he was chosen because he was black in an attempt by the prosecution to offset the defense's clear advantage with Johnnie Cochran. But at last one must ask: Why, out of nine hundred deputy D.A.'s in Los Angeles County, was Darden chosen to try the Simpson case, especially when he had not, by his own admission, "been in a courtroom for anything important in three years"? And deny as he did that this was a race case, no one finally made more of the racial issues in the trial than Chris Darden himself. No one devoted as much time to their implications, groused as much about them, raged as much about them—often with deep justification. However unjustly, he *did* become the Uncle Tom in the case. He *was* seen as a traitor to the cause of black people. But on the other hand, as Darden correctly saw it, the cause of black people could not have been better served than by a black prosecutor encouraging black jurors to use their power to convict the guilty, especially a famous guilty black murderer. Perhaps he was unable to say that quietly, thoughtfully, painfully, to the jury.

Still, after the trial, Darden continued to complain and to blame: How could he win such a case with lawyers on the other side flipping the finger at ethics and at truth, with a racist Cochran who was taking the case away from the "two slaughtered victims, to cry wolf . . . and turn a murder case into a bogus retribution for past injustices," and with a judge who let him do it? How could he win a case with a racist cop like Fuhrman and incompetents inhabiting the LAPD from top to bottom? How could he win with the defense lawyers playing to the media, and the media gone crazy and the tabloids buying up the witnesses as soon as they were identified, and the pundits second-guessing him to the end that the jury was probably infected with their crap? At last, and again, how could he win with a black jury that he felt would have, as he later wrote, "more sympathy for the gangsters than for the cops"?

Who, at last, can we blame for justice having gone awry in the O.J. Simpson case? If the jury did not believe the LAPD, who is to blame? Can we lay the blame at the feet of Willie Williams, the chief of police? Can we lay the blame on Fuhrman or Vannatter or Lange or the blinking witnesses who held themselves out as criminalists? Can we blame coyless Clark and her alleged paramour, who obviously had something to do with how the case was presented? In assessing blame we lose focus, because our attention is directed across the whole landscape of scapegoats. So let us refocus.

Like it or not, conventional wisdom to the contrary, political correctness notwithstanding, this was and is and always will be a race case. Race was the issue from the outset—a black man charged with cutting the throats of two white people. Drop over it as you wish whatever nonracist shroud, it was still a race case. If we are to lay blame, let us put it where it belongs: at the feet of the L.A. police, who appear in the black community as a daily reminder of white racism against black powerlessness. The truth of this assertion was obvious in the voir dire of the jury. Several black prospective jurors said outright that the police lie on the stand. One said, "It just seems like black men get picked on quite a bit." She didn't know anyone who'd had a pleasant experience with the police.

Think of it this way: When I was a boy in Sheridan, Wyoming, my mother used to tell me, "Gerry, if you get lost, or get in trouble, or need something, just find a policeman. He will help you." What black mother in East L.A. today, or anywhere else for that matter, would tell her son that? In black neighborhoods the police are seen as the enemy, and the enemy cannot be believed. To ask black people in the inner city to believe the white police is like asking Little Red Riding Hood to kiss the wolf dressed up in her grandmother's clothes. How, indeed, can we blame Little Red for refusing to believe the wolf even when he tells her the truth?

I agree with Darden, who believes that black people are fair. "Fairness," he wrote, "is a fundamental part of our nature. A black jury would convict if the evidence was there." But the state's case had to be honest. Although the state presented some of its facts, facts are like bricks: You can build anything you wish with them. And although the state's case was in most instances factually accurate, what it lacked was the painful, candid, let-it-all-hang-out presentation that is the stuff of credibility. What it lacked was the flat-out testimony of Faye Resnick, even though her credibility could be attacked. The case lacked the much ignored evidence in the hands of the LAPD, although its credibility could have also been attacked. As we have seen, the case lacked the testimony of Jill Shively, whose credibility as a seller of stories was at issue, and the testimony of Robert Heidstra, who heard an apparent altercation between a white man and a black man at Bundy at about the time of the murder. The case lacked much of the commonsense evidence: the money, passport, and disguise in the Bronco; the video and audio tapes made during the Bronco chase; the recorded interview of Simpson by Vannatter and Lange (even though their credibility, too, was at issue). Perhaps more than anything, the case lacked the presentation of Nicole as a whole yet flawed human being, instead of a helpless, battered saint. I say, present the facts and witnesses as they are. Tell the truth. Ultimately there is credibility in presenting the witnesses, whoever they are, whether their credibility can be attacked or not.

The prosecution lost its case not just once; as if once were not enough, it seemed bent upon making sure the case was lost at nearly every opportunity. I never go into court with a mob of lawyers to present the case. The storytellers, the chief trial lawyers, are the most important people in the trial. It is the storyteller who becomes the clear and familiar voice of his case. He relates to the jury. He becomes their friend. He becomes the state itself or he stands for the defendant himself. He is constantly building his credibility and thus the credibility of his case. He is the artist who paints the scene for the jury on the canvas. He is the captain who guides the jury's ship safely into port. He is the mountain guide who leads the jury through strange and foreboding forests and brings them safely into camp.

Marcia Clark divided up the work in the case as if it were pie: You take this witness, I'll take that one. She claimed she was tired. I have little doubt of that. Her principal energies were being diverted into nearly every creek, every rivulet, besides the main stream of the trial. The jury had no opportunity to attach itself to a lawyer, even if there had been one to whom they could have related. Cochran made the same error. Perhaps, given Clark's propensity to irritate the black women on the jury and, I suspect, others as well, she may have been wise in retreating into the background from time to time. But this only underscored the fact that she was the wrong attorney for the case. Darden took some witnesses and then days, even weeks, followed in which the drones droned on about DNA in words that no one could understand including the drones. It was as if the prosecution had intentionally set out to bore the jury into cruel submission. DNA is not difficult. I explained it to an American television audience in less than two minutes with a dozen paper cups. To put complicated testimony on through the auspices of "DNA lawyers" only signaled the jury that the evidence was too complicated to understand. I doubt that anyone understood the evidence, though it was not beyond understanding. But the highbrows of the profession, good for little else besides confusing a jury, had to have their chance to strut their stuff. If Clark could not understand DNA, how could she expect a jury to?

I saw this case roll on without a break for nine crazy months, a case that should have been briskly and clearly presented in a fraction of the time. In the meantime, jurors were becoming testy. Some were thrown off the case. Some were quarreling with one another. The marshals were snooping, investigating the jurors as if they themselves were criminals. The marshals were searching jurors' rooms without warrants. Obviously the state did not trust the jurors. Why, then, should the jurors trust the state? How would we react if this were the way the state treated us while we were under its complete power—if even we, the *jurors,* had no rights?

In retrospect, the case was clearly lost when Marcia Clark happened to stumble onto the stage and took over as chief counsel before the story of the case had been written and its audience defined. She was the wrong lawyer to try a race case before a black female jury, and I believe she knew it. Yet even then, she had a chance to win. She might have listened to people who were less arrogant than she and who knew more than she—the state's pro bono jury consultant, for one. She might have listened to her own witnesses and treated them with respect. She might not have been so headstrong, so intransigent. She might have learned something of humility before she promenaded back and forth like a high school baton twirler, in front of a very human and humble jury. She is a bright woman, a courageous woman, and probably, if she would only show us, a good woman. But she had become the iron shoe into which everything had to be stuffed. She was not, however—nor could she have ever been—the right woman to try the most infamous murder case in American history.

If blame is to be laid, let it fall at the feet of the prosecution. The case was not won by the foul of Johnnie Cochran playing the race card. He did not win the case. The case was lost by the prosecution. At last, the blame card should be laid at Garcetti's hand. He cannot stand pat. He had the power and the duty to determine what honest, simple story came out of the facts of this case and what audience would hear it. He had the power and the duty to select the best person to tell the story.

What the state's case lacked was a presentation of that "mountain of evidence" by prosecutors who were not game players themselves, who were presenters of the facts however they might come out, not clever iron-shoe strategists. What the state's case lacked was prosecutors who knew how to tell a story, simply, directly—the right story to the right audience. What the state's case lacked was prosecutors who were dedicated to their work, not enthralled in their newfound stardom and distracted by their under-the-table libidos, prosecutors who despised racism and fought an intelligent battle against it rather than somehow becoming symbols of its evils. Yet, more than all of this, the racial taint inherent in the case was never dealt with above the table, although the prosecution was on notice of it from the beginning and chose, instead, not only to ignore it but to play into it—like feeding a diabetic a sugar sandwich.

How did this verdict, this rupture in the promise of justice, come about? If we could turn back time and apply the wisdom of history, we would sink the first ship that landed on the shores of Africa to load its ignoble cargo for America. America's race issues have never been fully and honestly addressed, not in the history of the nation. The more the issue is suppressed by political correctness, the more people are oppressed by the force of the law; the more minorities are prosecuted and despised and held back from their fair share of the fruits of the land; the more they rise up, the more they hate back, and the more, as jurors, they distrust. The dynamic is so maddeningly simple that even a child, or perhaps especially a child, can understand it. And the police whose duty is to protect us from violence have become the symbol of a violent injustice imposed upon the black community by an equally violent and dominant white society. Given that, the blame lies not with the prosecutors or the defense lawyers, not with the witnesses or the police, who are, in the end, *our* police. The blame lies with us.

Nor have we yet learned anything from the disaster of this case. The victims and the families of the victims were not the only losers. In subtle but tragic ways, the American public has also suffered a loss, perhaps the greater loss. We have lost pride in our system. We have lost faith in our lawyers, who are our only warriors against the tyranny of the state. And worst of all, we have lost our understanding and our compassion.

CHAPTER 13

THE JUDGE

WHEN THE THROATS of the first criers finally dried and cracked, a new set took their place and began their own howling. This time the blame card was laid on the judge. Judge Ito, according to the pundits, was a wimp, a poor little emasculate who could not keep the lawyers in tow. He let Cochran run the court. He was a celebrity junkie himself. Clark called him "spineless." Both Clark and Darden irreverently referred to him as simply "Ito," refusing to acknowledge his office with the usual, respectful "Judge" preceding his name. Now the pundits and know-it-alls were serving up a new fare to the gullible. The latest conventional wisdom was that the judge had not been tough enough. He couldn't make a decision. He was a gutless pushover who let the defense use the judiciary as a doormat. He, and he alone, was to blame for this miserable miscarriage of justice.

Soon most Americans were echoing these sentiments. Ask anyone today what they think of Judge Ito. "He was too soft," they will tell you. "His courtroom was out of control." But how would the average man on the street know a good judge from a bad one? How would the pundits know? To hear them talk, a judge should be a tyrant, an irascible old devil who kicks lawyers around the way many people would like to kick lawyers around. Few members of the public understood the function of a good trial judge. Few had ever been in court. Few had ever shouldered the responsibility of providing a fair trial for an accused who was presumed innocent under the law. Yet the public seemed to believe that a trial judge was supposed to be mean and tough. They adored the image of the hanging judge. Get somebody up there who will raise hell and get the job done, get the case over with, shut the lawyers up, and get that murdering bastard convicted and hanged, forthwith.

Night after night on the talk shows, I heard criticism being leveled at Judge Ito. But I took a different position, born of years spent enduring the relentless abuse of tyrant judges, from having seen my clients' rights placed in severe jeopardy at the hands of blockheads in robes whose only claim to judicial excellence was their ability to scream and taunt and intimidate everyone who came before them. Ask trial lawyers who have been around the block even once, and they will tell you that many judges are mammal-eating monsters that feed on lawyers and their cases, trample over justice, and spew their venom randomly over the courtroom because they do not possess the intelligence or judicial temperament to preside over a fair trial.

Courtrooms are frightening places. Nothing grows in a courtroom—no pretty pansies, no little children laughing and playing. A courtroom is a deadly place. People die in courtrooms, killed by words. If you wake up someday in a courtroom and long to tell your story to someone who can hear and understand you, someone who will gave a damn, who will give you a just hearing, you will be shocked. You want to tell the jury that you are being railroaded? You aren't allowed to speak. Your lawyer isn't, either. Perhaps he can sputter a little. He can object. He can bow and scrape before the judge. If he's not too frightened of the despot up there, he can crowd into the half hour, arbitrarily allowed by the judge, an opening statement that should take at least two hours.

I have seen those judges pace back and forth across that little stage up there, smirking, peering down, hollering, interrupting. I have seen them nail lawyers to podiums like goats tied to a stake, or banish them to counsel table like lepers. Your lawyer cannot freely communicate tied to a stake or banished to a tabletop. I see judges who, the day before they ascended to the bench, couldn't ask the first intelligent question on voir dire, but who, the day after, sat up there as a judge, carrying on a voir dire for the litigants that, if I had conducted it, would have been adjudged as gross malpractice. Often the result is the selection of a jury riddled with prejudice or jurors who are predisposed to convict. I watch judges bullying prospective jurors into saying what the judge wishes them to say. I hear them read instructions to the jury that are critical to justice but that no one, not even the lawyer who submitted the instructions, can understand. I, and every other lawyer who has practiced more than a few years, have endured their intemperance, which so often leads to error and pain and injustice. I see them rule one way one day and another way another day, depending on what they had for breakfast. God help you if you come before such a judge after he has had a bad night under the connubial covers.

Judges are untouchable. You are at their mercy, and many have none. Your case is at their mercy. Your client is at their mercy. The only protection you have from a bad judge is an appeal to other judges, who will likely be of the same political bent, who will probably not have read the record, and who may or may not play golf with the tyrant at whose iron hands and stony heart you have suffered. If the judge has committed heinous error, the appeals court is likely to find that it was error, but harmless. Human beings tend to use all of the power at their disposal. I tell you, judges, on the whole— *laudable exceptions admitted*—habitually abuse their power, most often to the detriment of the accused. And these are the judges adored by the media.

Justice is dependent upon the ability of the parties in conflict to communicate. How do we enjoy justice if the people before the court cannot freely speak to the judge, to the witnesses, to the jury, to each other? When free speech is squelched by fear in the courtroom, justice is also squelched. Courtrooms, at best, are nearly impossible places to carry on a sensible dialogue, yet courtrooms are the designated places for the resolution of conflict in an intelligent and civilized manner. However, under the hand of a tyrant judge, courtrooms become places of horror in which human beings, with the most crucial need in their lives to speak, are frightened, emotionally tortured and abused, and, at last, prevented from crying out.

There you are, trying to explain what happened, and the opposing attorney interrupts your first sentence with an objection. Then come the arguments over the objection. The judge, if he is impatient, lays the judicial whip on your lawyer. The witnesses and lawyers recoil, intimidated. The mediocre minds that inhabit many of the benches in this country do not seek to make communication easier. They do not know how. They themselves could never communicate with a jury. That's why they are not successful trial attorneys but are, instead, judges. Many do not care to learn, and are not interested in justice. They want to clear their dockets. They want to fulfill the public's paradigm of the no-nonsense, tough-on-lawyers judge. They want to be reelected. They want to go play golf with certain lawyers. But they do not want to hear one more word from you or your lawyer. What they lack in wisdom they make up for with power, too often ignorant, arbitrary power. You cannot have a fair trial when your lawyer is afraid. You cannot get justice when the witnesses are cowed. Yet these are the judges most lauded by the media's talking wizards.

Judge Ito, they said, failed to exercise control over his courtroom, and that's why justice flew out the window. According to Vince Bugliosi, the judge was to blame "100 percent for allowing it all to happen, for permitting race to be a big issue at the Simpson trial." I watched this judge many a day. He was concerned; he listened. Sometimes, if anything, I thought him too curt with the lawyers. Yet overall he was the kind of judge I would like to try a case before. He would listen, and people must be heard. He had patience, and patience is the first requirement for any good judge. A judge without patience is like a bad parent who lashes out at his child before the child can spit out the first word, and then wonders why his child stutters. This judge had a sense of humor and a deep commitment to trying the case fairly. He got little help from the lawyers. Trying to stay on top of this case was like trying to herd a flock of wild turkeys. Cameras in the courtroom magnified the problem. With cameras ogling every word, every move, making every participant either camera-shy or camera-crazed, no judge in the history of jurisprudence could have done better without having done worse. He made mistakes, to be sure, but they were not the mistakes of a tyrant. If a judge is to err, he should err on the side of tolerance. Judge Ito was tolerant and a gentleman.

It has pained me much to see him pilloried by the vindictive and the hateful. I have never heard a criticism leveled at the man by anyone who had ever defended a murder case. The criticism steams up out of the bowels of ignorance. To have carefully and sincerely devoted endless days and long, ceiling-staring nights to the case only to have a cadre of featherbrains tell the world he was a bad judge must have cut deeply into the man. Yet I never heard him whimper or lash back. The blameworthy, the prosecution, the media, the disappointed American public, laid the blame card on this man. Too bad. Such only encourages the remainder of American judges to become meaner, shorter, less patient, more tyrannical—which will suit our fancies and please us greatly until we stand before them begging to be heard. To be sure, had the jury returned a verdict of guilty against Simpson, Judge Ito would have become the living icon of wisdom, symbolizing the finest the American judiciary had to offer.

I asked Judge Ito for an interview for this book. He refused, saying that the civil case, on appeal, was not concluded, and he thought it a violation of judicial ethics to be talking to yet another member of the media before the appeal was concluded—if, indeed, the case will ever be over. Why should it be? We would then be required to attend to such issues as the disintegrating environment that threatens the earth, the escalating racial strife that threatens our nation, the expanding poor who threaten us with even more crime, the deteriorating family that threatens the moral underpinning of the land, the corporate-government oligarchy that threatens our freedom.

Yet at times during the trial even I found cause to wonder if Judge Ito should be sitting up there, but for reasons that must surely have also troubled him. His wife was Captain Margaret York of the LAPD, and although she was not assigned to the case and supervised no one directly involved in it, I kept seeing this image: the judge slipping off his bunny slippers and sliding under the sheets into the arms of a police captain on the LAPD. How do you avoid images like that? How do you avoid hearing in your mind's ear her throaty whisper to the judge, murmuring words such as, "What kind of a day did you have, today, darling?"

"Well, it was hell. That Johnnie Cochran is trying to screw me good," the judge sighs.

"And he's trying to make the department look bad. I get a lot of heat about it all the time. People say, 'Captain, can't you put the reins on that husband of yours—guide him a little?'"

"Well, don't pay any attention to it. Like I tell the jury—you have to put that sort of thing out of your mind."

"How can you say that? I'm a captain. This is *my* career!" Her voice is above a whisper now. "My men—and a few women—are wondering what the hell is going on with this Fuhrman thing. You know Fuhrman. I know him. He's a racist, womanizing mother—"

"Whoo, there, honey, you can't talk to me like that. You aren't supposed to remember anything about Fuhrman, remember?"

"Well, this is *just us*, not *justice*."

"Well it is *just us*. But in the morning I gotta do *justice*. I gotta make some rulings."

Whispering again. "Well, remember, Lance, baby, the LAPD is paying the rent. You're just buying the groceries."

It's my damnable runaway mind that produces things like that. And then I'm on TV and I begin to say things such as, "This is the first case I have ever seen where the judge is literally in bed with the police." And everybody on the show frowns because that comment, too, is not politically correct. And, beyond that, the comment is not fair. I know that both sides were fully advised of the relationship between the judge and the captain, but still, the vision of these people—one a neutral arbiter of justice and the other a dedicated crime buster—cohabiting under the same sheets seemed to create an irresolvable conflict, if not in fact, at least in appearance. I could never understand why the judge, on his own motion, had not taken himself off of the case, the lawyers' waivers notwithstanding. When lawyers waive such an obvious conflict, there is usually an unspoken but powerful quid pro quo lurking in the background.

Why, then, had the lawyers on both sides kept Judge Ito on the case? Each side had a peremptory right to remove him. But what tyrant might they have gotten if he stepped down? I remember talking to Shapiro about it when I was in Los Angeles for my interview with him. Shapiro knew the judge's background. Judge Ito had been a prosecutor. But Johnnie Cochran had been in the same office as a fellow prosecutor with the judge, and that seemed to give the defense a leg up. On the other hand, prosecutors who become judges usually take their prosecutorial mind-set to the bench. Up there they forget they are judges. They still want to prosecute, and they do. Clark knew the judge's history. She knew about him sleeping with the captain. She knew the state's interests were certainly intact with Judge Ito on the bench. But when the jury laid their verdict on the world there was, thank God, the judge to blame, and shamelessly Clark and Darden, and all others who had axes to grind or venom to vent or excuses to peddle, didn't hesitate to lay that blame card on the judge.

Before the case was half over, along came the Fuhrman tapes, in which infelicitous references were made to Margaret York, who was not just the judge's wife, but also Fuhrman's old commander. Fuhrman claimed on the tapes that York had "sucked and fucked her way to the top." On the other hand, York had filed a declaration stating, in substance, that she remembered little if anything about this Fuhrman fellow, this racist, sexist miscreant who had been in her face for months. Fuhrman wrote, "The confrontations between York and me were not quiet conflicts. They were loud, frequent, and impossible to ignore. York was so antagonistic toward me that virtually everyone who knew her or me was aware of the situation. York made it clear that she detested me."

Bad memories are useful. The judge, being called upon to make a ruling on the Fuhrman tapes, was, as might have been foreseen by both sides, caught between the bench and the bedsheets, which is not a pretty place to be. At this point Cochran did not want a mistrial, because he thought he could win an acquittal, and never, if he tried the case a hundred times, would it again be as riddled with such prosecutorial blunders. Clark was afraid a mistrial might result in double jeopardy if the blame for the same could be laid at the feet of the prosecution. The judge, caught in this trap, one jaw of which was his wife and the other the law, was doubtlessly devastated.

"I love my wife dearly," Judge Ito said, speaking through thick emotions barely held back. "And I am wounded by criticism of her, as any spouse would be. And I think it is reasonable to assume that that could have some impact." Instead of recusing himself from the case, which would have likely resulted in a mistrial, he called in another judge to rule on the tapes.

The Ito-York-Fuhrman triangle only lent more fuel to the fire of racism, an inferno the defense claimed was burning out of control. Cochran charged that the race issue was being covered up in order to convict Simpson, that Fuhrman was a racist and everyone knew it, including York. Don Evans, a retired senior lead officer of West L.A., took to television to describe in some detail his memory of York's past negative comments concerning Fuhrman. Moreover,

Fuhrman claimed in his book that Johnnie Cochran received an unsigned statement from Evans that read, in part:

> Captain York was also directly involved in internal affairs investigations which centered on Detective Fuhrman that [concerned] alleged gender and racial bias. Captain York also personally counseled Detective Fuhrman regarding these issues while I was stationed with the two of them at West Los Angeles station, but I have read her declaration [that she remembers little or nothing about Fuhrman] and she is factually inaccurate.

Aside from the fact that the statement was unsigned, Fuhrman now wonders why it was not used in court. He speculates that it might have been because Cochran possessed information that the judge's wife had been less then truthful, that the judge knew he did, and that this provided Cochran some kind of hold over the judge. Fuhrman went on to lament, "For whatever reasons, personal, legal, or political, Ito chose the road most devastating to me, the one player in the trial who had an adversarial relationship with his wife. He allowed the trial of O.J. Simpson to become the trial of Mark Fuhrman." And so we see at once, and once more, that whether or not Judge Ito ever acted out of anything but the purest of motives, the appearance of impropriety permitted the blame card to be laid at his feet. But Fuhrman should not have wailed so loudly. Judge Ito did not allow the most pernicious portions of the Fuhrman tapes into the case, although they were eventually given to the public to fume anew over.

The scene was out of a brainless Hollywood comedy—something Eddie Murphy might have starred in. The white majority was ranting and raving that this supposedly stupid racist black jury had struck back at the system by turning yet another black killer loose. At the same time, the same people were aghast at the overt racism of Fuhrman, against which the black jury had reacted.

It was like being mad at the turkey who ate the snake. In short, everyone hated everyone, the accused who was the murderer, the defense attorneys who dared play the race card, the racist cop who lied, the race-sensitive jurors who were prejudiced, the Japanese-American judge who was a judicial marshmallow, and, eventually, the black and white prosecutors whose alleged copulation best expressed the public's view of the whole goofy affair: Fuck it!

———

CHAPTER 14

TRUTH

I HAVE OFTEN pictured this vulnerable creature, this mammal generously referred to as a human being, as an emotional, buglike entity with thousands of little feelers that curl out and around and probe and poke, always searching for evidence that the other— whoever the other may be—is not credible and is therefore danger- ous. To survive through the eons, this creature must know when those of his own species are about to do him in. Whom can he trust? Who will betray him? Who will lead him into danger? Who is not credible? Subliminally we ask these questions every day, and we answer them in the same way. At last we say, "I don't trust him. I don't know why, but I don't." We say, "There's something about that person that bothers me." Sometimes we are fooled; sometimes we have heard false signals or part signals, and sometimes we are paranoid. But more often than not, we are correctly warned, and if we listen carefully, openly, we are most likely to receive an accu- rate message that reveals whether the bearer of the message, who- ever it is, is credible. Through the ages we have learned over and over that juries have this power. As a consequence, jurors have been entrusted with determining who is and who is not telling the whole truth. Under the law, then, jurors become the *sole judges of the credibility of the witnesses.*

In the O.J. trial, the prosecution charged that Johnnie Cochran had laid out an incredible, evil case, and that a prejudiced jury had bought it. I agree that the conclusion Cochran asked the jury to adopt—namely, that O.J. had been the victim of a widespread conspiracy—was, indeed, incredible. But item after item, theory after theory of the state's case, when presented, was utterly void of credibility or laced with half-truths, and as we must know, *unless we tell the whole truth, half-truths become whole lies.* And further, lest we forget, the prosecution, not the defense, had the obligation of proof in the trial—beyond a reasonable doubt.

Once more, it was the undaunted arrogance of the prosecution's too smart lawyers that would cause this jury—indeed, any jury, black or white—to retch at the sight of the grotesque fictions being offered up as the whole truth in the case. Who was going to believe—you, me, anyone with a smidgen of common sense—that the officers left the scene of the crime, the bloody bodies, and the evidence exposed to the uncharted vicissitudes that become part of every crime scene; that they jumped the fence at Rockingham and, without a warrant, began their illegal survey of O.J.'s place, which was merely a fortuitous by-product incidental to telling Simpson that his wife was dead. That is like marching a legion into Nero's kitchen to explain to him that Rome is on fire. No one believed the over-the-fence excuse of the officers—surely not even Marcia Clark. And surely, absent the conjugal arguments of Captain Margaret York, not Judge Ito.

When the police fabricate and fictionalize rather than tell the simple truth, as damaging as it may be, the credibility antennas of the jurors are raised. These were the same police whom the jury would be asked to believe when the prosecution claimed Fuhrman did not plant the glove. These were the same police who asked the jury to believe that the socks in the bedroom had not been fiddled with, even when the blood on the socks was discovered to contain EDTA, the blood preservative—a magical substance that must get soaked up into one's socks out of thin air. These were the same police who could provide no satisfactory explanation for how EDTA, as if by divine miracle, meandered into the blood on the Bundy gate. And this was the prosecution that asked a dedicated, sincere jury to listen day after torturously boring day to the technical evidence about DNA, which, in the end, nobody understood, not even the scientists, who became entangled in their own mumbling, endless discourses before it was all over.

But remember, this jury was finally composed, in part, of eight black women. These are women who had lived beyond the pages of romance novels and the lollipop dramas of the *National Enquirer*. These were women who had had to survive in the walk-up apartments of hard neighborhood tenement houses, some of whom had known life as it is lived in the projects. These were women who knew about the frailty of the human species—that we sin, *all* of us, but some more than others, especially those who traipse through the upper echelons of the Hollywood set. If the black women on the jury had stepped over the line in their lives, they knew that Nicole had, too. They knew, from one source or another, that she was no stranger to the drug scene. They doubtlessly knew about Faye Resnick and her bout with drugs. They were likely aware of the rumors of her affair with Marcus Allen—"Driftwood," Resnick claimed Nicole called him, because in unsubtle ways he reminded her of that large hunk of wood lying on the beach. They must have known about Nicole's penchant for oral sex, as described by Resnick, about her living room assignation with one Keith Zlomsowitch, and all of the other morally tawdry stuff that Resnick had written about in her book (including their secret lesbian adventure), which everyone suspected had been leaked, in whole or in part, to that sequestered jury. Even if the Chinese wall that the court attempted to build around this jury held back all of the media, life-wise women on the jury knew that Nicole was not the pristine princess she was made out to be by Marcia Clark. They knew that if O.J. beat the hell out of her, well, she, too, brought prejudices and bigotry to their marriage. Spousal abuse has no excuse. None. But the prosecution made a serious error by portraying Nicole Simpson as a guileless princess. A.C. Cowlings later related an instance in which Nicole had once said to O.J. in the heat of battle, "I can't believe I married a nigger. I knew this would happen to me." In short, the jurors knew that Nicole was both a whole lot more and a whole lot less than she had been portrayed as.

What this meant to thinking jurors was that the state's case wasn't candid. They would have expected an honest prosecution to say something like, "Yes, this woman wasn't perfect. Some might even claim she wasn't even moral. She played the games of a woman looking for good times. She did things that maybe some of us have done but wouldn't want spewed out in a courtroom and carried in headlines in every newspaper in the country. She was a woman, but not better than most of us. She was a woman who, like the rest of us, might have lived her life differently if she had another chance. Do we not learn more from the mistakes we make than from all the preaching of all the preachers? Yet whoever she was, as imperfect as she was, yes, even as immoral as many might adjudge her, she was a human being who had the right not to have her throat cut and her blood emptied out of her body all over the front sidewalk."

I think ordinary human beings could relate to that truth. But when you have Marcia Clark in there twirling all over the courtroom and at the same time attempting to make Nicole out to be a battered angel, you have a credibility problem.

Then there was always the lingering suspicion, often not even whispered, that Ron Goldman was, in fact, Nicole's lover. Since this was not part of the conventional wisdom provided us by the talking heads, the public had not given that scenario much more than passing consideration. It was one that both the prosecution and the defense avoided. From the standpoint of the prosecution, such a tryst would fly in the face of their domestic violence schema. From the standpoint of the defense, it provided a clear, understandable motive for the killing.

Ron Goldman had been seen driving around in Nicole's white Ferrari. Moreover, Fuhrman claimed he had been talking to friends of his in Brentwood, and one lady, an acquaintance of Goldman's who wanted to remain anonymous, said Ron had told her that he had been seeing a thirty-five-year-old woman who had two kids. "She has a white Ferrari," he said.

"Isn't sex with an older woman great?" the woman asked.

"Yeah, it's great," Ron was said to have replied.

Fuhrman claims he delivered this statement to Lange and Vannatter, and that he never heard of it after that. He then says he was surprised to find the same information in Lawrence Schiller's book *American Tragedy*. "An LAPD source told Pavelic [an investigator for the defense] that they had interviewed a beauty salon attendant who said that Ron was straight and dating an older woman with two kids, presumably Nicole."

Darden had had a conversation with one Jennifer Peace, a porn star who had dated A.C. Cowlings. She claimed that Cowlings had wept on one of their dates, saying that Nicole didn't deserve what she got, and that just two nights before the murders, Simpson had been stalking Ron Goldman.

I remember one night on *Larry King Live* we were talking, as usual, about the case, and the murder scene came up. Simpson's kids were upstairs asleep. Warm water had been drawn in the tub. Candles were burning throughout the house, including the bathroom. I revealed my old-fogey-hood by confessing I had never heard of taking a bath with the lights down and the candles glowing except, perhaps, if the electricity had failed and I couldn't find the soap. But it seemed pretty romantic to me. I mentioned it to Imaging, my own fantasies aflame. But she was quick to point out that women take candlelight baths all the time.

"You never have—not to my knowledge," I said.

"Well, that doesn't mean that other women don't."

"I think she knew Goldman was coming over and was preparing a little romantic ta-ta for him," I said.

"I don't think that follows," Imaging said. "Don't fall overboard on that one." But I had already expressed my idea on *Larry King* and it had been pooh-poohed by the hip women. Yet it was hard for a country boy who took a bath at his grandparents' on Saturday night in an old washtub in the middle of the living room floor to get it through his head that modern women slip into the bathroom in a house empty of all but sleeping kids, draw a tub full of water, light the candles, and proceeded to fly off, solo, to a world I had never visited.

Whatever the facts, even if she could, Clark was not interested in connecting the two deceased romantically because, among other problems we have seen, it would also have sullied the battered-cherub image of Nicole she was creating. But here is what the jury was asked to believe: Ron Goldman, this young handsome fellow, just happened to be at the restaurant where Nicole was dining that night. The eyeglasses just happened to be left behind. This young hunk just happened to know Nicole, and her telephone number and her address, and he just happened to be the sort who, out of the goodness of his heart, would take the time to deliver, in person, these said glasses to a customer. And Nicole, at the same said time, just happened to have the kids in bed, the warm water in the tub drawn and the candles lit, when the buzzer rang. This was all just another of those coincidences of fate that drive and direct our lives, we are to believe.

We can forget the business about Goldman having been seen driving about in Nicole's white Ferrari. I mean, waiters usually drive their customers' expensive cars around town as an additional service, or something. We can forget the woman who mentioned that Goldman was having this good sex with a married woman with two kids and the white sports car, since that came from Fuhrman. But no one to this day, including the LAPD and the defense, seems to have been interested in this large glob of potential truth plopped out in the middle of their cases, and we know why they weren't interested.

That Goldman may have been seen driving Nicole's Ferrari and may have been directing his youthful rut to this older woman, with whom sex was an everlasting joy, would, if true, have afforded a more credible scenario than the one offered to intelligent black women jurors. These jurors were obliged to listen to such nonsense as was adopted by Clark from the psycho-jabber of the reputed domestic violence experts. These diviners insisted that Nicole's rejection of Simpson at Sidney's dance recital, coupled with Paula Barbieri's rejection of him with her "Dear John" message on his answering machine, irrevocably triggered his murderous intent. Listen to Clark's ridiculous rhapsody:

> [Simpson's] overweening ego and controlling behavior masked a fundamentally flawed, insecure, and extremely immature personality. To such an unstable man, violence would seem a justifiable means of reestablishing control. . . .
>
> But my guess was that Simpson's frustration over his inability to reach [Barbieri] that night had spilled over in rage against Nicole. The first time Nicole dumped him, he'd had Paula to catch him. The second time, he went into free fall.

Try selling that to a jury of sound minds. In the meantime, the prosecution not only had information that Nicole may have been having an affair with Ron Goldman, but they knew all about the living room assignation with Keith Zlomsowitch, who was supposedly the recipient of another of those "Brentwood hellos" while O.J. watched the whole thing through the living room window.

"I watched you last night," he told Nicole and Zlomsowitch. "I can't believe you would do that in the house. I watched you. . . . I saw everything you did." There wouldn't have been a man on the jury, or even a woman, who wouldn't have understood the bone-deep hurt a man would feel seeing the woman he loved (although also obsessively hated and abused) performing fellatio on another man—and with his kids upstairs? Wouldn't such a shocker, along with, say, the alleged Marcus Allen affair, a spree with Ron Goldman, and perhaps others—all or any of them—likely have motivated Simpson to kill? You cannot make up far-out stuff that flies in the face of the common knowledge of a jury. Psycho-jabber, if it is to be believed, has to conform to common human experience, not create it.

And so, by the time this jury took the case, the prosecution had no credibility left whatsoever. I saw Marcia Clark's final argument. She was sweet and kind, her eyes the eyes of the long-suffering Madonna. She turned it on and off like water out of a new garden hose. She spun her stories right out of the domestic violence manual, gilded with the flavor of Faye Resnick's tell-all. She told the jury to believe Mark Fuhrman, although she said he was a lying monster. She tried to woo this jury of predominantly black women, who likely saw her as just one more white female with an attitude who was hell-bent on neutering another black man. And the jurors weren't going to let that happen again.

And the glove: the bloody goddamn glove. The prosecutors had already placed the gloves securely on Simpson's hands without any in-court demonstration required. Nicole had bought two pairs of Aris Light gloves from Bloomingdale's in New York, the only store in America that sold these gloves. And the prosecution had the receipt. Not only that, they had a photo taken during a football game showing Simpson wearing the same style of gloves. So what more did it need? How many times as a young, inexperienced lawyer, when I had my point made with a witness, did I ask that one question too many, the answer to which sunk my ship? Young, eager lawyers do that. Experienced professionals rarely.

But Darden had to put the glove on Simpson. He simply *had to*. His first experiment would have warned him of the danger. You cannot put gloves on him who does not want gloves put on him. If you push the second thumb joint out—the one nearest the palm of the hand—you can't get even a too-big glove on. And since the sleeve of the glove is covering that joint, no one can tell you are pushing the joint out so that the glove won't slip on. You can pull and jerk at it and ask anyone around to pull and jerk at it and the glove will not go on. Only when you retract the joint will the glove slip over. Now add to the demonstration a pair of latex rubber gloves. You know how sticky latex is. There was no way that glove with Simpson pulling at it, could fit. The only way it would go on would be to put the man under anesthesia. Then, over a bare hand, it would probably still take a couple of other hands to pull it on.

I bought a pair of latex gloves and tried to pull my own leather gloves over them. No way. It was then that I learned the thumb-joint trick, which I demonstrated on NBC. But to this day, Darden still does not understand why the glove didn't fit. He thought it shrunk, and it wasn't his fault the goddamn glove shrunk. And besides, somehow the fault lay in the "defense team's trickery," which, when translated, means that Darden outsmarted himself.

Credibility. You lose it all when you say you are going to do something you do not do. It is like lying. If you lie once, people know you will lie again. If you don't keep your word with the jury, you will never be trusted. If you are going to show the jury that the glove fits, and it does not fit, well, what else can they believe from you? Such are fatal errors in a trial that only prove to the jury that you and your case are unreliable. It is called reasonable doubt. It usually exposes the false case. But sometimes, when an honest case is falsely presented, the jury is led astray. But that's not the fault of the jury.

You can lose nearly every battle in a trial and still win the war if you have kept your credibility. I'm not talking about acting. I'm talking about being genuine, being honest, presenting the whole case, the hurtful evidence along with the exculpatory. There is and never has been a perfect case, and you ought not try to make a perfect one. When the jury sees that you are telling the truth, it will understand when an occasional witness goes haywire. You, after all, have not gone haywire. If you are surprised in the trial, well, that happens to the best of us. The jury knows you can't force everything. If you have been honest with the jury and your case isn't as strong as it should be, often the jury will excuse you, make room for you, even fight for you. If your arguments are reasonable and fair, the jury will believe you, because you are entitled to be believed. But if you lie to the jury, fail to keep your word with the jury, well, jurors are hard-pressed to forgive a lawyer they have trusted who has betrayed them, even once.

Sadly, Marcia Clark and Chris Darden had little credibility left with this jury. They could blame whomever they wished. They could denigrate the jurors, attack the judge, and excoriate the defense team (who had earned little credibility themselves), but in the end, the case was over when this jury looked at Clark and Darden and asked themselves, "Can they be believed?" And the answer: Had they been guides at Disneyland, the jurors wouldn't have followed either one of them across the street.

CHAPTER 15

THE KNIFE

LET ME TELL you a true story. Good lawyers, we have seen, must be good storytellers. Once upon a time—actually, January 1, 1989, at nearly 4:00 in the morning—the police received a call from a screaming woman. She needed help at 360 North Rockingham, O.J. Simpson's house. Soon the police arrived, the lights blinking, the neighbors in their pajamas gawking out of their windows. A cop pressed the buzzer at the gate and the housekeeper came to answer.

"No problem here," she said. "You should go."

"Not going anywhere, ma'am, until we talk to the woman who made the call to the station."

Suddenly, out of the bushes behind the gate burst a woman on unsteady feet. She was blond, young, and dressed in only a bra and dirty sweatpants.

"He's going to kill me! He's going to kill me!" She beat on the gate button. The gate opened, and she ran to the officer, collapsing on him. John Edwards was the cop's name.

"Who is going to kill you?" asked Edwards. He's holding her. She's sobbing, hysterical.

"O.J."

"O.J. who? You mean the football player?" Of course she meant the football player—it was all in the record. The woman's lip was bleeding. Her forehead was bruised. Her cheek was scratched. Her right eye was black-and-blue and showing signs of swelling, and Edwards could see that on her neck was the imprint of a hand.

"You guys never do anything," she complained. "You've been here eight times, and you never do anything."

Then O.J. came out to the gate in a bathrobe, screaming, "I don't want that woman in my bed anymore! I got two other women. I don't want that woman in my bed!"

"I'm putting you under arrest," Edwards said to Simpson.

"I didn't beat her. Just pushed her. I don't want her in my bed."

"Well, you gotta come with us," Edwards said.

"What's the matter with you guys? You been out here eight times and now you're going to arrest me for this? This is a family matter." None of their business. But Edwards was going to make it his business.

"Go get your clothes on. You're going in with us."

Simpson went inside, and in a few minutes he came out again, dressed this time, and he began scolding the cops for messing in his private family affairs. By this time a second set of cops had arrived as backup. Edwards was briefing them when the officers saw a Bentley roar out of the other gate. Edwards, along with cops in four other police cars, sped off after him. But they couldn't catch him.

We leave the story here and fast-forward: The criminal trial is over. Simpson has been acquitted of the murders. The civil case in which Simpson has been sued by the Browns and the Goldmans is under way. It is 1996. A.C. Cowlings's deposition has been taken. From it we discover the rest of what happened that New Year's morning in 1989.

According to Cowlings, Simpson returned to Rockingham in a car belonging to Alan Schwartz a couple of hours after he'd given the cops the slip. He parked the car around the corner because he knew the cops were looking for him. He climbed over the fence of the adjoining property and entered his house through the back door. Then he stole upstairs. Why did he return to the scene of the crime? Cowlings claims Simpson came back to get some jewelry in a box.

Jewelry in a box? One risks arrest to come back to one's house to get a box of jewelry? What was in the box that was perhaps so incriminating that Simpson wanted to retrieve it before the cops came into the house, searching? Some have suggested it was O.J.'s stash of drugs. There is no evidence to support that speculation. But no one takes the risk of returning to the scene of the crime after a chase with five cars of cops in pursuit, probably with an all-points bulletin out on the car, to retrieve one's own jewelry out of one's own house, jewelry that was perfectly safe there. No one goes to the trouble to borrow another's car, hop a fence (or, as Cowlings said, a couple of fences), and steal up to the back door of the very house where one's beaten-up wife is hiding, all to retrieve some alleged jewelry. So what was in the box?

Still according to Cowlings, Simpson ran out the same back door and hopped over the same back fence to the car that he had parked around the corner. But fate is a troublesome interloper. He had lost the keys to the borrowed car, leaving Simpson, this black man in this white neighborhood, at an inauspicious time of night, carrying a bag (the box)—with whatever is in the bag. He had to get rid of the bag. And so what did he do?

Cowlings gave answers to John Kelly's questions at his deposition on April 17, 1996, as follows in part:

> COWLINGS: . . . he had hid [the box] at a neighbor's house in the garbage can. . . . He said he had jumped the [Von Wattses'] wooden fence that runs along Ashford, so I went over. . . . It goes maybe about five foot high, four foot. I don't know exactly. So I went to where he approximately said, and I looked around on the house side, inside the yard, and I didn't see it, and when I put my hands up to

jump over the fence, I kinda looked down, and I saw the keys had—[wedged between] the brick and the grass right there, there was two keys. . . .

KELLY: Tell me exactly what he told you in terms of leaving his house, what he did.

A. He told me that he had taken the jewelry and that he had dropped the keys.

Q. And then he told you what route he took also, didn't he?

A. Right.

Q. Tell me what route he told you he took.

A. He went across his tennis court, into the Von Wattses' backyard—

Q. Did he tell you how he got into the Von Wattses' backyard?

A. Then he told me that he walked up, jumped—walked up the steps, went across and jumped over the wood frame fence at the Von Wattses'.

Q. And how tall is that wood frame fence?

A. Could be five feet, for all I know. . . .

Q. Okay. All right. Tell me what you did after you found the keys.

A. I got the keys, and the house was on—the house where he hid the jewelry—the house was located on Bristol. It was two houses from the corner, going north. I got to Ashford and Bristol. It was two houses up from the corner. I went back there. I was thinking, I said, here I am jumping fences and stuff; I may get shot, some black guy jumping fences. I'm, you know, thinking to myself, and . . . So he said [what he deposited] was in the garbage cans down the driveway behind the house. So I went there, picked up the lid, and there it was. And I picked it up and brought the keys . . .

Q. And you never looked in the bag?

A. No.

Q. Was the bag heavy?

A. What do you mean by that, "heavy"?

Q. Well, was there some weight to it?

A. Yeah, there was some weight to it.

Q. Okay. More than a couple pounds?

A. I don't know.

So Simpson stuffs the bag with the box of whatever-it-was in a neighbor's trash can around the corner. Very clever, no?

At the civil trial, John Kelly, that handsome, clear-headed attorney for the estate of Nicole Brown Simpson, was thoughtful enough to ask Simpson about this incident his best friend described. Simpson denied it happened. But Cowlings had earlier admitted the story in his deposition, and at the civil trial, Simpson's faithful Cowlings testified to the story once again, contradicting his old friend when he told how the fence-hopping Simpson lost the car keys and how Simpson had disposed of the jewelry in the neighbor's garbage can.

During the deliberations in the civil trial, the last two jury requests for read-backs of testimony were for Kelly's cross-examination of Simpson and Kelly's examination of Cowlings. After the verdict was in, Kelly said he talked to several of the jurors who insisted that the testimony of A.C. Cowlings clearly showed Simpson's modus operandi. Simpson was not an inventive man. He was one who relied upon what he had learned from past experience rather than creating something new to fit the need of the moment. When it came to murder, as we shall see, he relied on past learned behavior as well. When the police were waiting to arrest him after the murder, as before on January 1, 1989, he attempted to escape, and, as before, not in one of his own vehicles, but in someone else's automobile, this time the 1993 white Ford Bronco belonging to A.C. Cowlings. And after the murder, when it came time to dispose of the knife and his bloody clothes, again he relied on old, learned behavior.

John Kelly, a very bright lawyer, had a very bright solution that explained perfectly how Simpson disposed of his bloody clothes and the murder weapon. Although a legion of officers in California and Chicago searched endlessly for this missing critical evidence, it was never found. As Kelly asked when I interviewed him, do any of us really think that Simpson took the bloody clothes and the knife with him? Must we suffer that silly scenario offered by the state at the trial—that Simpson insisted, when he loaded his baggage into the limo at Rockingham, that only he handled a small black duffel bag, and that at Los Angeles International Airport he was standing near the sky cap's check station by a trash container, into which he supposedly threw the bag? Are we asked to believe that a very famous national hero, with the victims' blood freshly washed from his hands, his own hand cut, and paranoid to the extreme—as would any guilty man be with a murder lodged but an hour in his memory—was actually taking *with* him the most incriminating evidence—his bloody clothes, the knife? Are we to further believe that he would dare dispose of this most incriminating evidence in plain sight of any of the hundreds of passers-by whose attention, under any circumstance, would have been drawn to this most famous of persons in airports? Or are we to believe the other equally fantastic theory—that Simpson brought the incriminating evidence back from Chicago in his baggage, and that Robert Kardashian or someone else disposed of it, thereby committing a blatant obstruction of justice, or thereby causing themselves to become accessories after the fact?

What murderer would attach himself to the most inculpatory evidence in the case by taking it with him on a plane, or worse, by bringing it back with him? Simpson would have thought that already the police were looking for him and would be waiting for him when he got off the plane in Chicago. Kelly believes that on that Sunday night the murder weapon and the murderer's bloody clothing were simply dropped in the neighbor's garbage can where Simpson had previously deposited the "jewelry box" early on January 1, 1989. His old behavior.

Let us pause momentarily to keep in mind, as Kelly pointed out to me, the very remarkable parallels between the deposit of the so-called jewelry box on January 1, 1989, and Simpson's likely conduct on the evening of June 12, 1994:

- In order to avoid detection, Simpson parked the car when he returned to Rockingham somewhere other than at the Ashford gate, where he always parked.

- He climbed over a neighbor's fence to get onto his property to avoid detection.

- He dropped the keys (just as he later dropped the glove) when going over the fence, and then couldn't find them.

- He took the bag he was carrying containing whatever it contained and hid it in a neighbor's trash can to avoid being seen with it—just as he probably hid the knife and clothes the night of the murders.

Kelly says, and I remember, that during his cross, Simpson was implacable in his denials that, on January 1, 1989, he had been climbing fences and avoiding the police. Kelly says, "I suspect Simpson was so adamant in his denials because his actions on January 1, 1989, including hiding items in a neighbor's trash can, were identical to the next time he thought the police were looking for him." That seems to me to be a very smart observation.

Most likely, then, on the morning following the murders, Monday morning, bright and early, a garbage truck came along and disposed of the incriminating evidence for Simpson, the crucial evidence that the police across the nation have been searching for ever since.

CHAPTER 16

THE RETURN OF
THE FROGMAN

I TALKED TO Faye Resnick, friend and confidante of Nicole, and author of the book *Nicole Brown Simpson: The Private Diary of a Life Interrupted.* In the days before the murder, O.J. was on the phone constantly with Resnick. She said that when the couple had earlier reconciled, Nicole had told O.J. about Marcus Allen, and the other men as well. Simpson told Resnick that Nicole and he had to clear the deck. They had to come back into the relationship with no secrets. They had to be honest with each other. He told Nicole about Paula Barbieri, who was supposedly the only other woman in his life, or at least the only one Nicole knew about, and therefore the only one he needed to confess.

Then Resnick said that O.J.'s series *The Frogmen* came up. Nicole was deathly afraid of frogs, a strange pathological phobia of some kind. According to Resnick, all of her friends knew how afraid she was of the little toothless creatures. O.J. thought it was funny:

"Hey, can you believe this?" he hollered. "It's just so ironic that my wife's biggest fear in life is frogs, and I've ended up starring in a TV series called *The Frogmen!*" He laughed. Then, according to Resnick, he jibed at Nicole, "I'm the Frog Man. Now, what do you think about that?"

196

The next day Simpson flew to Puerto Rico to begin filming *The Frogmen*. That same evening, Nicole told Faye she thought his joke about the "Frog Man" was cruel. And after that, Nicole said it was over for her, that she was afraid that O.J. was going to kill her. It was done. "I don't think he's changed," she told Resnick.

Faye Resnick said that while Simpson was in Puerto Rico he was on the phone with her almost incessantly. Why wouldn't Nicole answer his calls? Why wouldn't she call him? He was nearly insane over it, obsessive, I suppose the shrinks would say, this spoiled athlete who had always had what he wanted when he wanted it, and when he began to lose control over Nicole he lost, in the mirror of his neurotic mind, control of himself as well.

Did Nicole get back together with Marcus Allen? Resnick claims she saw Allen's car at Nicole's place a short time before the murder. And how about Simpson—did he know about the alleged assignation? Resnick couldn't prove what O.J. did or didn't know. She said she had her suspicions. But of course, the prosecution couldn't offer her suspicions as evidence. Still, Resnick said she thought the prosecution should have presented her friend Nicole as she was—real, with all the blemishes. Not fake it up. She thought the motive for murder was there, clear and clean: the other men. His constant threat—"If I find her with another guy, I'll kill her"—gave Resnick her certainty. I agreed with her, even if, in the process, not a few blemishes on Resnick would be examined by the defense, as well.

In *The Frogmen*, which was produced by Warner Bros. for NBC, Simpson starred as a character named Bullfrog. If you read the script you can see Bullfrog in his black wet suit, his black stocking cap, his long-bladed knife, sharp as a shark's tooth, strapped to his left ankle. He was a trained killer, a Navy SEAL, one who kills swiftly with the knife—cut the throat, the carotid arteries, the windpipe, no sound. It's all done so silently, efficiently.

Let me describe the scene from the TV movie shot as a pilot for the series:

NIGHT: EXTERIOR SHOT: THE DIVE SHOP. Bullfrog looks around. He recognizes all of the cars in front of his dive shop, all but one. He heads for the outside stairs that will lead to his apartment, checking behind him as he goes—habit, man. Almost to the top of the stairs, he hears a sound below. Now he eases himself down the steps, down, down. He moves silently, swiftly, along the perimeter of the shop, peering though the windows, stalking. Then, as silently as smoke drifting through a cracked door, he enters the dive shop, its lights out. He flips open the serrated knife, slowing, and cautiously, knife in hand, he searches for the intruder. Then he sees the shadow.

He moves past a wall covered with photos of his career in the SEALs, still silent, like silence moving. He's circled the shadow, and now he's behind it. Suddenly he lunges.

In one flash the intruder is on the floor, one arm twisting a head back. The knife poised to slash: Then he recognizes the woman on the floor.

Strange, inexplicable foreboding in the script. More: In the script, Bullfrog threatens to kill someone named Goldman. Jesus! Goldman? A cruel apocalyptic accident of fate? Still more: In the script he goes to his wife's grave and prays. When I heard of this I could feel a cold, eerie shiver.

No one could help but note the similarities in the murder at Bundy and the scene of the stalk and take-down from the script— both, I believe, played by Simpson.

It's night.

He's stalking.

He wields a knife.

He's wearing a black stocking cap.

He's in dark clothing.

His hands are covered with dark leather gloves.

His prey is a woman.

He lunges for her.

Had Simpson, at Bundy, reverted to the role of Bullfrog? Actors can get caught up in roles. Sometimes they cannot distinguish who they are from whom they play they are. Under stress they can revert to the role they've learned, for if they do not understand themselves, perhaps they can understand the character they have assumed.

I talked to Mark Lonsdale, the creator and technical advisor to the NBC series. Lonsdale is an expert on paramilitary tactics, a man who has written seven books on the subject. He said the major portion of the pilot was shot in Puerto Rico. One thing Lonsdale remembered: During the entire filming, both in Puerto Rico and during the last days of the filming in Los Angeles in March 1994, Simpson had his cell phone glued to his ear. Every spare moment he was on the phone. To whom? To Faye Resnick. To Nicole. He was compulsive about it, Lonsdale said.

But Lonsdale, an expert in the use of the tactical knife, insisted he didn't teach Simpson any knife techniques. Lonsdale believed the wounds reported by the coroner were not large enough to have been made by a knife the size of those on the set. And Lonsdale argued that the wounds on the victims at Bundy were not the kind a trained SEAL would have inflicted. The wounds were helter-skelter—stab, stab, stab, stab, as if the killer were enraged. Stab, stab, stab. The attack of a mad, inefficient amateur, not the trained, slick work of a man who knew his business with a knife, as one would encounter in a professional stalk and take-down.

But Nicole's wounds to the throat were clean, deep, and deadly. And Simpson was a killer, all right, who had learned some techniques, if not by hands-on instruction, then by observing the stuntmen or listening to the talk one can usually hear on such a set.

"Wanna stop the argument? Here's how you stop the goddamned argument"—tough talk like that goes on between the paramilitary types and the stagehands, and the stuntmen—the macho men of this world.

And then the men laugh, these stunt guys, these experts at killing; they laugh and drink coffee and wait. "Ya cut the throat to the bone. That stops the goddamned argument."

And remember, by the time of the murders Simpson had already done the scene, the last scene shot—the take-down, the knife in his hand, and then the woman on the floor looking up with horror into the eyes of the Frogman.

Lonsdale says the D.A. seized all the raw *Frogmen* footage. Clark and Darden must have seen the footage. Yet no one for the prosecution breathed a far word about the *Frogmen* series, nor about the eerie similarities between what was acted and what was real. Clark and Darden remained strangely silent throughout the trial about what appeared to be powerful evidence of Simpson's plan, his peculiar knowledge that would identify him as the killer, and they've maintained their silence on the subject to this day. One old hand I talked to at the D.A.'s office could suggest no rational explanation for why Clark and Darden hadn't offered the *Frogmen* evidence to establish Simpson's methodology for the killing. Such telling evidence was relevant. And once the *Frogmen* evidence was introduced, the mental comparisons between what was real and what was play-acted by Simpson would create powerful images not easily erased by the defense. That the technical personnel on the set could not or would not testify that Simpson had been trained in the subtleties of knife fighting did not disqualify the evidence of how Simpson's portrayal of Bullfrog carried over to the murder at Bundy—his dress, his stalking, his quick, silent, deadly slashing. Could the jury not see him, as Simpson surely saw himself, as a killer in the night, in that dark clothing, the gloves, the cap, the knife, and one neat, deep cut into the throat that would stop the goddamned argument once and for all?

The old hand in the D.A.'s office insists to this day that Nicole's wounds were the work of someone who had far more skill in using a knife than one would need to cut steak at Morton's. He believed Simpson, in the course of the *Frogmen* filming, must have learned plenty about the use of a knife. The wound to Nicole's neck, "the gaping incise wound, was a classic sentry killing wound," according to my source in the D.A.'s office. The killer comes up from behind, cups his left hand over the victim's mouth, snaps the head back, exposing the throat and the carotid arteries, and then, with a long slice with the right hand, neat and without splashing blood in himself, he cuts from the left side deep and clean to the right ear. Such was the mortal wound suffered by Nicole. Both carotids and her windpipe were severed. The veteran at the prosecutor's office, a man who had prosecuted many a murder, said, "The minute I took a look at that wound I thought, this is a trained killing technique."

And we recall the endless testimony about how Simpson got the cuts on his left hand. But put the Frogman killer at Bundy— see him in your mind's eye—the victim's head pulled back, the natural struggle in the dark, the slashing of the blade, the left hand up where the slashing is taking place. The first errant flick of a razor-sharp knife, and whatever it touches is cut—touch the finger with the blade and the finger is cut.

Wally Crowder, the stunt coordinator on the show, said Simpson had the knives used in the *Frogmen* in his dressing room for some time, but Crowder also claimed he knew of no one who had ever taught knife techniques to Simpson. And he was certain that the knives, six of them furnished by the manufacturer, were all accounted for. Most people believe that Simpson had a knife in his hand at Bundy. The question is, what knife? The knife, the long-bladed dagger used by Bullfrog that lay in Simpson's dressing room for many a day, there for him to fondle, to consider? The last scene shot was the scene with Bullfrog stalking in the dark through the dive shop clutching a Spyderco folding knife, one that in ways puts one in mind of the Swiss knife that must have fitted in the box Fuhrman discovered in the bathroom.

Lange and Vannatter, in their book, *Evidence Dismissed*, talk about Simpson and Swiss knives. They tell how they sent Detective Vic Pietrantoni to Shelton, Connecticut, on Friday, June 24, 1994, to talk to a chauffeur who had driven Simpson around just *three days* before the murders. Lange and Vannatter write that Simpson had attended a board meeting of the Forschner Group, a company that, among other things, markets Swiss blade knives and watches. Simpson was a member of that board. The board members visited a warehouse where the company kept its inventory, and Simpson was apparently given, in addition to some watches, about ten knives, three of which the driver said were, when fully extended, between twelve and sixteen inches long. Unlike the knives on the *Frogmen* set, none of these knives were later accounted for. The driver said that on the return trip Simpson took one of the knives from its cardboard box and began waving it around in the backseat. "This could hurt someone really badly," he said. "It could kill someone. It's real sharp." According to Lange and Vannatter, the driver passed a polygraph test.

One can imagine the killer, the knife in his hand. Which knife? It makes no difference. If one crawls inside the hide of the killer, explores his obsession, and becomes absorbed in the deadly fog of the assassin, one can perhaps feel it: In the eternally invading phantasm, he sees Nicole undulating in her affairs with the others, the men she has confessed to him, the men working at her naked body, her gnawing passion on them, this woman who, despite their divorce, belonged to him; he has stalked her, and now he sees her, the mother of his children, on her knees giving head to a man in the living room, the kids upstairs asleep; he hears the woman's confession of her affair with Marcus Allen—his best friend, some said—the woman who had refused to respond to his frantic calls while he was filming *The Frogmen*, the woman who had told him it was over, all over, the woman, his woman, who now shunned him publicly at the recital—how dare she? If one crawls into such a murderous place as such a mind, one can feel the lips beginning to move and the silent words beginning to form: "I oughtta kill the bitch. I oughtta kill the goddamned bitch." And the knife was in his hand. That much we know: The knife, whatever knife, was in his hand.

Simpson was not an inventor of murder scenes. He was not one to plan things in precise detail. He was a man of action, a runner, an actor, not a planner. He had already acted out the sequence—more than once. The stalking scene in *The Frogmen*. Did it get confused in the dark, endless corridors of his mind? The knife. The killer. The night. The stalk. The woman. Nicole . . . It would have been a different scene at Bundy. But in the mind of a man who had lost his hook to reality, who was swinging loosely, back and forth, on the thin rope of madness, one scene was easily transferable to the other. The night. The stalk. The black cap. The gloves. The dark sweats. The knife. He had done it all before.

Then he put on the black stocking cap—perhaps even the one from *The Frogmen*—and then the gloves. He took the knife into his hand. Oh, no. No. He was not insane, not as the law speaks of it, but of course, some argue, all killers are lost in a world of madness.

The hurt of it. The other men, the rejection. The hurt of it replaced by anger. The anger of it, the rage. He held back the rage like a person holding his breath until at last the terrible exhaling. And he smiled at all the people at the recital, still holding his breath. He smiled at his friends and talked casually with them at the recital, looked at Nicole, looked at her, the bitch—this is what she had done to him—before the terrible exhaling. And that night, there was nothing to it. It had been easy to exhale. The simple exhaling with the knife.

Whether Simpson was specifically taught how to wield the knife with such efficiency, whether he learned from his conversations with the experts at the filming or learned from watching, whether he already knew something about knife fighting from his early days on the street—some know it instinctively, I am told—

however he learned to use the knife, or whether he was even an expert with it, makes no difference. He knew what he needed to know to take down Nicole and Ron. And the experts agree: The killings could have been completed in less than a couple of minutes. An untrained man without the protection of his own knife is essentially helpless against a killer with one. In a knife attack, Lonsdale says, "there are no rules. This is primal man at his worst."

Whether or not your witness admits to having trained Simpson, you call the witness anyway. You begin to lay the foundation for the scene. You want the jury to see it in their mind's eye. You have the witness tell what the Frogman in the script was trained to do. To kill with a knife. To slice the throat. To cut the carotids. To sever the windpipe.

What were the Frogman's skills with a knife?

What kind of knife did he wield?

What did the Frogman wear?

What color were his clothes when he stalked to kill?

Did he wear a wool knit stocking (stalking) cap?

Did he wear leather gloves?

Did he cut the windpipe of the victim to silence her?

How much blood would the Frogman get on himself, cutting from behind?

Simpson was at the filming. Simpson played the part. Presumably he read the script. He could, after a fashion, act. He had done the stalk. He had a knife in his hand. He came up from behind his victim. He even did the take-down. How much more did the prosecutor's need? Lawyers, of course, might argue about the admissibility of such evidence, but the door can never be opened if you don't reach for the knob. *The prosecution slept.* Or, awake and bright, outsmarted themselves once more.

We could argue that perhaps Clark held back the *Frogmen* materials for her cross-examination of Simpson, a cross-examination that she was never given the opportunity to conduct since Simpson didn't take the stand. But she had no right to hold back, to take that chance. Still, perhaps she was ready. Let us see how it might have gone.

Simpson has taken the stand and told the jury that he wasn't at Bundy the night of the murders, that he was chipping golf balls; that he loved Nicole; and that such a horror as the jury has seen was something he did not commit or ever think of committing. He has wept. Nicole was the mother of his children. On cross, among other subjects, the Frogman business comes up like this:

"On direct examination, Mr. Simpson, you said that you never, not once, contemplated killing your wife. Do you remember that testimony?" Clark asks.

"Yes."

"You also said that you couldn't imagine such a horrid thing. You, of course, remember saying that?"

"Yes."

"But you didn't need to imagine it, did you, sir?"

"I don't know what you mean."

"Let's find out what I mean. You played the part of a Frogman in an NBC pilot for a television series?"

"Yes."

"You were a killer in that series?"

"Well, I knew how to kill. It was acting. You can act a lot of things."

"You wore a black knit cap in one of the scenes when you were stalking someone?"

"Can't remember."

Clark picks up the black knit stocking cap and holds it up in front of Simpson. "This doesn't refresh your recollection?"

"No."

"You stalked someone at your dive shop?"

"It wasn't my shop."

"It was your shop according to the script and the role you were playing, isn't that true?"

"I guess. It's been quite awhile."

"You're wearing dark clothes in that scene?"

"I suppose."

"And you wear dark leather gloves?"

"I don't remember."

"It is night."

"Yes, in that scene. But that was just a movie. Arnold Schwarzenegger didn't kill the thirty or forty people he terminated in his last film."

"That's exactly the point, sir," Clark says sadly. "Thank you. It is night in the scene?"

"Yes."

"And you have a knife?"

"I don't have a knife."

"What did you do with the dozen Swiss knives you were given in Shelton, Connecticut?"

"I don't know what you're talking about."

"You have a knife in your hand in this movie scene, isn't that true?"

"Yes. Although I think a stuntman did most of the scene."

"You know that a Frogman kills from behind, the quick, deep slicing of the carotid arteries, the severing of the vocal cords?"

"I don't know any damn such thing."

"You know that a Frogman cuts the windpipe so the victim can't scream?"

"What's the matter with you, man?"

"Did you talk about the art of killing with the stuntmen and the technical advisors on the set?"

"I never talked about killing with anyone."

"And you know that Nicole's windpipe was cut in the exact manner employed by Navy SEALs, isn't that true?"

"I don't know what happened to Nicole."

"She never screamed, did she, Mr. Simpson?"

"You are crazy, man. I never did any of that."

"And because you cut from behind, you don't get a lot of that gushing blood on you, do you?"

"That is way off, man. You are way off."

"Did you learn about cutting and slicing in the filming of the *Frogmen* series?"

"No."

"Did you read any of the books by Mark Lonsdale?"

"I don't read crap about killing."

"Did you talk with Mark Lonsdale, the expert on Frogman knife techniques?"

"I don't know the man."

"When you had your left hand over Nicole's mouth and you started to cut from behind with your right hand, that's when you cut the finger on your left hand, isn't that true?"

"No, that is not true."

"You had the knife in your right hand?"

"No, I did not."

"In the *Frogmen* series?"

"I suppose. I can't remember. It makes no difference. I didn't cut nobody's throat."

"And in the series, with the knife in your hand, you begin stalking whoever the intruder is in your dive shop, isn't that true?"

"You have the script. I don't remember."

"You don't remember circling the shadow and coming up from behind the intruder?"

"No."

"That's what you did to Nicole, isn't that true?"

"God no!" He looks to the judge for help.

"You don't remember the take-down of the woman in the scene?"

"This is crazy, man. I didn't hurt nobody."

"And when you decided to kill Nicole, you had already learned how from your experience in *The Frogmen,* isn't that true?"

"You off, man. You are making this up."

"You had practiced the stalk over and over for that last scene of the movie, isn't that true?"

"No. That is not true."

"And then in the same movie you go to your wife's grave and kneel down and pray? You surely remember that?"

"Not really. I did a lot of things."

"And, coincidentally, there was a man in the movie that you threatened to kill by the name of Goldman?"

"That's bullshit, man. I don't remember any of that."

"It is all just coincidence, isn't it, Mr. Simpson? Just pure coincidence."

"It's got nothing to do with me."

Such a cross-examination would likely have been riddled with objections, arguments, and perhaps some adverse court rulings. But despite the attack, by the time the cross was completed, the jury would have had the scene indelibly imprinted in their minds, and the fight launched by the defense would have only underlined the importance of the evidence the defense was trying to keep out.

The most interesting part is that nowhere in the self-serving tomes of Clark and Darden do we encounter any reference to their preparation for whatever cross-examination of Simpson they surely had planned. What were they intending to do with the man if he took the stand? Who had been assigned his cross-examination? Clark, presumably. Clark insists she believed up until the time of the Fuhrman tapes, which so devastated the prosecution, that Simpson intended to testify. Then came the Fuhrman tapes, and she concludes, "But after that windfall of racial obscenity from the mouth of Mark Fuhrman, Simpson had to know that juror sympathy was running so profoundly in his favor, testifying wasn't worth the risk." Such was nothing more than a wild, unfounded guess. Clark had no more reason to assume that Simpson wouldn't take the stand than she had to assume that he would. Simpson seemed to be in charge of his defense, and no one could predict the man.

Faye Resnick says she pleaded with Marcia Clark to tell the

jury about the *Frogmen* script. "That's how he learned to kill that way," she told me. "He learned it on the set. Practiced it. It got stuck in his mind. But no—Marcia Clark poo-pooed it." Resnick doesn't know why. "This is the way we do things around here" was Clark's attitude. "We know what we're doing." And Resnick says she begged Clark to come out with the Marcus Allen affair. "The motive," Resnick insisted. "You can't expect the jury to believe you if you don't tell them the way it was. We don't have to be perfect these days. Everybody knows that. The women on the jury weren't perfect. Nicole was in love with Marcus. It was the big thing to her, and O.J. knew about it." One of his best friends laying his wife. But Allen continued to deny having had any relationship with Nicole, and does to this day.

I reminded Resnick that Nicole was no longer O.J.'s wife when this all came down. "Makes no difference. She belonged to him so far as he was concerned. Always had, always would. He was compulsive about her." The shrinks like to put labels on his kind—a sociopathic personality, they call it, a personality disorder you often see in big-time athletes. They get special treatment. The captain of the football team rapes the cheerleader and he gets away with it, unpunished. The sheriff is not about to put the finger on the captain of the local football team; the fans would run the sheriff's ass out of town. The big-time athlete doesn't have to conform. He works within different boundaries than other people. He operates under different rules. He gets what he wants when he wants it. People flock around him, adore him. Men open the doors— women other things. Special man, special treatment. The universe, according to the sociopath, revolves around him. Everybody is there for him.

And when he breaks the rules, so what? He didn't do wrong. If the old lady burns the eggs and he kicks the shit out of her, well, she shouldn't have burned the eggs. He gets so he can't tell the difference between right and wrong. Sure, we all have some sociopathic traits. We drive five miles over the speed limit. Some cheat a little on their income taxes—well, the government has it coming; the government cheats on us. But the true sociopathic personality—that's something else again. He can kill and rationalize it: "The bitch had it coming. Look what she did to me" is his refrain.

"Jesus Christ, you fucking bitch, how can you do that *to me?*" the sociopath thinks. He has stalked her and now he watches through the window when the guy is getting head. She is doing it to the guy on the couch. But the sociopath personalizes it. She is doing it to hurt *him,* O.J. Simpson.

"Look at the bitch. How could she do that to *me* after all I've done for her? I took her out of fucking Hicksville and gave her everything, even the fucking car that Goldman asshole is driving. He is driving *my* car that *I gave* to her. I gave her money, kids, fame, a home, and she's sucking that guy's dick." She is the property of the sociopath. She is never free of him. Never a woman who has her own life.

"That is *my* woman, and the bitch is making it with Marcus Allen. I'll kill the bitch. She has it coming. Any motherfucker in my place would kill the bitch, too." Then the knife, the Frogman, the attack.

I think of the violent television culture in which we live, of blood, of death, of the splendor of killing, the great vicarious testosterone releases offered to us, we natural-born killers, now domesticated voyeurs grasping a Bud. The caveman on the couch is, nonetheless, still the genetic caveman. We yearn to rise above him, to abandon him, but the violence, barely under the hide, still lies lurking in savage veins.

The road back to our barbaric beginnings is to succumb to nascent urges. The road back is to the jungle. The way out is to alter the culture. The way out is civilization. Television and movies, bent on profit, target our underlying violence like any peddler who preys on the base appetites of his mark. "We're not responsible," argue the producers. "We give the people what they want. Give us a different audience with different tastes and we'll give them different programs. We're only trying to make a buck." I should think the same argument could be made with equal efficacy by the corner drug dealer.

Yet within the hands of an industry lies the most powerful tool ever imagined by which to elevate the species into the light—up into the airy divine. This tool is a universally compelling, mind-altering tool, indeed, a weapon, vested in the hands of an industry that dare plead "no responsibility." We fight against placing guns in the hands of the irresponsible, but the screen is a weapon with incalculable power to do harm. Yet the screen has an equal power to uplift and enlighten. Profit aside, could not the creative minds of the nation, the mighty heads of the media, responsible men and women of a nation, introduce our children to the sublime rather than instruct our children, yes, even our heroes, on how to cut throats with a knife?

Clark proved to be afraid of her own witnesses, the fact that they could be attacked, discredited, their dark underbellies, sometimes scummy, exposed. She was afraid of Resnick, afraid of Shively, afraid of the LAPD (sometimes with just cause), afraid of rafts of other witnesses, some of whom she was correct in not calling. But Clark did not hesitate to call the one witness, Fuhrman, who single-handedly could destroy her case, while she refused to call the tens who could have made it. I have stood there in the courtroom in many a trial dissecting the witnesses during cross-examination. Witness after witness comes to the stand, and you step up with the tender hatchet and begin to hack away. And when you are through, the witness steps down off the stand, and he is never the same in the juror's eyes.

But after you have destroyed enough witnesses, something begins to dawn on the jury: This man could do this to *every* witness. This man could do this to me. Not one single person has taken the witness stand and escaped. And then the jurors begin to look at you in a new way. What trick will he use against the next witness?

Is he fair? Is the witness lying, or is the lawyer just good at twisting things? A lawyer can lose his credibility by being too nifty with the blade.

Yet, observing Johnnie Cochran all those months, I never thought he had that kind of skill. His approach was different. He wrapped the witnesses up in conversation and fast words. He wasn't the wielder of the rapier, nor did he swing the bludgeon of Bailey. He laid the fog around the witnesses and did that little soft-shoe of his. Not a skillful cross, but a fast, skillful talk. Sometimes it worked. But even though he might have exposed the underbellies of all of the witnesses Clark was so afraid of, when it was over he would have had to attack each of them again in his final argument, and he would have begun to sound like the hooded inquisitor at a witch hunt: Everybody is a sinner, a liar, or a sellout. After a while the jurors say, "Well, they might not have been perfect, but neither are we, and we don't think *everybody* was lying or sold out, either."

The full Resnick story could never have been told to the jury—we know that. Much of it would have been excluded as blatant hearsay. But the pretty little exceptions to the hearsay rule that permit the judge to let in virtually anything the judge wishes the jury to hear would have cleared the way for much of Resnick's testimony. She could have told plenty. She could have brought Nicole to life. Her story would have been memorable, and told by a person who was interesting. She had her own underbelly. But sometimes the defense's attack on a truthful witness who has had a life, even if not one patterned after the sainted, shows us more about the bludgeoning attorney than about the witness.

I have heard the prosecutors in this case excuse their failure to put on certain witnesses by claiming the jury was getting tired after all of those months. Yes, you could get tired, ungodly weary, in only part of a day if you were being spoon-fed the deadly, unsalted Pablum of the DNA testimony offered to the jury by prosecutors who themselves sound more like the freshly exhumed than like trial lawyers. *The Frogmen;* the story of how a killer came to the method of his murder; the story of the knives and where they may have come from and where they likely went; the story of Nicole's life, perhaps of the affair between the victims themselves; the story of what was said by O.J. during the slow-speed chase and—the disguise, the money, the passport in the Bronco; Simpson's statement to the cops; the story that Shively sold to *Hard Copy* that destroyed O.J.'s claim that he was home at the time of the murders; Heidstra's story of the voices, the "Hey! Hey! Hey!" at the likely time of the murders, the suicide note—all of these stories, and many more, were never told. The stories didn't fit into the iron shoe. The mountain of evidence was mostly left unmined.

And surely nine hundred and some lawyers in the prosecutor's office could have found a way to let the jury see Bullfrog in his black knit cap come stalking, stalking in the night, a razor-sharp knife clutched in his hand, hands protected by leather gloves, the man in dark clothing, moving in the shadows toward his prey. And then the sudden, deadly take-down. That was the story of all stories.

CHAPTER 17

THE CAMERAS

AH, YES, CAMERAS in the courtroom: Why not? This is a free country, and the people want to watch. The First Amendment, you know. We have a right to know, to see. It is wonderful, this education we get from watching the trial.

We are educating America and at the same time selling diapers and hamburgers. That is what's so lovely about America and the Constitution and the First Amendment. The people want to watch. And the price of admission—well, the people are gathered up in the program nets by the millions, and then the people's eyes and minds are sold to the corporations who sell the razors and the potato chips. The advertisers—bless the advertisers—pay according to the number of people who have been caught in the net who will see the advertisements and buy the tampons and the deodorant. The cars. The headache pills. The beer. Oh, the pretty beer.

Now, let us not despair. This is all a part of free speech. This is the First Amendment. Remember, the Founding Fathers wanted us to be free to speak to one another. And the megacorporations out there speak to us. They are not citizens, of course. They do not vote. They are not even alive. But they are the ones who, under the First Amendment, are speaking to us. They say they have the right under the Constitution to say whatever they wish to us. Freedom of speech—these megacorporations who are not alive, but who have the rights of citizens. So what we have here are *non-humans* exercising their human right to speak to humans who own no newspapers and who own no television stations and who cannot speak back, who cannot even speak to one another, who have become but fish caught in the net, the listening, peering fish curled up on the couch who want to watch the O.J. trial, this new sporting event.

The strict constructionists up there on the Supreme Court—you see them sitting there all prim and long-nosed, all black-robed and stern, the great interpreters of the Founding Fathers' intent, like preachers interpreting the Bible. Religion, whether in the law or in the Scriptures, leads us into strange places, mostly places that are unfriendly to human beings. Can we not agree that our constitutional fathers must have intended that megacorporations would be the only entities who would have the right to speak to millions at a time? Do we not understand that free speech has become mainly the slickish peddling of mouthwashes and douches and deodorants? Perhaps we have missed something? That the First Amendment should be reduced to this net that traps the fish-people who swim into it to watch the O.J. case or the prime-time sitcoms, and are thereafter sold to the advertisers by the millions?

But we do not remember that the First Amendment had something to do with the right of people to communicate with one another, to carry on the lively, honest dialogues that are so essential for the maintenance of a democracy? Surely the Founding Fathers must not have intended that the people in a democracy would remain silent, that they would only listen, curled up on the couch drinking Bud, never to speak, only to listen, glued to their sets while they watch whatever freak show is offered to lure them into the nets. Surely the Founding Fathers must have intended that the megacorporations speak to the people like clever snake-oil salesmen, their beguiling spiel crafted by the psycho-devils on Madison Avenue, those geniuses in the advertising agencies whose sorcery even sells death to the youth of our nation with a idiot camel named Joe. Surely free speech and the First Amendment were intended as mere commodities that could be purchased only by those who want to sell Japanese cars and shampoo. That is free speech, all right, is it not?

Should cameras intrude into the courtroom? Whose cameras? In what courtroom? Will the cameras of ABC and CBS and NBC be trained on the mundane murder case down in the Bronx where some poor wretch is hauled into court in his orange suit and chains to be represented by a public defender with five more cases to present the same day? Will we be amused while we watch him plead guilty even though he was defending himself when he killed his attacker? Honest defense. Get the case out of here. Get on to the next case. Offer the guy twenty to life. Good deal. If you want to take him to trial he'll get the chair. Next case. Come on! move it!

What about the woman who has worked for a company thirty years and one day is laid off? The boss replaced her with a blonde with something—something the faithful woman who had worked for him all those years didn't have. She can't hire much of a lawyer. No funds for experts or research assistants. The case comes to court. Her attorney has to take it. He knows he can't win against the phonied-up company witnesses who will say his client was incompetent, even though she was the hub around which the entire department revolved all those years. Witnesses have to keep their jobs, too. Survival of the fittest. The company lawyer says give her the amount of money we would spend to defend the case. Nuisance. These fucking nuisance cases he says. But the cameras in the courtroom? Who'd want to watch this poor woman's case on TV?

Who makes the decisions about the trials, the cases, that will attract the fish into the nets? No one, I tell you—no one. The *unalive* make the decisions for the living people and tell the living people what they will see. The unalive are the numbers. They are called ratings. If the case creates ratings the trial will be shown on TV. Do you think we are fools? Do you think we would show a disgusting, everyday divorce case, a bankruptcy, one of those maudlin age-discrimination cases? Do you think we are going to show you cases against our advertisers, against the pharmaceutical company who peddled its drug to American mothers after false testing, and the babies were born without any arms or legs? Do you think we are going to show you the lawsuits against the car manufacturers who knew that their gas tanks would explode and burn whole families to death? You must be crazy. We will show the American people what we want to show them. But it has to have ratings. We are not in this business to educate, we are in this business for business. God bless business.

Cameras in the courtroom? Cameras in what courtroom, determined by whom, for what purpose? Talk to Thomas Jefferson about it.

"Mr. Jefferson, sir. Do you think it would conform with your intent that we put television cameras in the courtroom?"

"What are you talking about, son? What are television cameras?"

"Well, we can transfer live images from one place on earth to another. I don't know how to explain it if you haven't seen it. You are a little behind the times, sir, if you don't mind me saying so. But what I want to know is, would it be all right with you if we brought a jury trial into the homes of the people and they could watch and, of course, be sold shampoo by the sponsors? I mean, the First Amendment and all . . ."

"You mean you people are selling shampoo at a trial?"

"Well, yes. What's the matter with that? We also sell lipstick and running shoes. Nike. Oh, God, Michael Jordan—he is it! And he wears them, too!"

"What are you talking about? A jury trial is the single most powerful deterrent against tyranny known to man. It is a sacred institution. How dare you!"

"Now, now. Don't personalize this thing. We are only trying to educate the people. And besides, we have to take a break. We'll be back right after this, with more from Thomas Jefferson."

Ratings.

Money.

When we let *ratings*—not educators, not living human beings with minimum human values still attached—decide what will be shown to the people, then we play to the lowest level of human interest. The elite like to say they rise above it, but we all suffer pinches of the ugly and the raw and the prurient. We are all cut from the same multipatterned human cloth. We all have a little of the lecher, the murderer, the wife beater, the victim, the bigot, the sexist, the racist, stamped on us. We must deny it, of course. We fight against it. But the advertising gurus on Madison Avenue know the truth about us, and the ratings show it. We want the filth. The dirt. The murder. The blood. The sex. The intrigue. The decadence. Give us the bloody sex, the horror, the pain, the tears. But don't forget the sex. We want to be shocked. And when we are sated, we want to be shocked even more so we can still feel something, just *something*. Shock us and prove that there is still life in there. Amaze us and astound us and prove to us that we are alive. Cameras in the courtroom, as an educational device? We do not watch that which is educational; we watch only that which is entertaining. Entertainment, not education, drives ratings. Anyone knows that. Get the educators off the screen. Get in the knives, the blood, the murder, the sex, the perversions.

Cameras in the courtroom? Let us put cameras in the operating room instead. Let us watch and leer as the surgeon removes some celebrity's hemorrhoids. Why not let us watch a cancer operation, the removal of the horrid tumor, the blood all over, the children of the mother pacing in the waiting room, their faces drawn? Let us have a close-up now, please. Shoot up tight. Let us actually see the diseased, severed breast in the surgeon's hand. Let us follow the hand as he drops the bloody breast into the garbage can.

He dusts his gloved hands, as if to say, "That's that." We will return right after this brief word from our sponsor. They are selling insurance on this spot. And anti-itch powder. Why not? Free speech. This is America.

But have you forgotten the right of privacy? You cannot take the cameras into the operating room, because we have the right of privacy. But a trial is a public affair. True, but what kind of a public affair? There are seats in the courtroom for public attendance. The trial must be public to make sure that the rights of the people are not eviscerated behind closed doors. But it is the *defendant's* right to a public trial. It is a right that inures to the people only to the end that the people can assure themselves that justice is being delivered and that important rights are not being abrogated. The public trial was not intended to *entertain* a nation. To many a defendant, his trial is painfully private. He is hauled before the court by his wife to hear her tell of his epicurean preferences. The process must be open enough to ensure that the process is fair. But what about putting citizens' private lives on national television? International television? To sell fertilizer and lawn mowers? Who is being used? The parties, the witnesses, the judge, the system. Yes, the system. It is the cheapest production the networks have ever enjoyed. You don't have to pay those millions for those feckless stars. You don't have to pay for any special effects. You just walk in, set up the cameras, and shoot. You get the players free. You throw their asses up on the screen of every home in America and we get to measure everything from the size of their souls to the length of their private parts—for free. God bless the First Amendment. And in the meantime, Mrs. Smith, would you rather go to court with cameras in the courtroom, or would you rather take this very reasonable plea bargain I am offering you? The fact that you had sex with your fifteen-year-old nephew may be irrelevant, but I guarantee you, it will seep into the case. The tabloids, you know. They also have your medical records on your recent breast implants. Size 38D, right?

Ask anybody, even lawyers and judges, what they know about the American justice system, and they will relate it to that abomination called the O.J. Simpson case. It was a freak, an anomaly. It stood for very little of the good of the system and emphasized most of the bad. Indeed, it created most of the bad. The players were more aware of the media battle than the courtroom battle. Marcia Clark's hairdo, for Christ's sakes. The length of her hems. Darden, all ecstatic about the stars showing deference to him: "Jack Nicholson, Warren Beatty, and Michelle Pfeiffer knew who I was," he said. "We were recognized everywhere." Lawyers who in many ways were still mere apprentices were suddenly celebrities. They became best-selling authors, even though they couldn't write. They became the final word on the justice system to many, but they hadn't learned to work successfully within it as professionals. The media, part of the ratings game, peddled the wrong ideas to everyone and educated hardly anyone about what was *right* with the system.

Cameras in the courtroom? The media is a strange beast. It feeds on itself. But instead of consuming itself it grows on a diet of itself. It becomes an uncontained tumor that eats away at itself and grow larger and larger. A few cameras in the courtroom to start with were eventually seeded into over two thousand reporters who took part in the case—myself among them. There were 121 feeds coming out of the courtroom and 80 miles of cable. Nineteen television stations, 8 radio stations, and 23 newspapers and magazines took their seats in the courtroom. The public had a seat or two, Mr. Thomas Jefferson, in case you are interested. But most of the room was occupied by the media. Free. In the twelfth-floor pressroom there were 250 telephones. I have only scratched the tiniest itch on the pimpled skin of the O.J. media. Across the street CBS had five trailers, ABC four, and NBC three. I hung out in one of them. How can anyone say that this was an education? That this was free speech? This was the most insane happening ever invented by man.

I remember walking to the porta-toilets trying to rehearse the precise words Brokaw would hear from me on the evening news. The ten porta-toilets were always full. Had something to do with my wordy performance, some would say. In the meantime people wanted any story, even about the storytellers who told stories about anyone. Give us something, as if what was going on in the court-room were not enough. Tell us what was going on in the porta-toilets. Tell us anything!

All the while people were accusing each other of being media hounds. Darden charged Ito with being camera-struck. He was the kind, Darden said, "who invited actors Richard Dreyfuss and James Woods back to his chambers, who gave network anchors and authors the best seats in the courtroom." Well, cameras do that to people—some people. Darden said he "hoped that Judge Ito would yank the cameras, but he never had the courage to do it. 'Go ahead,' I dared him once, 'take them out.' It would have cut the length of the trial by at least 40 percent," Darden wrote. But Darden never seriously insisted that the cameras be removed. If they had been, who would have ever known Darden?

The cameras encouraged the media leaks, the lawyers swearing against each other, pointing, blaming, becoming the laughing-stocks of the nation. Heroes became fools. I know, they were al-ready fools; the cameras just confirmed it. There they were, however, standing before the cameras, shamelessly preachifying about the law, hawking their case, blistering the witnesses, the judge, each other, carrying on their private feuds in public. The cameras ate up ethics, digested decency. The cameras became the proctoscope of the system, showing the dreary, the obscene. I con-tend there are parts of the system that ought to be private. Nothing to hide—we can inspect those parts if we must. We simply do not run around this world with our pants off.

In the end, cameras denuded the justice system. They showed us our own justice system at its worst. They showed us a freak, the bastard child of the media, the progeny of the continued media rape of the judicial process. And the media asked America to gasp over this freak—over its own child! And of course, it asked Americans to come on into the fish nets to be sold to the advertisers. And then along came the reformers and the jury haters and the lawyer hates and the closet fascists, and they cried, "You see! The whole justice system is a mess. The lawyers are shysters. The judges are incompetent. The witnesses can be bought. The jurors are prejudiced. We have to do away with this system! We told you so." And we all went home ready to trash the one last safeguard we still wield against the despots. Because we had been educated by the media? God bless the media, the holy media and the First Amendment by which it stands. And God bless you too, Thomas Jefferson, sir.

CHAPTER 18

CELEBRATING MURDER

OUGHT WE NOT celebrate the verdict in the O.J. Simpson case? The media should, the prissy authors of conventional wisdom should, the talking puppets on television should, the intelligentsia of the rumpled brows should—yes, everybody should. Why do we celebrate the bloody murder of two people committed by a knife-wielding monster? We celebrate the verdict because it stands as proof not that there is something wrong with the system, but that it can be made to work, even under the most extravagantly bizarre conditions. We celebrate the fact that we can still swim, even though the surface of the pool is floating three feet thick with garbage. We did not drown. *That the justice system functioned at all is the miracle and the cause for our celebration.* This case, this grotesquely freakish case, tested the justice system to the maximum and still, in the end, the system functioned as it was designed.

So are we to celebrate when justice was beaten up and thrown out of the place, when we feel so cheated, so frustrated? Well, what is justice? Justice to us is seeing the murderer hauled off in chains. Justice is retribution. And we know what justice is *not.* Justice is not permitting a grinning, unrepentant, arrogant murderer of two to laugh in our faces while he chases little white balls all over celebrity golf courses with his amoral pals. That's what justice is *not*—to us.

Yet no one can define justice in the abstract, neither you nor I nor all the sages of old. All have tried and failed. Justice is not something that we buy at the grocery store, two bundles for a quarter. Justice—does it redress, does it avenge, does it teach, does it make us feel all warm inside, does it make us say, "There! That will teach you!"? Does it punish? Does it lead the wretch to the gas chamber to teach him a lesson? Is it logical, even-handed, consistent, predictable, something we can understand? What justice is to one is likely injustice to another. To put the murderer on the gurney and stick the executioner's long needle in his arm may be justice to some but a horror to the innocent parents of the condemned. At last, justice can be defined no more than truth, or God.

But I am not talking about the failure of the justice system to deliver justice in the O.J. Simpson case. I am talking about how the justice system *functioned,* despite the fact that it was populated with lawyers who were more qualified to preen before the cameras than stand before the jury, with a judge who was inherently disqualified to sit in the case from the beginning, and with jurors, in a race case, who likely were possessed of their own brand of racist demons. The miracle of the case is that despite a crazed media that chewed up critical witnesses and permitted us to examine the full length of the small intestine of every lawyer, every party, the survivors, the dead, to the end that we were sickened by the whole affair, somehow the system worked. It may not have delivered justice, but it worked, and it worked as it was designed to work, and we must stand back now, look at it with awe and respect, and celebrate the verdict.

Let us consider why. No case is ever tried with flawless lawyers of equal ability on both sides and a wise, impartial, patient judge ruling on the evidence and instructing a totally unbiased, thoughtful jury. In over forty years of trial work in the courtrooms across this land, I have never seen such a case, nor heard of it. I have seen good lawyers make horrid errors. I have even seen them physically fall, and I have also seen them collapse mentally. I have seen judges cry, explode, and run from the bench. I have seen witnesses have heart attacks on the stand, and police officers perjure themselves. I have seen riots in the street and panic in the jury box, but in case after case—none of which were, as a whole, as preposterously aberrant as was this case—the system was eventually made to work. There is something in the way the legal system is constructed, its inherent checks and balances, that causes it to function despite the extreme and often impossible task it may be given.

The system had its roots in trial by duel, the premise being that the contestants on both sides would be equally competent and that the winner would be chosen by God. The king's champion, better equipped, usually stronger and more skilled with the sword, usually won over the less experienced, weaker champion of the wretched accused, and thus God was habitually on the side of the king. Today, for the same reasons, God is usually on the side of the government with its unlimited power. But there *is a duel* in the courtroom, and despite the differences in the inherent skills of the lawyers and their resources, the truth is also a powerful leveler, for truth in the hands of an incompetent is more powerful than all of the tricks available to his most skilled adversary.

Moreover, the judge—if the judge is a judge, and not a retired prosecutor who continues prosecuting from his higher perch on the bench—often evens things out with his rulings. And when the judge fails, as he often does, there remains the jurors—not one but twelve, who together present an awesome intelligence often not fully understood or appreciated by the public.

Aside from the combatants in the courtroom, we have witnesses under oath, witnesses who, to be sure, lie from time to time. But we have cross-examination to reveal the lies. We have jurors to detect the lies, jurors who are instructed that they, and only they, are the final judges of the credibility of the witnesses. Jurors, the parties, work in an atmosphere of decorum and order and are usually provided time to think and consider. And when all else fails, when the judge makes a fatal error, when one of the attorneys steps over the line with a foul to the irrevocable injury of his opponent, when fairness is lost, we still have an appellate process with all of its own checks and balances. And beyond all of that, the public, advised by a responsible media, stands as the final arbiter with the final power to change the law.

This is a near perfect system that sometimes fails to deliver perfect justice, whatever justice is; a near perfect system that sometimes stands by helpless as the truth eludes it, whatever truth may prove to be. But the system usually provides justice, at least to some, and when it fails to do so, it still stands as perhaps the greatest bastion against tyranny yet invented by man. I do not write these words out of a need to inject empty rhetorical splendor here. I write them out of love of a system that is often hated, often abused, and often misunderstood by the uninformed, and universally hated by the enemies of a free people. I do not write these words without realizing that the system can be improved, mostly by streamlining its processes so that the weak and the poor have equal and fair access to it, and by improving the quality of the judges and lawyers who function in it. But the structure of the system itself is sound, even blessed. And to mess much with it, to join the braying hounds who wish to deform it under the guise of reforming it, is dangerous to our freedom and to the freedom of our grandchildren to come.

But the verdict—why celebrate it? Let me show you why. Suppose that you are a juror in the O.J. Simpson case. You are not one of those know-it-all talking heads who must say something and scrapes the bottom of a very shallow pan every day to come up with something intelligent to say in six seconds. You are not a member of the public who has heard the pundits until your mind is washed as empty as theirs and you mimic their conventional wisdom by saying this jury was dumb and biased. You are, instead, a reasonably intelligent juror, harboring your own life experiences. And the thing that distinguishes you from the rest of the world that is out there carping and complaining and conjecturing is that you have taken an *oath,* an oath to listen to the evidence, all of the evidence, and to apply the law of the case as it is given to you.

Under these circumstances, suddenly you are different from all those outside the courtroom who occupy the remaining space in the world. You have heard all of the evidence in the case, nine long, lonely, loony, loathsome months of it, while those who criticize have listened only to sketches of it on television from time to time while they drank their beer and trimmed their toenails. And what they missed of the in-court proceedings on TV they filled in with the vacuous comments of those yacking-yappers, who themselves were not under oath and who had their own agendas to advance, which usually had something to do with ratings. As a juror, under oath, you took notes all during the trial. The rest of the world took nothing except their afternoon nap in the middle of a crucial ruling by the judge, who told you, the juror, to disregard certain evidence that had wrongfully slipped into the trial. You, the juror, were permitted to consider only evidence that was lawfully presented. They, out there, heard it all, the Fuhrman tapes ad nauseam, the Resnick book, the wailing of the Goldmans, the angry cries of Geraldo and Grodin. They heard it all. You were sequestered. But the most telling difference between you and the public out there who so quickly and easily criticized your verdict is that you not only had the responsibility to decide the case, but you had the responsibility to also *preserve the system for them,* your most vocal critics.

Now let us assume that you think that O.J. was probably guilty. You can see him behind Nicole, see the knife in one hand, his other hand jerking back her blond head to expose her naked throat, and now you can see him slashing, the blood gushing out on the sidewalk. You see him overcome the weaponless Goldman. You see the bodies lying there and you are sickened and angry and you want to do justice. What do you do?

You and your fellow jurors have been charged by His Honor that you are the sole judges of the credibility of the witnesses. That means you are the sole judges of whether they are telling the truth or not. In making that determination, you are to take into account your own experiences in life, as the judge has instructed you. That means you are to determine if Fuhrman was telling the truth, if Vannatter and Lange were telling the truth. You don't have to look at the defendant's witnesses yet, because the state has the burden of proving the case. The judge has instructed you on this as well, and you, under your oath, have sworn to follow the judge's instructions.

Your judgment on the witnesses' credibility doesn't sprout out of a putrid bed of prejudice; it grows out of your *experience*. If we were to interview you as a reasonable juror, black or white, male or female, old or young, on your not guilty verdict, what would we hear? Perhaps this would be the dialogue:

"What did you think of the testimony of the police?"

"Well, if you obey the law that the judge has laid out as to the credibility of the witnesses, you can come up with only one conclusion: The police have proven themselves *not credible.*"

"Why?"

"The lies about the search without the search warrant. The N-word racist lies of Fuhrman. The EDTA in the blood on the socks and the gate. The blood carried around in Vannatter's pocket. There is something seriously wrong here. I don't know what it is. I think O.J. is probably guilty. But the prosecution has been less than open and honest with us."

"There was a lot of evidence offered by the police that was never refuted."

"I know, but the defense doesn't have to refute anything. The state has to prove its case. And prove it beyond a reasonable doubt. And the judge instructed us that, if we believe that a witness has lied about *any* material fact, we are at liberty to disregard *all* of his testimony."

"So what?"

"So applying that rule of law, we are left in no-man's-land. How did the glove get there? Only Fuhrman can say, and we think we should disregard his testimony. How did the EDTA get in the crucial evidence? No one has told us."

"What about the DNA?"

"The DNA is only as good as its foundation. No one explained to us the missing blood from the blood that Vannatter had carried around in his pocket."

"Do you believe there was a conspiracy among the police?"

"No."

"Do you believe some lied?"

"Yes. But exactly when and how often and about what we could not tell."

"But even if everyone lied, the blood evidence was overwhelming. So what about that?"

"What about that? *You* explain it to me. No one else has. You tell me about the details of the science of DNA so I can understand it. I have already learned not to accept the conclusions of these so-called experts. They make mistakes too."

"Well Marcia Clark and Chris Darden explained it in their closing."

"They didn't understand it, either. And the judge said their arguments are not evidence, which they obviously are not. Even the experts didn't agree. They were sloppy. What about that expert for the state, that Bruce Weir fellow, who got up there and told us one thing one day and the next day got up there on the same witness stand and told us he had made a mistake in his calculations? You can't make mistakes and ask us to believe the testimony beyond a reasonable doubt. It is reasonable to make mistakes, but they create doubt. I know that that was probably O.J.'s blood. But my suspicions are not proof."

"Do you think the DNA evidence showed what it was supposed to show?"

"Who knows? The experts themselves seem confused."

"You listened to the arguments of Clark and Darden. Do you believe their take on the evidence?"

"No. They are hiding something."

"What?"

"Who knows? The case wasn't totally credible."

"If you had to bet your life on whether O.J. Simpson was guilty or not, how would bet?"

"Guilty, of course. There is too much smoke for there not to have been a fire. But can you convict on suspicion? Even on probability? No. And how do I know? The judge said so in his instructions. The case must be proven beyond a reasonable doubt. You cannot convict Simpson even though you suspect, perhaps even more than suspect, that he is guilty."

Although we may feel that justice was aborted in this case, we celebrate the jury's verdict because, even though it may have released a guilty man, it preserved a system that can also protect the innocent. If a jury can convict the guilty Simpson on *less* than evidence beyond a reasonable doubt, the same jury could convict us, the innocent, on insufficient evidence as well. We celebrate the jury's verdict, not because a guilty man escaped, but because that jury has taken the brave and irreversible step in the most notorious of all cases, to preserve *our* rights against the tyranny of the state. Without jurors who will release those suspected of crimes when the crime has not been proven beyond a reasonable doubt, we would be left to the horrors of a system where we could be incarcerated, even executed, on mere probability, put away on perjured testimony, or our lives terminated on whim and speculation, on the hatred of the mob, on the implacable power of the state against us, the powerless people.

It comes down to this: If the government can put any criminal away on less than proof beyond a reasonable doubt, it can put us away as well. The safeguard applies to every case, not just *their* cases. When the safeguard is lost in their cases, it is lost in ours as well.

We may disagree with the jury, believing as many do that proof beyond a reasonable doubt was there. But the witnesses were tested by the experience of *that jury,* not by our experience. That jury heard only the evidence that was presented to it. How would we like to have a jury that was trying us take into account all of the garbage we heard on national TV from the jabberers who filled the airways? We judge the O.J. jury on our entire fund of knowledge gathered from every source, including the tabloids, gossip, rumors, and talk shows. How would we like a jury to judge us based on such "evidence"? I say we must celebrate the verdict in the Simpson case, and honor the jurors for their wisdom and the unappreciated gift of freedom they have delivered to us.

Some worry about O.J. having gotten away with murder. Do not worry. There is a saying among old criminal defense attorneys who occasionally see a known murderer walk out of the courtroom free. "You can't beat the big one," the old lawyers say. "You cannot." What happens to the freed murderer? He is freed to live a life of misery and guilt. He is freed to drink himself to death. He is freed to face the banishment of his community, the rejection of his neighbors, the trust of his loved ones. He is freed to be killed by his enemies, to live a life in hell—his own hell.

I remember Joe Esquibel, who shot his own blond wife in the presence of nine eyewitnesses, including a deputy sheriff standing there with his gun drawn. I remember the long years of my work to save him, and the three trials that led to the jury's final verdict that this Mexican-American had not intended to kill, that he had killed out of a desperate, raging insanity, and that, having thereafter spent years in a mental institution, he should be set free. Within days after his release, against my fatherly begging, he returned in the same old rotten hole that had spawned him, where a bartender promptly shot him to death. He had been drawn back to that place, compelled to return, and, perhaps, compelled to die. I can think of many others who are dead too soon, or worse than dead, the lost, wandering souls who are trapped in their fear of life and their fear of death and their fear of whatever may lie beyond death. I have never known a guilty killer who, acquitted, was ever freed. The trial of the guilty is mostly for the innocent, for victims, for a people demanding an orderly, peaceful society. The judge's sentence cannot further injure the killer. Unless he is the sociopath, the psychopath, the already living dead, he cannot be punished further. We reap our own gifts. Love begets love. Mercy begets mercy. Murder kills the murderer.

You can never beat the big one. And despite what we see, the golfing, his dwindling state of celebrity, in the end, O.J. Simpson will never beat the big one, either. Never. It is one thing to be celebrated as the greatest running back of all time; it is another to be remembered as the man who, as everybody believes, cut the throats of two human beings and got away with it.

But O.J. Simpson didn't get away with anything. The system worked. It revealed his guilt and, at the same time, preserved its safeguards for us. We complain about the system, but Simpson has felt the hard judgment of the people upon him. He will bear it without relief, reminded of it wherever he goes. He can no more escape the judgment of the people than he could escape a tattoo on his forehead reading KILLER. And that, perhaps, is the greatest punishment of all for a man whose worth is reflected only in the quantum of adoration he can glean from his fans. The fans are gone. Only the oglers at the sideshow remain. The people smile and holler, "Atta boy, O.J.," but he knows. He is the freak. The freak that escaped from the cage in the circus tent.

Yet we lament the verdict. We rant against it like children deprived of their dessert, having cleaned up our plates and eaten our spinach. But the system did not fail justice. The system failed only to provide us our vengeance. We were cheated out of our chance to cheer as Simpson was dragged off to live out his life in concrete and steel. Still, if justice includes a search for the truth, then this trial provided the truth, one that all America knows: Orenthal James Simpson is a murderer.

CHAPTER 19

THE PUNISHED

WE MUST DELIVER a better kind of justice to the people, about that there is no debate. But why do the people care about justice in the O.J. Simpson case? Why do we care when Nicole, of the long blond pampered body, of candlelight, sleek sports cars, and sweet, high times, is murdered, but not care when the bag lady is smashed down on the concrete, raped, and her old, dirty head bashed in? The police don't look for her killer, the newspapers don't carry the story. Her body is sold to the medical school, and kids learning to do autopsies cut her up while they make jokes and throw her severed parts in the garbage can.

Do we care or not care because, when we compare their souls, we find one more worthy than the other?

Why do we care when the Menendez brothers, languishing in decadent excesses, blow the head off of their mother, but we pass the hungry children on the street without turning our heads? We want justice. But what is this justice that we want? Do we want justice for the Menendez mother, whom we did not know? We never met the woman, never laid eyes on her. But we saw the hungry children on the street and we turned away.

We want justice, but for whom? We want to punish someone, but for what crime? I say we are an angry people. Our demand for justice is a demand for punishment. We confuse our longing for justice with our unrequited anger. If only we could punish more, strike back more, squash the gangs, imprison more felons, kill more killers. If only we could line the criminals up in long lines, lines that extend from San Francisco to Boston, and stick the needles in their arms, all of their arms, and incinerate their bodies. In our hearts we want to kill O.J. Simpson. So in our hearts, are we not killers as well?

But in the morning, after Simpson has been executed, and on the same morning, after the bodies of the Menendez brothers have been hauled off, do we feel better? Does this justice salve our hearts? Do we feel light and sweet and airy? Has this justice brought us happiness? Do we feel safer? No. We do not feel safer. And we have not escaped the urchins on the street. They are coming along on the endless conveyer belt of crime.

Why do we shout so loud and rage so incessantly when Jon-Benét Ramsey is murdered in her home—this case of baby porn, as some call it—while we utter barely a whisper of concern for the millions of children in the nation who are consigned to a life of drugs and poverty, and who die in ignoble anonymity, whose bodies are found in alleys and garbage cans and Dumpsters? Something is wrong here. We want justice, we say. But for whom? And what is the justice we want?

We need to punish. We will kill Timothy McVeigh for having killed the 168 in Oklahoma City. Will the families of the 168 feel cleansed, relieved? Will their lives grow better out of revenge? If we could kill the Menendez brothers and whoever killed JonBenét, we would kill them, too. And O.J. Simpson. But will that satisfy us? What is it that we want? O.J. Simpson and JonBenét and the Menendez brothers are only symbols upon which we focus. The media shows us these symbols. It does not show us the old bag lady and the babies born amid a cradle of crack vials. The media shows us Simpson and the other celebrity crimes and we are angry. Yet Simpson and the others mean nothing to us. We never met them. The killers, the victims—we never knew them. Still, they stand for our sorrow. They stand for the child we lost, the maiming of our bodies, the loss of our dignity, our sense of enslavement, our continuing fall from, as the Puritans dreamed of it, "the American city upon the hill." These celebrity cases stand for our injuries, whatever they have been, for our loneliness, for the injustices rendered upon us by God and the ungodly, against which we are helpless. And we are angry. And we want justice.

But these symbols—O.J. and Nicole—the others, also stand for our fear. We are not afraid of O.J. Simpson or the Menendez brothers or the killer of JonBenét. But we have our own fear, and they stand for it. We are afraid of the criminals out there. We are afraid of our spouses. We are afraid of our own private demons, whatever they are—it makes no difference. When O.J. Simpson is acquitted, it reminds us of our fear and we are angered. Anger stands in front of pain, and the pain is fear. Once more we demand justice. And we do not receive it. Once more we demand punishment. But even if the punishment is meted out, it will not make us safer. It will not diminish our fear. It will not bring us peace. In the morning we will be afraid all over again.

O.J. Simpson stands, as well, for whatever we hate. We do not know O.J. Simpson. He did nothing to us. It makes no difference how our hate was engendered. It comes to us from as many different sources of injustice as there are rays from the sun—from abuse, from injury we can no longer remember, from forgotten slights, from deep disappointments. If only we can punish Simpson, somehow our hate will be diminished. But in the morning, even if he is executed, we will still hate as much. Nothing will change. We will still be angry. Justice and anger are blood brothers, but like Cain and Abel, they are at odds with each other. One will kill the other.

I think we must begin to ask why we are so afraid. Why do we hate so? If we can understand our fear, our hate, perhaps we can better define the justice we require, for unless justice renders good, unless it ameliorates our terror, unless it brings about change and elevates the human condition, it is worthless. Revenge is worthless to all but the victim, and for the victim it only poisons the heart. And will we be safer having punished all of the criminals? Will they have learned their lessons and, when released, become friendly, helpful citizens whom we can embrace as our neighbors?

I say punishment cures nothing. We have been punishing from the beginning of time and have learned nothing of benefit from it. From the beginning we have confused punishment with justice. And if punishment is justice, justice cures nothing. We have already punished the child born in squalor. We began punishing the child the day he was born. You were a bad child, Willie, an evil child for having chosen such parents, that blank-eyed welfare mother, that unidentified sperm-planter who drops his seeds into any available crack or crevice. You should have known better than to have chosen such parents. Your punishment is to live like a human cockroach until you grow old enough to join a gang. And then we will get you, you cockroach transformed by the evil hand of hate into a juvenile rat. We will get you. And we will get you again when you rob us or kill us. We will punish you from the day you are born until the day you die. And that will be justice. Our punishment is our justice.

I see Willie. I see him walking along in old shoes and blemished clothes. He sees the others as well. He sees them in the pretty automobiles and the pretty clothes. He sees the long green yards, the brick homes with fluted columns set back from the road. He sees the women in the red convertibles with their hair blowing behind them and the wind in their faces. What did he do to deserve feet stuffed in those old shoes he found in a garbage can? And when we punish Willie for whatever it is that he has done lately, what has he learned? Has he learned that we are just? Has he learned not to hate us? Has he learned that crime does not pay?

Has he learned what he needs to learn in order to get a job? Has he learned of our compassion?

When we dump him out of that pen of concrete and steel, back into the concrete streets, what has he learned from the punishment? He has learned that the world out there, our world, is the enemy. That it is a savage, punitive world. He learns that *They*, whoever *They* are, hate him. Hate begets hate, and he hates back. Have we forgotten? We hated Willie first. If we had not hated him the day he was born, we would not have let him be carried off to that filthy hole. Only people we hate are thrown into such ugly places. He will be tortured there. We know that. He will be beaten, terrorized, injured. We know that as well. He will grow up tough and full of hate. Crime is his only choice because it is his only vision. He will rob. And kill. And that is because Willie is bad, is it not? He was bad the day he was born, was he not? And we must punish him for that.

I have never known any criminal who was the object of our punishment who felt it was justly rendered against him. Yes, he was caught. He is receiving his just dues for being stupid he thinks. "If you are going to be stupid, man, and get caught, you deserve what you get." That is justice. But was his punishment justice?

Justice has something to do with fairness, with equality, with opportunity, with a vision for one's life other than slogging through a jungle of hate and crime, of drugs and merchants of drugs, of killers and killers of killers.

So what are we afraid of? We as a people are afraid of our own progeny. We as a people are afraid of the children we have abandoned on the endless conveyer belt of crime. We want to be safe from them. We want them eliminated. We want them hurt so they will not hurt us. We want them punished without them punishing us back. Poverty is the breeding hole of crime, poverty both of the body and of the undernourished spirit. The impoverished children are coming along on the endless belt, coming to rob us and to kill us. And we pass them on the street, our heads turned.

We, the nation of people, are the body. We know the body is diseased. It breaks out in sores. We call it crime. Crime injures us. The sores are ugly and painful, and we see the sores, and they make us afraid. We cannot rid ourselves of them. It angers us that the body is ill. We hack away at the sores. But more come in their place. Always more. We have the power over the body, but in our anger and our pain we only dig at the sores. We leave many scars on the body. The boils, the carbuncles—their roots extend deep into the flesh. The sores drive us to madness, and in our madness we strike out at the sores and injure the body further.

The children are coming along, the impoverished ones on the streets, in the projects, the ones we do not see because they are "over there on the other side"—the ones who, at five years of age, steal to eat, and who survive like sewer rats. And on the other side of town, those whose bellies are stuffed, who live in disgusting opulence, who are pampered like yapping, perfumed lap dogs, search for meaning in empty affluence, and blow their parents away with a twelve-gauge shotgun. It is only a different sort of poverty that also leaves sores on the body.

Punishment will not free us of crime. It only creates it, exacerbates it, spreads it, forces the roots into deeper flesh. Crime will end when punishment ends. When we no longer punish the innocent child. When we are willing to be just by being fair. When we care for an old bag woman as much as we care for Nicole. When we care as much about the millions of children in America who live below the poverty level as we care about JonBenét. Crime will end when we no longer commit our own crimes of banishment and greed against the weak and the poor. Then we will no longer need to be afraid, our anger will subside, and a calm will begin to set in. A blessed calm.

CHAPTER 20

A NEW JUSTICE

THE O.J. SIMPSON case is a classic example of how we judge by anecdotal evidence. If we were visitors from Mars and captured the Hunchback of Notre Dame and made the same error, we would proclaim that all human beings looked like this poor freak. Do we adjudge all of mankind by Charles Manson? Do we adjudge all of mankind by the midget in the sideshow? But we judge the American justice system by this aberration called the Simpson case.

We have a right to hate the case but not the system. The case was not born of the system. It was, as we have seen, hatched, fed, and mostly feathered by the media. Yet the case reveals much of the worn-out and weathered elements of the justice system. And having been given the opportunity to review that which is learnable from it, we ought not ignore it.

Let us get to it: America's corporate oligarchy would be more comfortable with judges trying our cases rather than jurors, and the oligarchy, through its voice, the corporate-dominated media, has been successful in convincing many of the people to give up their right to a jury in favor of trials conducted by panels of professional judges. Could we improve the system by substituting the jury with a jury of judges? God, please help us if we do. Who would appoint the judges? Judges are not the representatives of the people, of us. Judges are the minions of the state. Do we want to be prosecuted by the state and adjudged by it as well? Judges are hand-picked by those in power. And those in power pick their own kind. Do you want the political judge-pickers to pick those who will judge us—judge us for those who picked them?

And who are the judges who sit on these cases, anyway? How many of them have ever labored for a living? How many have known poverty? Judges do not love. Judges judge. Judges do not harbor compassion, they harbor judgments. Their souls are not the tender souls of people. Their souls are like the callused feet of men who have walked many a mile over the gravel of human misery. Their innocence has been used up. Their psyches have lain in the rot too long. There are exceptions, and I respect the exceptions greatly. But we will not be tried by a panel of the exceptions. We will be tried by a panel of judges.

I was recently speaking to a group of trial lawyers in Seattle. On the panel was a federal district judge. I made the argument that juries as a whole are very wise. Take the woman who has cleaned up around the judge's toilet, I said. She walks home at night, alone. She is weary. Slowly she climbs the three flights of stairs to her little two-room apartment. She opens up a can of tomato soup, and then curls up, exhausted in her bed. She reaches over to touch the spot where her husband used to lie. He died last year. The bed is cold. She weeps alone in the covers. Then, one day, she is called for jury service. She joins the plumber, the schoolteacher, the retired telephone company repairman, the businessman, and the farmer. These are the jury. Who knows the human condition better, this jury or a panel of three judges selected by the governor?

After I finished speaking to the group, the federal judge got up. He said, "Yes, I agree with Mr. Spence. I've sat up on the bench and seen thousands of jury verdicts. And I say, 'Well, they got it right again.' Over and over juries have a magical intelligence. I see it every day. They get it right. They see things I do not. Their melded minds bring on an exponential intelligence that exceeds the intelligence of the twelve."

Ah, yes, it is argued, but the judges can understand the technical evidence better than laypersons—the DNA in the O.J. case, for example, the subtleties of medical and other scientific evidence. After all, this *is* the technical age. Yet I know few judges who can understand how the engine in their car works or who can fix a leaky faucet. Most judges are judges precisely because they were not beckoned by the sciences that would have propelled them into engineering or biology. They are judges because they were lawyers first. Most judges don't understand the technical evidence that is presented to them any better than the computer operator who is on the jury. Most judges don't know a RAM from a goat. President Bush didn't know anything about the price scanners at the grocery store. I can't operate an ATM machine; if I lose my credit card I can't buy supper. Alan Dershowitz, that brilliant Harvard professor, admits that much of the technical evidence in the Simpson case "was incomprehensible to *me,* and I have been teaching law and science for a quarter of a century." No, judges are not better equipped to unravel complicated scientific data. As a matter of fact, the scientists themselves can no more agree on a given scientific issue in a case than the lawyers can agree on the law. The best truth-sorting mechanism yet invented by man is a jury of twelve.

When the pompous pundits sound off, claiming that the evidence was "above the heads of the jury," they are only saying that the lawyers and the witnesses who were attempting to communicate with the jury failed in their task. Explaining technical facts requires the ability to speak in clear, understandable language. Lawyers who do not know, and do not want anyone to know that they do not know, use big words. The same goes for the expert witness. Albert Einstein was able to explain the theory of relativity in a simple, straightforward way on a few handwritten sheets of paper that any high school physics teacher could understand. And if the high school physics teacher can understand it, he can, if he is a reasonably successful teacher, explain it so that we can understand it. The problem is not the failure of the jury to understand, but the failure of the lawyers and witnesses to make it understandable. We ought not do away with the jury system because lawyers and witnesses cannot communicate effectively. The most difficult, the most complicated issue, legal, technical, scientific, or otherwise, can be made understandable by those who understand it themselves and who are able to speak in plain English. We don't need judges to stir around in an already addled pot. They would only be pouring mud into the soup.

Well, then, what about changing the requirement of a unanimous verdict? And how about changing the burden of proof that the prosecution must meet, holding prosecutors to a lesser standard than proof beyond a reasonable doubt? But what are we trying to accomplish? Why, in view of the near 90 percent conviction rate in this country, are we attempting to make it even easier for the prosecution to prosecute us? By ensuring that no more O.J.'s can ever again escape, do we want to make it so the innocent, too, will more often be convicted? Most of us, once charged, will not likely survive a criminal case brought against us, even if we are innocent. Countless innocent people populate the penitentiaries. Some sit on death row. Some are in their graves. But it is our overriding belief that we or our loved ones will never be the ones prosecuted. It is always *them*. It is "the murdering O.J.'s" who get away with it. It is the drug dealers and the gangs we so loathe and fear. But if it is only *they*, and never *we*, the innocent, why have trials at all? The police must be right most of the time, no? "That's close enough for government work," as the saying goes. Why not just leave justice in their hands? Let them deal with it. Let them take the miserable miscreants out and murder them back and keep us safe.

But if we have given this business of justice a modicum of thought, we know that once our rights have been taken from us, once we have, in disdain for them, given them up, they are gone forever. America then is no longer a blessed land of people with rights. We are no longer free. We are a police state, a junta, and the police, as always, are put in place by those in power and serve those who hire them. We have forgotten the inevitable process: By giving more and more power to the police, we extract more and more liberty from ourselves. When we throw the net over those malefactors who so plague us, we throw the net over ourselves as well. We are in the net. And when the sorting is done, it will be done at the hands of the police—not by us, not by our neighbors, not by a jury, but by the servants of power.

It takes a certain amount of courage to live in a free state. It also takes a modicum of patience. It takes understanding, and mercy. It requires us to recognize that as long as people are free, they are also free to commit crimes, to frighten us, and to hurt us. But I will take my chances at the hands of my fellow citizens, who include those who are free to hurt me, over the hands of the police, who are empowered to imprison me, even, at last, to open the oven doors and herd me in.

I remember talking to the head of one of the nation's leading networks one evening. Here is roughly how the conversation went:

"You are way too liberal for me," he said.

"What does 'liberal' mean?" I asked.

"It means your knee jerks every time somebody holds out their hand or whimpers a little."

"No," I said, "I'm not a liberal. I'm a conservative."

"Kid me not," he said. Sounded like Captain Queeg.

"I am against giving over the power of the state into the hands of the few," I said. "I want to *conserve* the right of the people."

"Well," he mused, deep into his third martini, "if I had my way we would be ruled by a benevolent dictator."

"Yes," I said. "But you would want to choose the benevolent dictator who would be the most benevolent to you, isn't that so?"

Then he laughed and ordered another martini and raised hell

with the waitress about the quantum of vermouth the bartender had dared inject into that dubious art form.

We ought not make decisions without first becoming students of history. Generation after generation, the human race falls blindly into the same error, claiming new remedies for the same old social problems that reappear, like the storms of winter, in each new season of history. Let the judges render justice? Have we forgotten the Bloody Assizes of James II and his chief justice, George Jeffreys? In 1685, James sought to capture and execute all those who had joined the duke of Monmouth's rebellion, as well as those who sheltered any such rebel. Judges then, as now, were and are the servants of those who elevate them. The Lord Chief Justice Jeffreys was a very bright man by all accounts, as are some of our judges today. But, as is sometimes the lure of power, Jeffreys loved cruelty, and just as we observe in some courtrooms today, he covered his sadism under a cloak of self-righteous sanctimoniousness.

One of his most infamous trials was that of Lady Lisle, a widow over seventy years of age, and frail, who had given shelter to one Hicks, a Presbyterian minister who had been a Monmouth accomplice. No evidence could be found that she had been a supporter of Monmouth, only that she had been a woman of generous and kind concern for Hicks and had given a night's lodging and food to him, and so was she charged. Jeffreys used her innocence to instill fear into the citizenry of the countryside, and vowed that her execution would be the most terrifying death imaginable.

His conduct in court was said to be outrageous. He browbeat the witnesses, terrorizing them and raging at them like a maddened beast. It is said that under one assize, as many as 250 persons were tried and executed at his direction, many of them tortured, some skinned alive. Nothing, it was said, excited him more into a high state of exhilaration as when he explained to Popish priests that they would be disemboweled alive to watch their own entrails being burned.

Lady Lisle was without an attorney. She was ignorant of the

law. She was afraid and alone. But she interrupted the opening statement of the prosecutor by saying, "My Lord, as for what is said concerning the rebellion, I can assure you, I abhorred this rebellion as much as any woman in the world."

The chief justice mocked the poor woman, and he frightened the witnesses until they finally testified as he willed. Yet three times the jury returned a verdict of innocent and three times the judge, in a passion, sent them back, threatening them with "an attaint of jury." Finally the jury gave in, and he sentenced Lady Lisle to be burned alive. As an act of charity, and in response to a powerful petition, the king permitted her to be beheaded instead of burned. Posthumously, by act of Parliament, the infamous trial was declared null and void, and the judge himself eventually died in prison.

The point of the story, of course, is that bad judges, cruel judges, occupy the benches in some of our courtrooms today and sit alongside their brothers and sisters of the bench, some of whom provide service to the nation's judiciary of the most honorable and dedicated kind. But as the power of the jury is eroded little by little, law by law, the potential for judge-made justice creates the possibility of more bloody assizes, or variations on the theme, some of which we suffer in more sophisticated versions even today. And the people, unaware of the danger of an unfettered judiciary, encourage more and more those judges who are "tough on crime" rather than tough on *injustice,* to the end that many judges, seeking to curry favor with a people who exhibit a national pathology of anger, slash away at the rights of the accused, truncate his day in court, treat his lawyer as if he too were a rogue, and, by their conduct, lead juries to unjust convictions, after which they level cruel and undeserved sentences.

I remember watching a judge in a Southern state presiding over the hearing of a boy condemned to death who sought a new trial because of various errors in his case, including the fact that his lawyer, a member of the good old boys' club, had encouraged him to plead guilty even though he had a good defense. The judge wasn't listening to the boy who was pleading for his life. Instead, I was shocked to see the judge wave to the people meandering in and out of the courtroom, hollering down to them from the bench, interrupting the boy's testimony.

"Hi there, Billy Joe," he would shout, drowning out the condemned's weak voice. "Come on in. Glad to see you. How is Patsy? Tell her to come on down."

His rulings on the evidence were empty-headed and mean. As the boy pleaded for his life in his own quiet way, the judge would at times lean back and drift off into slumber. Sometimes he would awaken only to shout or jeer at one of the defense attorneys. He had no respect for the lawyers, the law, or the procedures of justice. A few years later the boy was executed, although he had a perfect record before he had gone off on this murderous spree under the influence of PCP. The judge—of course, one of those "tough judges" we have come to adore—was later elevated to the state's high court, and there, I am told, he sits today, sorting through the appeals of other poor wretches who claim to have been railroaded by the state.

I say that any movement toward a brand of justice rendered by judges rather than by juries is one that all those who are even faintly infatuated with freedom must resist with all vigor. Yet I agree that the justice system needs improvement. We need better lawyers and better judges. That the justice system sometimes gets into a wreck does not mean that we should discard the vehicle. We don't need a new car, we need new drivers.

Let us consider for a moment how we select our judges. We would witness rioting in the streets if the Dallas Cowboys' front office appointed the referees for the Super Bowl. Yet for some reason we do not question the fact that the judges in the federal system are appointed for life by the party in power. "For life!" we say with pride. Judges appointed for life don't have to pander to the voters to keep their jobs, and they can call the jurisprudential shots as they see them. But even though we can take the judges out of politics, we can't take the politics out of the judges, most of whom were hoisted to their high place because in some way or another they, or those close to them, did service of some description (often money donations) for the party in power that saw to their appointment. We are who we are. And the judges are appointed to the bench because of who they are. Although there are wonderful stories to be told—such as the story of Chief Justice Earl Warren, who was supposed to be the savior of the conservatives but who instead became the saint of the liberals—nevertheless, exceptions always acknowledged, judges rarely change as radically as did Warren. Judges, like the rest of us, are creatures of their own experience. And when a federal judge grows moldy and mean and has lost his connectedness to human beings, we cannot get rid of him. Every trial lawyer can furnish endless horror stories of federal judges who should themselves be strung up for the cruelty they inflict on those who stand helplessly before them.

On the other hand, the people would also riot in the streets if we *elected* our referees for the Super Bowl and it was discovered that the largest contributors to their campaigns were the same Dallas Cowboys. When we elect our judges, we, the people who appear before them, are not the ones who have paid their campaign costs. Again, mostly lawyers from the large firms who represent the banks, insurance companies, and multinational corporations foot the bill. Moreover, laudable exceptions still acknowledged, these judges do not test the law; they test the wind. They do not put their fingers on the pulse of justice; they put them on the pulse of public opinion. They are the worst of all politicians. They can put someone away for life on the wrong evidence or on a faulty interpretation of the law, if such will serve them in their campaign for reelection.

We must find a better way to select our judges. Judges should be neither appointed for life nor elected. Judges should be chosen by *lot,* as jurors are chosen. Here's how: Since the judge must be "learned in the law," as the law requires, we will place the names of all active trial lawyers in good standing in a box, in much the same way that the names of citizens are placed in a box. When we need a judge on a case, a name will be randomly selected, as jurors' names are picked. That judge, so chosen, will hear the case and probably several other cases, and will do his judicial duty just as jurors perform their jury duty. He will be paid a modest fee. When he is done with his assignment he will return to his practice until he, by chance, is chosen again.

A panel of appellate judges will be called up in the same way to hear appeals. The appellate panel will be chosen from a second box, in which the names of lawyers who have served as trial judges have been placed. This panel of judges will hear several appeals and thereafter will also be returned to their private practices. The great advantage of such a system is, of course, that we have taken politics out of the process. We have been provided a wider demographic base that more accurately represents our citizens. We may get a few bad judges, but we are not stuck with them for life. We will also get some of the best legal minds, because the best often do not seek the judiciary. Lawyers who have served as judges will have learned the difficulty of being good at it, and will thus become better lawyers. Judges who have had to become lawyers again will become better judges because they have experienced the responsibilities of the trial lawyer. We will no longer have to wait two years or five years for a trial or an appeal while some old judge fiddles around with his docket and no one can make him go to work. We can call as many lawyers as we need to clear the docket. On the other hand, we will avoid the problem of the overworked judges who desperately try to keep up with their dockets but sometimes shortcut justice and are often short of patience and lack circumspection, traits that all good judges require.

We need better lawyers, lawyers for the people, lawyers trained to fight for the ordinary citizen, rather than those who leave our law schools best suited to serve the corporate and governmental overload. But how should they be selected, and how should they be trained? I have begun a pilot program for training such trial lawyers, a nonprofit school in which young lawyers of every race and origin, men and women who have already demonstrated a dedication to the delivery of justice to people, are taught how to win against the giant corporations and the government monster that despoil justice in this country for so many. In short, the new trial training emphasizes not only the basic skills of the courtroom, but also the conversion of the lawyer from a law-book automaton to a human being who can feel, who cares, and who understands that justice is the most sought-after of all human experiences, coming, as it does, even before love and health and money.

At the Trial Lawyer's College conducted at my ranch at Dubois, Wyoming, we teach trial lawyers the simplest things: We teach them the power of being real. We teach them the staggering weapon that is theirs when they tell the truth, even when it seems to hurt their case. We teach humanness and candidness over strategy. Young lawyers learn to sing again and to tell stories, because the voice, used in connection with the storytelling, is the ultimate instrument used in that ultimate art of the trial lawyer. At Trial Lawyer's College, lawyers learn from the best trial lawyers in America, who without fee give of their time and share with the younger warriors the skills they have learned from years of hard and painful experience in the courtroom. The young lawyer does not leave until he has tried cases from every perspective of the case. He has crawled into the hide of the opposing lawyer. He inhabits the judge's skin. He finds out what it is like to be the witness, and he becomes the juror. He learns that communication is the skill of being open and genuine. He is given the opportunity to rediscover who he is. At Trial Lawyer's College, he is given the opportunity to become the new, powerful horse of old Uncle Slim Spence.

I do not believe I overstate when I say that the transformation is nearly impossible to believe. These young lawyers go out, and as if by magic, they begin to win justice for their clients in cases that many saw as hopeless before. They have learned that it is permissible to care about their clients and that caring is contagious. The jury catches caring, and the judge as well. The courtroom comes alive. It becomes a sanctuary of humanness where justice is born, and the participants are once more caught up in the highest calling of the trial lawyer: the search for justice.

In the law schools, the new law student will no longer be trained "to think as a lawyer," as was the admonition of George Washington Langdell of Harvard Law School nearly a century ago, whose foolishness has been followed ever since in the law schools of America. Instead, the new law student will be trained *to think like a human being,* and to communicate like one. We need lawyers who care deeply, who care more about justice than money, who care more about people than the nonbreathers, the dead corporate entities, that, at last, have become the power elite in America.

Today, young lawyers are cheated of their legal education—an education that prepares them to represent people in their search for justice. When they emerge from the law schools and have passed the Multistate Bar Examination, all nicely sanctioned by the American Bar Association, most have lost contact with the humanness that distinguishes them from the machine. They are empty-souled and empty-headed, except for the multitude of rules and laws and the nice word games played with them that too often are unrelated to any human experience. The American people are justifiably angry with the legal profession. Never in the history of the United States have there been so many lawyers and so few competent ones available to represent the ordinary citizen.

In order to improve our chance at justice, we must have economical court procedures. Today a lawyer representing a person who has been severely maimed or killed by the negligence of another may spend hundreds of thousands of dollars in pretrial discovery depositions. He will live under an avalanche of motions, all concocted by "litigators" thrown against him whose business is not to resolve the legal dispute, not to assist their client to an economic conclusion of the case, but to keep the hourly billing going at up to five hundred dollars an hour. Lawyers who bill their clients by the hour have an inherent conflict of interest with their clients. The longer the case takes, the more money they make. The more motions, the more depositions that are taken, the richer the lawyer. On the other side of it, the injured party's lawyer, say, a lawyer for a mother who needs medical care and assistance for her child negligently injured in birth, often cannot afford to keep up with the bottomless pit of money that the insurance companies throw at the case. I am convinced, after my more than forty years in the courts of this country, that many insurance companies would rather pay their lawyers two dollars rather than pay a just claim of a dollar on behalf of their insured. When you buy an insurance policy, too often you do not buy protection; you buy a lawsuit.

Something is wrong with a system that, during the trial of a case, allows the appearance of lawyers positioning themselves to make big money selling their stories to the media. I do not accuse any lawyer in the Simpson case of having done so. But I do say that all of the lawyers who have now written their apologies in that case, their dissertations of blame, their finger-pointing epistles, who have become immensely rich from having sold their "inside stories," do so leaving the question open: What effect did the lure of the sale of their books and their stories have on their performance in the case?

Lawyers should have the right to free speech as well as any other citizen. But when, before or during the trial? Lawyers should be prevented by professional disciplinary rules from selling or contracting to sell before or during a trial, and for, say, two years following the conclusion of the case, any rights to any stories arising out of the case. By that time public interest in most cases should have cooled sufficiently to prevent the rush to print with all of its insanity that was so ill advised in this case and which left the clear impression that the sale of rights was more important than the rendering of justice.

Lawyers are already prevented by the ABA's Disciplinary Code from making any statement to the media "that would have a substantial likelihood of materially prejudicing" the case. Because lawyers are strategically situated at the core of every in-court conflict, they can affect the outcome of a trial through the use of the media. And to get a story, the media is only too happy to be used. Lawyers can poison the well. They did so in the Simpson case. They can be distracted from their in-court responsibilities to their clients by the out-of-court lure of self-promotion and self-praise. They often did so in the O.J. case. As a consequence, even more stringent, all-encompassing gag rules on attorneys during trials should become automatic and strictly enforced. Unethical lawyers bring the system into disrepute. Lawyers are the guardians of the system, the Knights of the Round Table of justice. They must be held strictly accountable to that sacred trust.

The jury system cannot survive facing the specter of jurors who, as they deliberate in the jury room and as they come to their verdict, may be considering big payoffs for the sale of their stories to the media. We may not be able to stop irresponsible members of the media from buying their stories—the First Amendment, you know—but surely we can keep jurors from selling them. Again, the legislatures of the fifty states and the U.S. Congress can make it unlawful for a juror to sell his or her story for a stated period of time following the conclusion of the trial.

Further, witnesses ought not be able to sell their stories before they have testified. If a person has been subpoenaed as a witness to either a grand jury, a preliminary proceeding, or a trial—as Jill Shively was—the witness ought not be permitted to sell or contract to sell his or her story, again, until after a set time following the conclusion of the case. Such laws would, no doubt, be attacked as in violation of First Amendment rights. But the First Amendment is not the only right citizens possess. And the courts are not strangers to the balancing act required to preserve our right as citizens to a fair trial, our right as citizens to due process under the law, and our right as a people to maintain a high level of faith in our justice system.

In criminal trials, a procedure should be made available to test the efficacy of the prosecutor's complaint before the accused is dragged into court to defend himself. In civil cases, a motion for summary judgment tests whether the minimal elements of a just claim in fact exist. In the criminal process, any prosecutor, incompetent, vindictive, or ignorant, or all of these, can haul the most innocent person before the dock, charged with whatever fanciful charges may itch the prosecutor's whim. The accused, almost always overcharged, faces the possibility of going to prison for many a year, perhaps for the rest of his productive life, on a groundless charge, or he can plea-bargain—that is, plead guilty to a crime he has never committed. Many citizens in this country stare out from behind bars, having pled guilty to crimes they did not commit, only because they feared they would suffer a worse fate at the hands of the system if they went to trial. The bloody assizes still wields its terror in America today.

The O.J. Simpson case has both taught us much and taught us little. It has taught us that if we are to enjoy justice under the best system yet devised, we must take steps not to erode it, not to chop away at it to quiet the hue and cry of its opponents. Instead, we must act to protect the justice system from the enormous corrosive forces that a modern, amoral media, too often representing its enemies, has dumped upon it. We must protect the system against money-grubbing players in the system, and reinstall by law those ethical standards that have heretofore been taken for granted by lawyers and jurors and witnesses alike.

The Simpson case has taught us what we already knew: that even the best of us are still only human and, to some degree, embody all of the human frailties that plague the species; that the lawyers from whom we have expected so much are not perfect, perhaps not fully competent, perhaps not always ethical, and surely not entitled to our adulation as heroes. We have learned anew that the media is not to be trusted to think for us. The media is not a substitute brain for the masses. It is surely not the voice of the people. It is only the sound and the fury of money-driven producers in the business of jacking their ratings. The media, like the ringmaster at the circus, brings on the great show. But the ringmaster is not sworn to tell the truth. He is not even interested in the truth. He is interested only in his ticket sales under the big top.

The Simpson case has taught us that this great American judicial machinery of ours, as old and doddery as it may seem to be, is still working. It can be regenerated. It can be made to labor magnificently for us if we take from it all of the rotten baggage it has been asked to carry, if we give it dedicated, honest operators who are more concerned about justice than money or celebrity. In the end, if we care enough of justice to protect it and honor it, it can keep us from falling under the iron fist of those who hate the system.

So why, Mr. Spence, have you, too, written one of "those O.J. books"? I have believed that the quality of justice in a nation, like the quality of coffee at a restaurant, often reflects the establishment. I have wanted to demonstrate that we can never be free if the opportunity to enjoy justice has become a commodity that can only be obtained by those sporting the wherewithal to purchase it. If the justice system is nothing more than that which can be bought and sold like pork bellies and sides of beef, then democracy has become a mockery, a cruel joke. If the justice system does not function *for the people* in a society that purports to be a nation *of the people*, our democracy is only a myth. If our rights, our lives, and our liberty, are protected with the efficacy of a blind old man on the porch in his rocker, there is nothing to keep the thieves and the tyrants from our door. And if we judge the system by the freak show known as the O.J. Simpson case and, on account of that case, attack the system, undermine it, and destroy it, we will one day awaken to find we are no longer safe because the system, the heart of which is the jury, has been negligently, mindlessly cut at and hacked at by those who have the power but not the knowledge or the skill or the caring to repair it. Then, too late, we shall discover that the system protects only those with the power to manipulate it. We shall discover it will no longer protect us, not only from our errant neighbors, but also from the greater threat, which is a government that serves mostly those seated in power. In the end, that is why the Simpson case is important. It has provided the one great opportunity not only to tell the truth about that aberrant case, but also to expose the greater truth about how justice is, and too often is not, achieved in America, and what we may do about it.

The last word on the Simpson case, this canker on the justice system of America, will never be written. But these have been mine.

SOURCES

THIS BOOK IS based on my observations of the trials, both civil and criminal—I attended both in person—and filtered both through my nearly forty-five years in the courtrooms of the country. I have also relied on what the participants in this case have said in court, the public record, and what they have written in their various books on this trial.

I was in frequent contact during the trial with many responsible and insightful writers, reporters, and TV personalities. I had numerous conversations with Ira Reiner of NBC, the former D.A. of L.A., whose observations were nearly always on the mark, and I spoke from time to time as well with Jack Ford of NBC, Jim Moret of CNN, Linda Deutsch of A.P., Andrea Ford and Henry Weinstein of the *Los Angeles Times,* David Margolick of *The New York Times,* Dominick Dunne of *Vanity Fair,* Professors Peter Arenella and Laurie Levenson, and other bright and perspicacious writers, observers, and citizens who were in regular attendance at the trials.

My observations of the media came from my own exposure to it, my appearances as both guest and host on *Larry King Live* and CNN, and my comments made on the various programs carried on NBC, including the *Today* show and the *Nightly News.* I also appeared frequently on *Rivera Live,* and other programs on CNBC and elsewhere.

Marcia Clark has spoken often, and in unstodgy language in her book, *Without a Doubt* (New York: Viking, 1997). Unless otherwise noted, when she is quoted the words are from her book. The same is true of Christopher Darden, who tells his story in his book, *In Contempt* (New York: Regan Books, 1996). I have also had passing private conversations with both Clark and Darden. I had numerous lengthy conversations with Robert Shapiro, as noted in the book, and passing conversations with Johnnie Cochran, and O.J. Simpson, both in person and by telephone.

The most comprehensive and complete book on the criminal trial is Jeffrey Toobin's *The Run of His Life: The People v. O.J. Simpson* (New York: Random House, 1996; paperback edition published by Simon & Schuster). I have relied on it heavily. I was with Jeff Toobin in the courtroom from time to time as well as on various television shows. His competence in reporting the events of the trial, his research, and his independent view of this case make his work the standard.

I have had occasion to both agree and disagree with my old friend Vincent Bugliosi, the prosecutor's prosecutor. His forthright book *Outrage: The Five Reasons Why O.J. Simpson Got Away with Murder* (New York: W. W. Norton, 1996; paperback edition published by Island-Dell) has been the source of the Bugliosi positions and quotations I have commented upon herein.

I have referred to the books of the detectives. Mark Fuhrman's *Murder in Brentwood* (Washington, D.C.: Regnery Publishing, 1997) gives his perspective on the so-called race card that was allegedly played by various participants and reveals other information that heretofore somehow escaped public attention. Most of the quotes from Fuhrman are from his book, some are from Toobin and Clark. I have also found valuable information in Tom Lange and Philip Vannatter's book, *Evidence Dismissed: The Inside Story of the Police Investigation of O.J. Simpson* (New York: Pocket Books, 1997).

I have read Alan Dershowitz's intelligent book *Reasonable Doubt: The O.J. Simpson Case and the Criminal Justice System* (New York: Simon & Schuster, 1996), and I have quoted from Lawrence Schiller and James Willwerth's *American Tragedy* (New York: Random House, 1996), an intimate view not provided elsewhere.

I have both interviewed Faye Resnick and quoted from her book, *Nicole Brown Simpson: The Private Diary of a Life Interrupted* (Beverly Hills: Dove Books, 1994). Her book has the ring of truth and supplied the script for much of the prosecution's case.

The story of the Bloody Assizes is from *Famous and Infamous Cases,* Patrick Hastings, Theodore Brun Limited, London, a Limited De Luxe Edition, and from *Lord Macaulay's The History of England,* reprinted by Penguin Classics in 1986.

Chapter 1: The "Dream Team"

The writer who had "never heard of Cochran ever winning a murder case before a jury" was my friend Vincent Bugliosi, in his book *Outrage*.

Chapter 4: Race Card Fever

Robert Shapiro's quote about Mark Fuhrman's getting up in the morning to kill some "niggers" is from Jeffrey Toobin's *The Run of His Life,* as are the story about Joseph Britton's suit against Fuhrman and Shapiro's quotes concerning the race card. Fuhrman's admission about shooting Britton is from Fuhrman's book. The history of Fuhrman's fight for disability and the Ronald Koegler quote are also from Toobin.

That black women thought Marcia Clark was "a bitch" is from her book, *Without a Doubt,* as is her complaint that Cochran said the prosecution had "hired a token black man."

The quotes about the Lincoln-Douglas debates and the other antebellum quotes are from that most wonderful account of the Civil War, *Battle Cry of Freedom: the Civil War Era,* by James M. McPherson (New York: Oxford University Press, 1988).

Chapter 7: The Needle

Statistics on the criminal records of death penalty inmates are from *U.S. News & World Report,* June 16, 1997.

Chapter 8: The Media Monster

The quote from Commander David Gascon is from Toobin, as is the story of how Jill Shively came upon Simpson at Bundy and San Vincente.

Chapter 9: *People* v. *John Wayne*

The quotes from the Fuhrman tapes were found in Toobin and were doublechecked against transcripts of the tapes on the Internet.

Chapter 11: The Iron Shoe

The statistics on wife batterers who become murderers are from Alan Dershowitz's *Reasonable Doubt.*

The reference to Clark having been seen as a "bitch" as well as the quote from Gil Garcetti are from Clark's book. References to Don Vinson's advice to Clark and his findings, as well as the statement that black women saw her as a "castrating bitch," are from Toobin.

Chapter 12: The "Blame Card"

The Donald Dutton and Angela Brown suggestion that the prosecutors might end up sleeping together is from Chris Darden's book, *In Contempt,* as is his memory of an LAPD photo showing dark clothing near a hamper in the bathroom. Also, his complaint about Johnnie Cochran's comments to the media and Cochran's quotes about his being in the case, as well as Darden's and the black community's reactions, are all from his book. His book is the source of his quoted complaints and his intended method of handling Fuhrman's testimony.

The black women's observation concerning Resnick as another white bitch trying to bring down O.J. is from Clark's book. Also, Clark's claim that Vinson didn't have a clue and simply wanted to be on national TV, and that Darden's chain was jerked by Cochran, are from her book, as is her account of her conflict with Darden over the presentation of the glove experiment to the jury, as well as her conclusion that he wanted to "score a coup" with the demonstration.

Fuhrman's comparison of Darden to Cochran and his request to have Clark handle his testimony are from Fuhrman's book, *Murder in Brentwood*.

Darden's book is the source of his complaint that the pundits gave Marcia good reviews but paid little attention to him. His book is the source of Clark's argument to him that he should apologize to the judge as well as his quotes about how he should keep his emotions in check and the juror's observation about how black men get picked on.

Chapter 13: The Judge

Clark's characterization of Judge Ito as "spineless" is from her book. Bugliosi's claim that the race card was 100 percent the fault of the judge is from his book. The quote about York having "sucked and fucked her way to the top" is from Toobin's book. Don Evans's unsigned statement is from Fuhrman, as is Fuhrman's claim that the judge permitted the case to become a trial against Mark Fuhrman.

Chapter 14: Truth

The quote from Nicole about having "married a nigger" is from Darden's book, as is his claim that Jennifer Peace, a porn star, had told him of Simpson's stalking of Ron Goldman. That Darden thought the glove fiasco was a result of the defense's trickery is also from his book.

The material about Keith Zlomsowitch is from Toobin's and Clark's books. The "Driftwood" reference to Marcus Allen is from Resnick's book.

The quote from an unnamed source about Goldman having

sex with an older woman is from Fuhrman's book and is confirmed in a similar passage in Lawrence Schiller's *American Tragedy*.

The quote setting out the psychological theory of why Simpson exploded into murder—that he was in a "free fall"—is from Clark's book.

Chapter 15: The Knife

The story of Simpson's 1989 abuse of Nicole is from Toobin's book.

Chapter 16: The Return of the Frogman

The quotes from Nicole concerning Simpson's joke about the frog and *The Frogmen* and that he hadn't changed, that it was over, are from Resnick's book, as is Simpson's quote concerning the irony of his starring in that series and his wife's fear of frogs.

Reference has been made to *The Frogmen,* a TV series pilot produced by Warner Bros. for NBC, authored by Carol Mendelson. The script reveals that this is a Magnum Television effort, and my references to it are from the revised April 6, 1994, version, together with information provided me by Wally Crowder and Mark Lonsdale, who were on the set from time to time.

The statement about knife fighting being primal man at his worst is from *CQB: A Guide to Unarmed Combat and Close Quarter Shooting,* written and published by Mark Lonsdale (Los Angeles, 1993).

Simpson's statement to the limousine driver about the large Swiss knife being sharp and that it could kill someone is from Lange and Vannatter's book, *Evidence Dismissed.*

Clark's analysis about whether O.J. would take the stand is from her book.

Chapter 17: The Cameras

Darden's statement about the stars knowing who he was is from his book, as are the facts concerning the media's presence at the trial. The statement from Darden to Judge Ito about jerking the cameras from the courtroom is from his book.

ACKNOWLEDGMENTS

CAROLE JEAN FLECK, Imaging's and my long-time friend, has read all of my books and has tried, sometimes in vain, to keep me consistent where consistency is often not my wont. I thank her for reading this one as well, and for her caring suggestions.

In May of this year Garvin Isaacs, that great Oklahoma City trial lawyer, and I drove through Oklahoma, Texas, and New Mexico on a photo trip. I read the books of the various participants in the O.J. case out loud as we drove, and we hollered, and argued the case all over again, and I made notes, and in between times we took photographs of worn-out places and great clouds and crumbling missions. It was during this outing that I outlined the book.

I give my thanks to Wally Crowder and Mark Lonsdale for their memories of the filming of *The Frogmen,* and to Faye Resnick for her assistance in helping me understand Nicole's state of mind during the time that series was being filmed as well as her own take on Marcia Clark. In this regard I also thank an old hand in the D.A.'s office in Los Angeles who knows who he is and who gave me his own take on this same subject.

Jeffrey Toobin's book *The Run of His Life* is the complete and standard work on this case. I thank him for his generous, offered cooperation as I wrote this one. Martin Garbus gave me time and thought concerning the First Amendment issues in the last chapter. I needed to bounce my ideas off of the leading First Amendment lawyer in the country, and I did so with Martin. He does not agree with some of my recommendations, and gave others I have not included, but I am confident that what is contained herein, if enacted, would pass constitutional muster.

I thank John Kelly, attorney for the Browns, for his generous assistance in understanding how the knife and bloody clothes were disposed of. Thanks, as well, to our long-time friend and counselor, Sheila Sandubrae, for lending me insight into the workings of the mind of the sociopathic personality.

Bob Weil, my editor, my friend, one of the most gifted, ethical and caring men I know, has always provided the guidance and encouragement that one such as I require. It has been his demand that I work to the extreme ends of my potential, and if occasionally I should succeed at that, it is because of his vision for me. As usual, he came to Wyoming and worked the long, tedious hours of the skilled and thoughtful editor, and he has nurtured and cared for this book as if it were his own, for which gift, among many others, I again thank him, and his powerful and quiet associate editor, Becky Koh, whose unacknowledged work is on these pages. I also thank Beth Pearson for her thoughtful and thorough copy-editing.

I am grateful to John Sargent, the head man at St. Martin's and another Wyoming man, for his faith in this book and his trust and patience in seeing it come to fruition. I remain at this house because of the dedicated people who work well and faithfully beyond any of the reasonable expectations that have been set for them.

I thank Imaging, my mate, my love, who is always at my nucleus. I could not write the first or the last word without her.

INDEX

ABOUT THE AUTHOR

BORN, RAISED, AND educated in Wyoming, Gerry Spence has lived in small Wyoming towns all of his life. He is a consummate country lawyer. Yet from these rural places he has conducted a national law practice and has tried and won some of America's most famous cases including the defense of Imelda Marcos, Idaho separatist Randy Weaver, and the renowned Karen Silkwood case, in which the jury awarded his client a verdict in excess of $10 million. He has obtained a series of multimillion-dollar verdicts including a $52 million verdict against McDonald's for a small bankrupt ice-cream company, a $26 million verdict against *Penthouse Magazine* for Miss Wyoming, and a settlement in excess of $40 million for the workers against U.S. Steel.

Spence's court work has changed the face of trial law in America. He has not lost a criminal case in his entire career of over forty years and he has not been denied by a jury in a civil case in the past twenty-five years. For over twenty-five years Spence has refused to represent banks, insurance companies, big business, big corporations, and, unless, as in the Imelda Marcos case, there are overshadowing public issues, he also refuses to represent the rich and famous.

Spence, the author of seven other books, is an accomplished

photographer, painter, and television host and commentator. He is the founder of Trial Lawyer's College, a nonprofit school, where he and the nation's leading trial lawyers teach young trial lawyers how to win against government and larger corporations on behalf of the individual. He is also the founder of Lawyers and Advocates for Wyoming, a public interest law firm devoted to public interest cases. His agenda: to promote justice in America for the "little guy" and to make the American justice system work for the "average citizen."